Foundational Concepts

Walking in the Way of Christ & the Apostles

Theological Reader Part 1

Peter Briggs

Copyright © 2017, Daystar Institute / NM, Inc.

2nd Edition

All rights reserved. No part of this publication may be reproduced, except for brief quotations in printed reviews, without the prior permission of the publisher.

The Two Ways cover picture was created by Louis Pecastaing of Albuquerque, NM. Used by permission.

Unless otherwise noted, all Scripture quotations are taken from the Holman Christian Standard Bible®, Copyright © 1999, 2000, 2002, 2003, 2009 by Holman Bible Publishers. Used by permission. Holman CSB®, and HCSB® are federally registered trademarks of Holman Bible Publishers.

Scripture quotations marked [ESV] are from The Holy Bible, English Standard Version®, Copyright © 2001 by Crossway Bibles, a publishing ministry of Good News Publishers. Used by permission. All rights reserved.

ISBN-10: 1-947642-07-3
ISBN-13: 978-1-947642-07-2

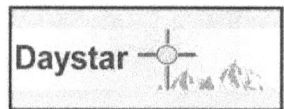

Published by:
Daystar Institute / NM, Inc.
P.O. Box 50567
Albuquerque, New Mexico
87181-0567 USA
www.DaystarInstituteNM.us

Distributed in Africa by:
Daystar Institute / Africa
P.O. Box 3989 00200
Nairobi, Kenya

www.DaystarInstituteAfrica.org

TABLE OF CONTENTS

Testimonials . . . . -vi-

Foreword. . . . . -vii-

Preface . . . . -ix-

Acknowledgments & Dedication . . . . -xv-

Chapter 1. Introduction and Overview of the WitW Study 1
    Keynote Scripture Passage. 1
    Overall Learning Objectives 1
    Learning Objectives for this Chapter. 1
    Doing Theology and Building a Biblical Worldview 3
    Theology as a Verb: Some Initial Definitions 9
    Integrative Study Process 10
    WitW Study Overview: Summary of Each Chapter 13
    Overview of the Appendices 20
    Achieving the Overall Learning Objectives of
        the WitW Study. 22
    Questions for Discussion 23
    Notes & Reflections. 24

Chapter 2. Storyline of the Bible:The Bible as True Narrative 25
    Learning Objective 25
    The Bible as a Representational System 26
    The Bible as True Narrative. 26
    The Storyline of the Bible: A Thematic Guide for
        Doing Theology. 35
    Keynote Scripture Passages. 37
    Questions for Discussion 50
    Notes & Reflections. 51

Chapter 3. The Bible as a Representational System. 52
    Chapter Overview. 52
    Learning Objectives. 52
    Some Definitions. 53
    Two Ways of Representing Reality 55

Life-Critical Importance of Embracing a Godly
  RW Mental Filter............................. 62
Representations in the Christian Scriptures.............. 69
Guarding the Heart..................................... 77
Questions for Discussion............................... 91
Notes & Reflections................................... 93

Chapter 4. Discovering the Meaning of Biblical Books
  and Passages... 94
The Importance of Rightly Handling the Word of Truth..... 94
Learning Objective.................................... 94
Structure of the Canon of Scripture.................... 94
The Primacy of the Bible's Story...................... 98
Biblical Principles of Biblical Interpretation............. 100
Implications of Biblical Principles..................... 106
General Principles of Biblical Interpretation............ 108
Interpreting Biblical Narrative........................ 111
Interpreting Hebrew Poetry........................... 118
Interpreting Didactic Literature....................... 126
Interpreting Apocalyptic Literature.................... 135
Interpretation Tools.................................. 140
Concluding Comments Regarding Biblical Interpretation... 141
Questions for Discussion.............................. 142
Notes & Reflections.................................. 143

Chapter 5. Torah: The Fountainhead of Wisdom............ 144
  Chapter Overview.................................... 144
  Learning Objective.................................. 144
  Overview of the Fourteen Integrative Motifs.......... 144
  Progressive Development of the Integrative Motifs.... 153
  The Invasion of Evil, Sin, and Death................. 154
  The People of the New Way........................... 169
  The Gospel.. 181
  Sovereign Election and Human Responsibility.......... 189
  The Covenant of Conditional Blessing................. 202
  Questions for Discussion............................ 214
  Notes & Reflections................................. 215

Chapter 6. The Two-Part Christian Gospel 216
    Chapter Overview. 216
    Learning Objective. 216
    Discovering the Christian Gospel 217
    Introduction to the Christian Gospel 233
    The Gospel of the Kingdom of God. 234
    The Gospel of God. 235
    The Four-Faced Living Creatures 236
    Perversions of the Christian Gospel: A Brief Summary 236
    Proclaiming the Christian Gospel 238
    Questions for Discussion 238
    Notes & Reflections. 239

Endnotes 240

LIST OF FIGURES AND TABLES [1]

Figure 1-1. Doing Theology Over Supper. 6
Figure 1-2. Integrative Study Process 10
Figure 2-1. Time Line of the Biblical Narrative 26
Figure 3-1. The Workings of a Godly RW Mental Filter 57
Figure 3-2. The Workings of a Worldly RW Mental Filter 59
Figure 3-3. The Tabernacle in the Wilderness:
    A Rich Biblical Representation 66
Figure 4-1. True Narrative Supports Doctrine. 97
Figure 4-2. Delineation of a Chiasmic Structure. 124
Figure 4-3. Multiple Fulfillments 137
Figure 5-1. The Progressive Development of the
    Integrative Motifs. 153
Figure 5-2. The Tower of Babylon 160
Figure 5-3. Vessels of Mercy = Bowls and Vessels
    of Wrath = Jugs 198
Figure 5-4. Prophetic Chain. 206
Table 6-1. Summary of the Two-Part Christian Gospel 220

Testimonials

"The *Walking in the Way of Christ & the Apostles* (WitW) series by Dr. Peter Briggs is a powerful tool for fulfilling Jesus' universal mandate to make disciples. WitW is theologically sound, conceptually brilliant, and life-changing for those who are trained by it. The impact of WitW is not only personal transformation into the image of Christ, but also a profound influence on families, churches, and the larger culture, whether in America or Africa or anywhere else. Peter Briggs is a theologian of substantial import, but he has not merely plied his theological craft in the halls of academia. With God's enablement, he has managed to translate biblical truth and disciple-making principles into something that actually works in the real world! Those who embrace and employ *Walking in the Way* in their own lives will find themselves part of a movement affecting generations to come."

Steven Collins, PhD
Executive Dean, Trinity Southwest University

"*Walking in the Way of Christ & the Apostles* (WitW) is a magnificent literary work in biblical theology that offers the student an education in practical Christianity. The WitW study was first introduced in November 2011; since that time we have been using it to instruct ministry leaders and rural pastors at a low cost, and the transformation of lives is phenomenal. Learners get to understand the message of the Bible and are able to study it effectively. In my own interaction with the material over the past five years, I have come to realize that Jesus Christ is using it to revive His remnant in Kenya and other parts of Africa, teaching us how to think in a biblical way and be successful in all spheres of life. I am convinced that the WitW material holds the key to Africa's revival, and, in Yahweh's hand, it is a mighty tool for returning the continent back to Him."

Michael Mutinda
Team Leader, Daystar Institute / Africa

Foreword

Walking in the Way of Christ & the Apostles (WitW) is a study in uncompromising discipleship, practical Christian theology, and building a biblical worldview. It is designed for use by adult, self-motivated learners who are proficient in English. The content and structure of the WitW study are summarized in the following paragraphs.

The **WitW Theological Reader (TR)** is the principal textbook for the WitW study. The TR consists of seventeen chapters and is structured in four parts as follows:

- **Part 1** (TR 1) is entitled Foundational Concepts and consists of chapter 1 through chapter 6. Thus, the material presented in Part1 is foundational to understanding Parts Two and Three. It concludes with chapter 6, which introduces the two-part Christian gospel. The two parts or aspects of the Christian gospel are the **gospel of the kingdom of God** and the **gospel of God**. These are in nowise two different gospels. Instead, they are like the two sides of a single coin, in that they are two interconnected and mutually complementary aspects of the single Christian gospel.

- **Part 2** (TR 2) is entitled The Gospel of the Kingdom of God and consists of chapter 7 through chapter 12. The discussion of the gospel of the kingdom of God is based primarily upon the Synoptic Gospels and the Book of Acts. It emphasizes the kingly authority of Jesus Christ, and it confronts man's prideful rebellion against that authority.

- **Part 3** (TR 3) is entitled The Gospel of God and consists of chapter 13 through chapter 17. The discussion of the gospel of God is based primarily upon the Pauline Epistles, especially the Book of Romans. It confronts our bondage to evil, sin, and death, and it sets forth God's complete solution to that problem.

- **Back Matter** (TR 4) consists of the List of Resources and appendices. Appendix A presents a glossary of theological terms used throughout the WitW study, and the rest of the appendices complement and support the discussion in the body of the TR. You should at least browse through the appendices so as to familiarize yourself with their contents. Then you should study the appendices more carefully when appropriate to understanding the discussion in a given chapter of the WitW study.

The **WitW Study Guide (SG)** consists of seventeen booklets, each corresponding to a chapter in the TR. TR 4, the WitW Back Matter, supports both the TR and the SG. The SG is designed to enable and facilitate discovery of insights directly from Scripture, and achievement of chapter by chapter learning objectives through a study and discussion learning process.

Preface

Purpose of the WitW Theological Reader. The mission of Daystar Institute of Biblical Theology and Leadership Development is to advance the kingdom of God by training and equipping pastors and church leaders to be, themselves, fully devoted followers of Jesus Christ, and to then reproduce this training and equipping in the lives of their families and church members. [2]

My objective in the TR for the WitW study is to produce a concise but comprehensive theological resource that is suited to adult, English-proficient learners who are studying in a church-based setting. The principal target audience of the TR consists of apostolic messengers, pastors, and church leaders who are proficient in English and who, in turn, are training disciples of Christ to become church leaders in Africa and throughout the 10 – 40 window. [3]

My Approach. In preparing the WitW study, I have taken seriously the teaching priorities of the Apostle Paul in his early epistles. Even a casual study of Paul's life and ministry places in evidence his burning zeal for establishing new disciples in the way of Christ and the apostles. This is especially evident in two of his earliest epistles, the letters to the fledgling church in Thessalonica. I therefore approach this subject, which was so vitally important to Paul, with fear and trembling. In fact, I recognize that I am but a child in understanding and practicing the way of Christ and the apostles – that is, the way of wisdom that leads to life. This is true even though I have been endeavoring to walk in that way for over 50 years.

My Theological Journey. Allow me to briefly summarize the trajectory of my theological journey. I came to Christ in 1960 while engaged in graduate studies and research in mechanical engineering at the Massachusetts Institute of Technology. Some of my colleagues, who were beginning their spiritual pilgrimages in parallel with mine, felt that God was directing them to transition immediately into seminary training leading to full time ministry. However, I took my direction from 1 Corinthians 7:20, which states, "Each man must remain in that condition in which he was called." Moreover, passages like Ephesians 6:7-8 and Colossians 3:23-24 clearly indicated to me that working in a so-called secular vocation "heartily, as for the Lord," was good and acceptable before God. With this firm conviction, I completed my graduate work at MIT and entered into a career as a defense avionics systems engineer with General Electric and then Honeywell. My engineering career continued until the late summer of 1992 when my wife, Rosemarie, and I determined that God was directing me to leave engineering and enter into a second career as a minister of the gospel. In December 1993, I enrolled as a doctoral student at Trinity Southwest University (TSU), which at the time was the Albuquerque branch campus of Trinity College & Seminary based in Newburg, Indiana.

Peter & Rosemarie Briggs

My First Exposure to Representational Thinking. As I commenced my studies at TSU in January 1994, my life was powerfully impacted by new insights in theology, discipleship, apologetics, and biblical archaeology. In the summer of 1994, Michael Strawn, one of my fellow graduate students, presented a lecture on the results of his research in biblical representations. This lecture marked a turning point in my career as a student and as a Bible teacher. From that point onward, I came to regard the Bible as a representational system which defines reality for the disciple of Christ. This was a life-transforming insight that I set about to factor into my own research and teaching from that point onward. [4]

Introduction to the Theory of True Narratives. In 1996, I was introduced to the Theory of True Narratives by John W. Oller, Jr., who was then serving as Professor of Linguistics at the University of New Mexico. He broached the idea of applying this theory to testing the factuality of a portion of the biblical narrative – in particular, the story of the conquest of Ai recorded in the 7th and 8th chapters of the Book of Joshua. I was excited to address myself to this research, which occupied me for five years. During that time I served as Surveyor & Research Scientist for the Khirbet el-Maqatir excavation project the under direction of Bryant G. Wood.

The Criterial Screen Method of Analysis. The key analytical concept that I pioneered in my research, and applied to testing the factuality of the conquest of Ai narrative, was the **criterial screen**, which is based upon the correspondence property of true narratives. That is, a true narrative corresponds to the material time-space context in which the episode represented by the narrative is alleged to have occurred. I successfully applied the criterial screen method of analysis to a demonstration of the factuality of the conquest of Ai narrative.

Generalizability Property of True Narratives. Another property of true narratives that is significant to any study in the sphere of Christian theology is that of **generalizability**. If, and only if, a narrative is true is it able to support and sustain valid generalizations. In particular, the biblical narrative is only able to support and sustain valid generalizations in the form of normative theological, moral, and ethical principles if it is true. No wonder then that those who are hostile to the Bible's message have directed such intensive and fierce attack on the historical authenticity of the biblical narrative, thereby endeavoring to undermine its theological integrity.

Countering the Attack of Critical Scholars. While it is important to comprehend the views of critical scholars vis-a-vis the historical authenticity and factuality of the biblical narrative, it is also necessary that we refute their arguments wherever possible based upon the scientifically objective criterial screen method of analysis. Because of the importance of the historical authenticity and factuality of the Bible, an entire chapter of one of the resources cited in the List of Resources is devoted to a discussion of this vital subject. [5]

Inclusive Language. In view of the postmodern obsession with political correctness and the careful use of inclusive language, a word is in order concerning the use of personal pronouns throughout the WitW study materials. Generally, "he" and "his" are employed in their traditional, inclusive sense, which accords with their use in Scripture. Accordingly, I assiduously and unabashedly avoid the stilted and cumbersome "he or she" or "his or her". Therefore, the context determines whether "he" or "his" refers to a specific male individual, such as an author of a text to which I am referring, or whether it is intended to be inclusive. Personal pronouns which refer to God are capitalized.

Motivation for the WitW Study. Before leaving this Preface, I need to clearly state the motivation for the WitW study, which is to confront and counteract the peril of nominalism. Note well Paul's stern warning in the 3rd chapter of 2 Timothy:

> But understand this, that in the last days there will come times of difficulty. For **people will be lovers of self**, lovers of money, proud, arrogant, abusive, disobedient to their parents, ungrateful, unholy, heartless, unappeasable, slanderous, without self-control, brutal, not loving good, treacherous, reckless, swollen with conceit, lovers of pleasure rather than lovers of God, ^{5} **having the appearance of godliness,** but denying its power. **Avoid such people.** [2 Timothy 3:1–5, ESV, emphasis added]

From the characterization in the 5th verse, I believe Paul is describing nominal Christians in this passage – people who are Christian in name only (CINO), and who, therefore, have only the outward appearance of godliness. Since we are told to avoid such people, clearly we are to avoid **being such people**.

Moreover, we need to do all in our power to ensure that the members of our churches are disciples – that is, fully devoted followers of Jesus Christ. It has been estimated that as many as 75% of the people who attend the average evangelical church are CINOs. If this is true, then there is an enormous, and largely overlooked, mission field within the very walls of our churches! I conclude this section with the following three warnings.

> *First, the peril of nominalism is constantly lurking to overwhelm and render fruitless every Christian community. In fact, any given Christian community is, at most, two generations removed from becoming CINO.*
>
> *Second, evangelism without discipleship guarantees nominalism.*
>
> *And third, in accordance with Revelation 21:7ff, citizenship in Christ's eternal kingdom is reserved for those who overcome. Therefore, nominal Christians will be excluded. (In this regard, refer to Jesus' stern warning in Matthew 7:22-27.)*

Jesus Christ emphasized that His sheep hear His voice, and those who are not His sheep do not. And how do we hear the voice of our Lord? In his seminal study entitled *Experiencing God*,[6] Henry Blackaby asserts that God speaks to His people through four channels or modalities. First, He speaks to us primarily through His **word** – that is, the language of Scripture. Second, He speaks to us through **listening prayer**. Third, He speaks to us through **godly counsel**. And fourth, He speaks to us through **circumstances**.

Disciples of Christ are intent on listening to the voice of God and receiving direction and guidance from Him. In particular, disciples have an irrepressible appetite for the language of Scripture. On the other hand, for those who do not belong to Christ, reading the Bible is a duty and a struggle. Indeed, according to Paul in the 2nd chapter of his first letter to the church at Corinth, Scripture is foolishness to the non-disciple.

As we embark upon the WitW study, I admonish you with the command that Yahweh, the God of Israel, issued to Joshua so many centuries ago.

> This book of the Torah shall not depart from your lips. But you shall meditate and audibly muse upon it day and night, that you might be careful to practice everything written in

it. For then you will make your way prosperous, and then you will experience good success. [Joshua 1:8, adapted from the ESV]

If Yahweh were to speak this command to us in our day and time, I am convinced that He would embrace the entire Bible in the command rather than only the books of Moses. Therefore, in keeping with this passage, I encourage you to join me in devoting ourselves to God and His word as a lifelong pursuit.

                                  Your fellow servant,

Peter Briggs

Acknowledgments & Dedication

At the outset, I discussed how best to acknowledge contributions with members of the course development team. We considered two principal options, which were, first, to declare multiple authors, and, second, to formulate an Acknowledgments section to list significant contributors and their contributions. We decided on the second approach, since I would continue to function as the principal author and general editor. In addition to listing significant contributions below, footnotes in the TR place in evidence the chapters and sections which benefitted from substantial inputs from members of the course development team. Accordingly, I want to acknowledge with profound gratitude each of those who have helped and supported me in the development of the WitW study.

I am especially grateful to Louis Pecastaing for creating The Two Ways cover art used throughout the WitW Part 1 materials.

Dedication

The WitW study is dedicated to the Wanje family, who have been serving Christ and advancing His kingdom in Kenya, East Africa. It is especially dedicated to Rev. Morris Wanje and to his son James, together with James' wife, Chao.

Peter with Rev. Morris Wanje

Rev. Morris Wanje. As I learned during our visit to Kenya in August 2012, the WitW study is God's answer to the diligent prayers of a faithful servant of Christ, Rev. Morris Wanje. In the adjoining photograph, Morris is sitting next to me at a luncheon that was prepared in our honor in connection with our attending the morning worship service at the Fellowship Baptist Church in Malindi, Kenya on August 12th, 2012. During his many years of ministry, Morris Wanje planted over 60 churches in the coastal region of Kenya. Many of the pastors and church leaders who have been participating in our WitW training seminars are serving at the churches which Morris founded. As we sat together, he spoke to me as follows: "I have been praying for God to send someone to help our pastors learn to preach; thank you for being the answer to my prayer."

James & Chao Wanje. In the mid-1990s, Chao Mwachofi was a star student of mine at TSU. She later married James Wanje, and she and James have been working in Kenya under the auspices of Campus Crusade for over 10 years. During all that time, James has had a vision and has felt called of God to serve in an instrumental way to train and equip village pastors and church leaders to walk in the way of Christ and the apostles. This was so that they, in turn, could train and equip their families and the members of their churches to be fully devoted followers of Jesus Christ. It was at the invitation of James & Chao that we commenced development of the WitW study in 2010. James, supported by Chao, served as Director, WitW Project / Pan Africa from the inception of the project until June, 2014.

James & Chao Wanje with their sons, Morris & Francis

Michael & Antoninah Mutinda. Following our visit to Kenya in August 2012, Michael and Antoninah Mutinda joined our leadership team, and they have been contributing to the development of the WitW course materials and leading WitW training seminars since that time. Beginning in June 2014, Michael assumed the role of overall project leader for the

Michael & Antoninah Mutinda with Ezra and Debra

WitW Project / Pan Africa, and Antoninah assumed the role of overall training leader. We rejoice in the Lord greatly over their collaboration with us, and we express our gratitude for the contributions they have already made to the WitW Project / Pan Africa. Of particular note, Antoninah prototyped the chapter by chapter booklet format for the WitW SG, which we have now adopted as the publication format for the SG.

Project Team Structure

I have organized the WitW project into three teams, the participants of which are listed in the paragraphs which follow.

Theological Reader Development Team. As the principal author of the WitW TR, I express my profound gratitude to Rosemarie Briggs, Wu-Ching Cheng, Ruthanne Hamrick, Marcie Kinzer, Marian Meyer, Stephen Patterson, Rod Pauls, and Ron Rammage for assistance with various sections of the TR. Their specific contributions are acknowledged by means of footnotes.

Study Guide Development Team. My wife, Rosemarie, and our daughter, Ruthanne Hamrick, have been leading the development of the WitW SG, and we want to express our profound gratitude to Marcie Kinzer and Stephen Patterson for helping them in its development.

Consulting, Editing, and Proofreading Team. In addition to those already named, we want to express our gratitude to Darienne Dumas and Emily Fuller, who have served as proofreaders.

Chapter 1.
Introduction and Overview
of the WitW Study

Keynote Scripture Passage

The keynote Scripture passage for the entire WitW study is Colossians 2:6-7, in which Paul issues the following command:

> Therefore, as you received Christ Jesus the Lord, **so walk in Him**, rooted and built up in him and established in the faith, just as you were taught, abounding in thanksgiving. [Colossians 2:6–7, ESV, emphasis added]

We will have occasion to refer to this passage at several points in our study. My purpose in bringing it to your attention at this point is to place in evidence the clear biblical mandate that every disciple of Jesus Christ needs to acquire skill in **walking in the way of Christ and the apostles**, which is equivalent to walking in the Spirit and discerning and doing the will of God.

Overall Learning Objectives

The overall learning objective of the WitW study is to establish the disciple of Christ in the way of wisdom that leads to life. A second, and equally important, objective is to help the disciple to learn how to initiate and sustain the lifelong project of building a Christian worldview; [7] that is, a way of representing persons, circumstances, events, and things in his material time-space world that accords with Scripture rather than being derived from his natural intuition and lived experiences apart from God.

Learning Objectives for this Chapter

The learning objective for this 1st chapter of the WitW study is fivefold as follows:

- To grasp the significance of the biblical phrase **the way** as signifying our way of life or our lifestyle. In this connection, we briefly explore the history of the **way of Yahweh**, which is the way of wisdom that leads to life.

- To grasp and internalize the fact that there are two contrasting ways presented in Scripture: the way of the righteous or the way **wisdom** that leads to life; and the way of the wicked or the way of **folly** that leads to ruination and death. There is absolutely no middle ground or grey area between these two ways. You and I are either walking along one way or the other.

- To grasp and internalize the fact that theology – the study of God and His ways – is not just something that we believe, but rather it is **something that we both believe and practice**.

- To grasp and internalize the fact that theology should be **done in community**, not just in personal study. Moreover, **every disciple** of Christ needs to be trained in the doing of theology.

- Finally, to grasp and internalize the fact that every disciple of Christ needs to persist in the lifelong project of constructing a biblical worldview – that is, a **way of perceiving** persons, events, circumstances, and things through the eyes of Jesus Christ, which is to say through the lens of Scripture.

Biblical Basis and Motivation for Learning Objectives

In the following paragraphs, I bring forward the biblical basis and motivation for each of these learning objectives, including brief commentaries.

Walking in the Way. First, what is the biblical basis for the title of this study, *Walking in the Way of Christ & the Apostles*? In this connection, what is the history of the biblical concept of **the way**?

The phrase "the way of Yahweh" appears first in Genesis 18:19 in connection with Abraham. This phrase denotes a pattern of conduct – that is, a lifestyle which is in harmony with the nature and character of

Yahweh, the God of Israel. The 1st Psalm contrasts the way of the righteous – those who walk in the way of Yahweh – with the way of the wicked – those who refuse to walk in that way on account of their prideful rebellion against the righteous rule of God. Isaiah 26:8 speaks of "the path of your judgments," which links the way of Yahweh to the Torah. In Matthew 7:13-14 Jesus contrasts the narrow, restricted, and difficult way that leads to life with the broad and inviting way that leads to ruination and death. In John 14:6 He declares that He is "the way, the truth, and the life." Not only is He the singular way by which we can approach the living God, but His life uniquely defines the way of Yahweh.

The Way of Christ and the Apostles. Beginning with Acts 9:2, "the Way" is a technical term that designates the proper lifestyle for a disciple of Christ. As will become evident as our study unfolds, the way of Christ and the apostles is counterintuitive.

> *In fact, if we rely upon our natural intuition, lived experiences, and feelings apart from God we will fail!*

Only by patterning our lives in accordance with Scripture can we successfully navigate the way of Christ and the apostles. Thus, the WitW study is devoted to helping a disciple of Christ initiate and sustain his journey in this radically counterintuitive way.

Doing Theology and Building a Biblical Worldview

Theology is a word derived from two Greek words: *Theos* = God, and *logos* = a word or discourse. Thus, theology literally means **a word or discourse about God**. It designates a field of knowledge that derives from a study of God and His ways as revealed primarily through the inspired writings of the Bible.

I believe the short epistle of James provides an adequate biblical basis for my assertion that theology is to be practiced, not just believed, and that building a biblical worldview is critical to our success in walking in the way of Christ and the apostles. Allow me to briefly touch upon a number of assertions in James that motivate the WitW study.

Overview of the Epistle of James

Bible scholars have asserted that the structure and pattern of James' epistle is such that it corresponds to the Book of Proverbs in the Hebrew Scriptures. In his epistle, James moves from one principle of practical Christian living to the next without any apparent ordering. In fact, he may introduce a principle and then return to it later in the epistle. One needs to observe the amount of attention given to a particular principle in order to gauge its relative importance in the mind of the apostle.

Faith Without Works is Dead. This assertion is found in James 2:14ff. According to James, the kind of faith that brings salvation **invariably and necessarily engenders a Christian lifestyle** – that is, a pattern of behavior that accords with the Christian gospel. I would claim that this is James' thesis statement, the principal focus of his argument. Following is a concise statement which summarizes James' teaching in regard to the vital connection between saving faith and the works of faith:

> **"You only truly believe that which activates you."**

I heard this statement from the lips of a missionary leader forty years ago during a missions conference at our church. I encourage you to memorize it as I have, and keep it continually before your mind as a reminder that **saving faith necessarily engenders righteous behavior**.

Demons' Faith. To further establish James' assertion that theology is to be practiced, not merely believed, consider the 19th verse in the 2nd chapter:

> You believe that God is one; you do well. Even the demons believe – and shudder! [James 2:19, ESV]

The faith of demons is only an intellectual faith – merely a mental assent to facts concerning God. Their belief is not linked with behavior at all; in fact, they persist in behaving in a way that is contradictory to their theological belief. Accordingly, the disconnection between theological belief and behavior is the essential characteristic of CINOs – those who are Christian in name only.

Everyman's Theology. A corollary to my assertion that theology must be practiced is this: every disciple of Christ must be trained to do theology. While it is true that some of us must be trained more deeply and more rigorously in accordance with our calling from God, the idea that only the professionals, like pastors and seminary professors, need theological training is both false and damaging to the advancement of God's kingdom.

Where in Scripture might we turn to find a biblical mandate for my assertion that every disciple of Christ needs to be trained to do theology? In the 2nd chapter of 2 Timothy we find this command from the Apostle Paul to his disciple, Timothy:

> ... And what you have heard from me in the presence of many witnesses entrust to faithful men who will be able to teach others also. [2 Timothy 2:2, ESV]

In the opening verses of the 6th chapter of Hebrews, the apostle expresses the desire to take his audience beyond "the elementary doctrine of Christ and go on to maturity," thereby implying that the natural and normative progression of the Christian life is to become versed in the deep things of God. In the 3rd chapter of 1 Corinthians, Paul expresses the same desire. In each case, the apostle was concerned over a spiritual impediment in the lives of his audience that was preventing them from making progress toward maturity. The clear message derived from both passages is that for a Christian to remain stuck in "the elementary doctrine of Christ" is an **abnormal condition**. Like a baby, who progresses from his mother's milk to solid food, a disciple of Christ should progress from elementary doctrine to an ever deepening understanding of God and His ways.

Doing Theology in Community

My favorite passage in support of the assertion that theology should be done in community is found in the 3rd chapter of Malachi:

> Then those who feared Yahweh spoke with one another. And Yahweh gave attention and heard them, and a book of remembrance was written before Him concerning those who feared Yahweh and who esteemed His name. They shall be

> Mine, says Yahweh Sabaoth (= LORD of hosts), in the day
> when I make up My treasured possession, and I will spare
> them as a man spares his son who serves him. [Malachi
> 3:16-17, adapted from the ESV]

What were these people discussing that caused Yahweh to pay attention with pleasure, even delight? I suggest that they were speaking with one another concerning God and His ways. In other words, they were doing theology in community. A corresponding passage in the Christian Scriptures is Matthew 18:20, where Jesus promises to be present through the Holy Spirit wherever and whenever "two or three are gathered" in His name. Another passage in the Christian Scriptures which touches on doing theology in community is found toward the end of the 2nd chapter of Acts:

> And they devoted themselves to the apostles' teaching and
> the fellowship, to the breaking of bread and the prayers.
> [Acts 2:42, ESV]

It seems that the 1st century Christians did theology around the supper table, as depicted in Figure 1-1.

Figure 1-1. Doing Theology Over Supper

It is difficult to identify a clearly prescriptive and normative biblical mandate for doing theology in community. However, based upon years of teaching in accordance with this method, my assessment is that its benefits are both rich and plentiful.

> *This is what I have repeatedly experienced: when the people of God gather to discuss with one another the things pertaining to God and His ways, a synergy develops whereby insights and concepts emerge which exceed the sum of the individual contributions of the group members. This is undoubtedly the result of the powerful ministry of the Holy Spirit.*

Therefore, the WitW study is designed around theological discussion as the principal environment for achieving the learning objectives of the study.

Building a Biblical Worldview

This is the focus of chapter 3, which is entitled The Bible as a Representational System. A principal objective of that chapter is to establish from Scripture that our embracing and practicing a biblical worldview determines whether we are walking in the way of wisdom that leads to life versus the way of folly that leads to ruination and death. Thus, my purpose in this introductory chapter is only to touch upon the biblical rationale for building a biblical worldview.

Returning to the epistle of James, consider the unit of thought in James 1:2-18. As is typical of James' argument, this paragraph-length passage moves from one principle to the next in a way that challenges our recognition of a single idea that runs through the entire passage. The ESV Study Bible proposes that the integrative idea upon which the passage is focused is **the testing of our faith**. While I would embrace this proposal as helpful, I want to focus on the **trajectory** of James' argument in the passage. In particular, let us take note of James' statements that mandate a biblical worldview – that is, a way of seeing persons, events, circumstances, and things in accordance with the power, love, and promises of God as contrasted with our natural intuition apart from God. I observe seven representational statements in this short passage as follows:

- **James 1:2-4**. Trials and testings should be represented as beneficial rather than grievous. This is true on account of the progress toward spiritual maturity that they bring about.

- **James 1:5-8**. God is represented as the sole source of wisdom, and He will give it to us abundantly in response to our prayers of faith.

- **James 1:9-11**. In God's economy, those who are poor and lowly in this life should be represented as exalted, and those who are rich should be represented as abased.

- **James 1:12**. Remaining steadfast under trial – that is, patiently enduring in the face of adversity – gives rise to heavenly treasure, which reinforces James' first point.

- **James 1:13-16**. Temptations – that is, solicitations toward evil – should be represented as originating in our fallen natures and not from God.

- **James 1:17**. In contrast, gifts that are good (that is, beneficial) and perfect (that is, giving rise to spiritual completeness) should be represented as coming down from God. Moreover, God should be represented as steady and constant in His desire to do good on behalf of His people who love, fear, and trust Him.

- **James 1:18**. God Himself should be represented as the source of true life, for He has brought us into being by the instrumentality of His word. Moreover, we, as His people, should represent ourselves as a firstfruits offering unto God. In other words, we are like the firstfruits offering prescribed in Exodus 23:16. Under the terms of the old covenant, as God's people presented their firstfruits offerings unto Yahweh, He responded by consecrating and blessing the entire harvest.

The density of representational ideas expressed by James in this short passage should be sufficient to convince you that our building a biblical worldview is critical to our success in walking in the way of Christ and the apostles.

Theology as a Verb: Some Initial Definitions

I believe we have adequately established a biblical basis and motivation for pursuing the five learning objectives for this introductory chapter that were stated at the outset. Allow me now to offer up four important definitions that will form a framework for the entire WitW study.

- **Doing theology**. In the WitW study, I define theology as a set of concepts and principles that govern **behavior**, rather than merely **belief**. Accordingly, I define **doing theology** as the **discipline** of deriving theological, moral, and ethical principles from Scripture through proper hermeneutical procedure and skillfully applying those principles to the practical issues of life and ministry in community and in culture. [8]

- **Theological education**. Moreover, I define **theological education** as the learning process by which those who have embraced Jesus Christ as Savior, and have placed themselves under His authority as Lord and King, acquire skill in doing theology. The scope and rigor of theological education required by a disciple of Christ is a function of his **ministry identity**, defined as the unique profile of talents and endowments that determine the particular set of ministry arenas in which he can perform with great power, impact, and fruitfulness.

- **Theology as habitus**. I define **theology as habitus** as the desired outcome of theological education whereby the disciple habitually applies theological principles to all aspects of life and ministry, and he thereby walks in the way of Christ and the apostles; that is, the way of wisdom that leads to life, as opposed to the way of folly that leads to ruination and death. [9]

- **Theology for every disciple**. In accordance with the foregoing definitions, **every disciple of Christ needs to acquire skill in doing theology**. In fact, to live and minister as a disciple of Christ requires the doing of theology. The reason for this is that the way of Christ and the apostles is **radically counterintuitive**. Only by habitually aligning our thinking process to the language of Scripture are we able to live and walk as disciples of Jesus Christ.

Integrative Study Process

The **Integrative Study Process (ISP)** presented in Figure 1-2 describes the pattern and flow of the biblical theology method practiced throughout the WitW study, especially in the formulation of the SG. As delineated in Figure 1-2, the ISP consists of three major stages: **Study the Scriptures**, **Share Learning in Community**, and **Apply the Principles**. In the following paragraphs, each of the stages in the process is briefly described.

Study the Scriptures

This is the first of the three major stages in the ISP. We emphasize Scripture as the **primary source** of theological information, which has been exemplified by our establishment of the biblical base for this chapter's learning objectives. Moreover, we study and interpret the biblical text according to the methods of biblical and exegetical theology

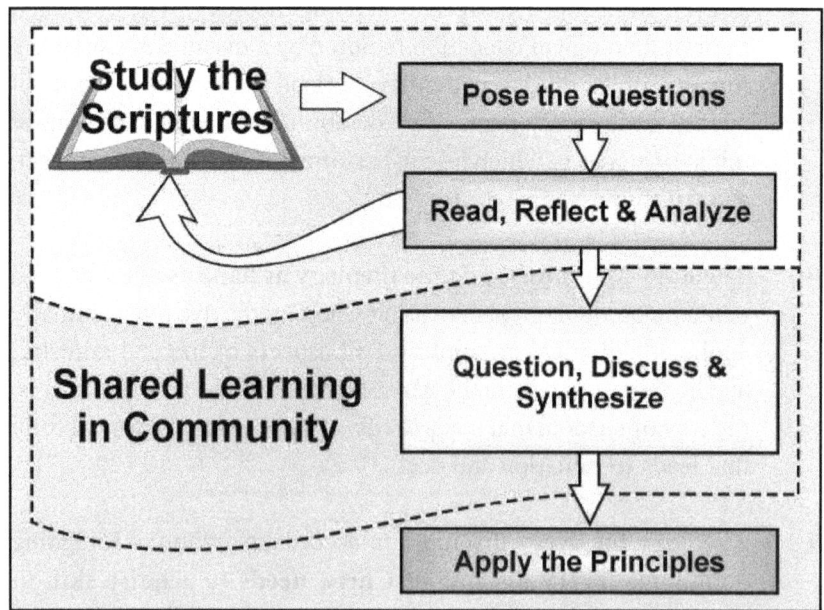

Figure 1-2. Integrative Study Process

whereby the meaning intended by the author is sought by paying careful attention to the theological, historical, cultural, canonical, and linguistic context of a given book or passage. [10]

Each of the SG booklets consists of a number chapters or sessions, with each session being directed toward a specific learning objective. As delineated in Figure 1-2, in each of the SG sessions, the Study the Scriptures phase follows a cyclical pattern. Scripture readings are interspersed with questions and commentary for reading, reflection, and analysis. In general, the commentary included in the SG is derived from the TR, and, of course, each student can access the entire TR as well. A summary is included at the conclusion of each session to ensure that the learning objective for the session is attained.

Shared Learning in Community

This is the second major stage in the ISP. The principal learning environment for the entire WitW study is Socratic group discussion facilitated by a trained teacher / leader. The preferred venue for such discussion is a church-based setting. As explained in Appendix C in TR4, I prefer to characterize the group discussion as **Shared Learning in Community (SLIC)**. Earlier in this chapter, I have quoted one of my favorite Scripture passages from the 3rd chapter of Malachi, which expresses the delight that Yahweh experiences when His people gather to discuss with one another the things pertaining to Him and His ways – that is, when they gather to do theology in community. In the same context, I also referred to Jesus' promise that He would be present by means of His Spirit when even two or three meet in His name. **Accordingly, the most important and powerful factor in the SLIC discussion is the presence of the Living God.** By means of His Spirit, He enables group insights to emerge that transcend what the individual participants – even the teacher / leader – bring to the discussion.

Apply the Principles

As delineated in Figure 1-2, the third and final stage of the ISP is to apply the principles learned from each chapter of the WitW study – in other words, each SG booklet – to the practice of life and ministry. The teacher / leader is responsible for helping each student tailor and shape an application project that is best aligned with his ministry identity.[11] The application project should correspond with the learning objectives for a given chapter, and, to the maximum extent possible, it should reflect answers to the questions addressed throughout the chapter. The application project selected for a given chapter can be tailored and shaped from the following five typical application modules:

- **Preaching application module**. Under the supervision of your teacher / leader, prepare a sequence of messages that teach the content of the chapter to your congregation. Arrange for a select group of three or four members of the congregation to prepare written assessments of your messages that places in evidence how well they present the main points of the chapter.

- **Teaching application module**. Under the supervision of your teacher / leader, prepare a sequence of lessons, such as for a children's Sunday School class, that teaches the content of the chapter to the class members. Arrange for either your teacher / leader, or another qualified person, such as an elder of your church, to observe your teaching and prepare a written assessment that places in evidence how well the class members seemed to internalize the main points of the chapter.

- **Apologetic interaction module**. Under the supervision of your teacher / leader, package the content of the chapter into a set of talking points for either an evangelistic conversation that you will have with a family member, friend, neighbor, or work associate, or an exhortatory conversation that you will have with a weak or erring disciple. Work out a means for obtaining an evaluation of the effectiveness of your conversation which is mutually acceptable to your teacher / leader and the person with whom you are to converse. For example, a fellow student who understands the chapter content could sit in as an observer.

- **Personal development module**. Under the supervision of your teacher / leader, map out and execute a path for deepened discipleship that entails practicing the content of the chapter in your life and ministry. Evaluative feedback could be obtained through your teacher / leader or one or more of your fellow students, who know the chapter content, to observe your life and ministry over a period of time.

- **Research application module**. Under the supervision of your teacher / leader, map out and execute a research project that would entail a deeper engagement with the content of the chapter. Evaluation of your project by your teacher / leader could be accomplished either by your preparing a written paper, or by your presenting the results of your research orally.

WitW Study Overview: Summary of Each Chapter

I have included in the WitW study only that teaching which I consider to be essential for the disciple of Christ to grasp in order to successfully navigate his pilgrimage in the way of Christ and the apostles. I have been guided in my selection of what material to include by the following two factors: first, the teaching priorities of the Apostle Paul, especially in his early epistles; and, second, the teaching that is needed for the disciple to have and to be governed by the mind of Christ.

The WitW study is divided into three major parts with a number of chapters included in each part. The paragraphs which follow summarize the content of each of the seventeen chapters.

Part 1 – Foundational Concepts

Part 1 of the WitW study consists of six chapters, which are summarized in the following paragraphs. SG booklets 1 through 6 correspond to the six chapters of Part 1.

Chapter 1. Introduction and Overview of the WitW Study. The 1st chapter includes the overall learning objective for the WitW study, the five learning objectives for the chapter, the establishment of a biblical basis and motivation for these learning objectives, a presentation and discussion of the Integrative Study Process, and a chapter-by-chapter summary of the entire WitW study.

Chapter 2. The Storyline of the Bible: the Bible as True Narrative. A principal thesis of the WitW study is that we must always engage with the text of Scripture within the framework of the storyline of the Bible – that is, the overall message of the Bible. In this connection, we need to recognize that most of Scripture is narrative. In fact, I assert that the Bible is **true narrative**, and its property of being true narrative means that valid generalizations in the form of theological, moral, and ethical principles can be derived from it. Therefore, the stature of the Bible as true narrative is crucial to our doing theology in the manner defined above. The 2nd chapter includes Scripture quotations that support the proposed storyline formulation and provide the context for defining a number of important theological terms.

Chapter 3. The Bible as a Representational System. The point of the 3rd chapter is twofold as follows:

- **Understanding the Bible as a representational system.** The Bible is a representational system that defines all reality, and it is absolutely normative for all people, periods, and places. As embraced by the disciple of Christ, it governs all of life and ministry.

- **Life-critical importance of embracing the Bible's representation of reality.** It is of life-critical importance for the disciple to embrace the Bible's representation of reality. In fact, to do so is the key to the **way of wisdom**; God bestows blessing upon those who walk in this way, and its end is eternal life. To do otherwise is the **way of folly**, and those who walk in that way are subject to the cursing of God. Moreover, its end is ruination and death.

Chapter 4. Discovering the Meaning of Biblical Books and Passages. If our walking in accordance with the Bible's representation of reality is life-critical, and if the Bible is the primary source of godly representations, then our rightly handling of the biblical text as disciples of Christ is also life-critical. In the 4th chapter I summarize the principles of rightly handling the biblical text with a view toward deriving from it normative theological, moral, and ethical principles to govern all of life and ministry. This is done not only in general, but also for the four principal literary genres found in Scripture, which are narrative or story, Hebrew poetry, didactic or teaching literature, and apocalyptic literature

– that is, prophetical text which is dominated by figures of speech, symbols, and word pictures.

Chapter 5. Torah: The Fountainhead of Wisdom. Not only is the Torah – that is, the five books of Moses – the fountainhead of wisdom, but also there are fourteen integrative motifs or themes that surface in the Torah and that run through all of Scripture. Even as the storyline formulation affords an overall interpretive framework for understanding the trajectory of biblical teaching, each of the integrative motifs affords an interpretive framework for tracing important strands of teaching from creation to the end of history.

Chapter 6. The Two-Part Christian Gospel. The Christian gospel sets forth God's purpose and program for completely obliterating the effects of the invasion of evil, sin, and death into the cosmos. It consists of two equally important, mutually complementary, and interconnected aspects or components.

- **The gospel of the kingdom of God**. The gospel of the kingdom of God dominates the Synoptic Gospels (i.e., Matthew, Mark, and Luke) and the Book of Acts. It confronts human prideful rebellion against the righteous rule of God, and it appeals most strongly to the Jewish mind.

- **The gospel of God**. The gospel of God is actually introduced in the Gospel of John, and it dominates the epistles, especially those of Paul. It confronts human bondage to evil, sin, and death, and it appeals most strongly to the Gentile mind.

Part 2 – The Gospel of the Kingdom of God

Part 2 of the WitW study consists of six chapters, which are summarized in the following paragraphs. SG booklets 7 through 12 correspond to the six chapters of Part 2.

Chapter 7. Authority of the King. The preface to the Great Commission in Matthew 28:18 is Christ's assertion of His kingly authority over the entire universe, which was evidently conferred by God the Father in connection with Jesus' resurrection according to Psalm 2,

Acts 13:33, Romans 1:4, 1 Corinthians 15:27ff, Philippians 2:5ff, and Colossians 1:15ff.

Chapter 8. Called by the King. Chapters 8, 9, and 10 form a trilogy on the biblical representation of Christian discipleship:

- Chapter 8 answers the question as to what Christ's call into discipleship and a person's response to that call should look like.

- Chapter 9 answers the question as to the meaning of discipleship in terms of the fruit that we would expect to see in the disciple's life in two areas: life thrust toward Christlikeness and ministry identity.

- Chapter 10 answers the question as to what developed and sustained disciplines should characterize the disciple's life from the instant of his responding to Christ's call until the end of his life.

In the 8th chapter I examine each of the calling episodes recorded in Scripture in order to derive from them normative principles governing the proper response to the call of Christ into discipleship. In particular, the following four normative factors are identified: (1) recognition of the supreme value of relationship with Jesus Christ; (2) immediate and unequivocal obedience; (3) attunement to the King's voice; and, (4) life thrust toward Christlikeness.

Chapter 9. Meaning of Discipleship. There are two aspects to discipleship that are discussed in this chapter. First, the disciple's life should clearly manifest the development of Christian virtues. Second, Christ's call is not to a religious experience of salvation, but rather to a **specific ministry identity**, which means each disciple is endowed with a unique set of gifts that enables him to operate in a corresponding set of ministry arenas with great power and fruitfulness.

In the first major section of this chapter, I unpack Peter's teaching in 2 Peter 1:3-11 under the heading of Manifestation of Christian Virtues. The necessary result of the personality of Jesus Christ being reproduced from within the heart of the disciple is that his life begins to look like the life of Jesus Christ. In Galatians 5:22-23, Paul represents the reproduction of the nature and character of Jesus Christ in terms of the ninefold fruit of the Holy Spirit: love, joy, peace, patience, kindness, goodness, faithfulness, gentleness, and self-control. And, in 2 Peter 1:3-11, Peter represents the reproduction of Jesus' nature and character in terms of the seven virtues of the Christian life: moral excellence, experiential knowledge, self-control, patient endurance, godliness, brotherly kindness, and self-sacrificing love.

In the second major section of the chapter, I unpack the concept of **ministry identity**, including practical tips for discovering your ministry identity.

Finally, by way of a summative overview of both the manifestation of Christian virtues and the disciple's ministry identity, this chapter concludes with a section on **walking in the Spirit**.

Chapter 10. Disciplines of the Kingdom. The following seven disciplines of the Christian life are emphasized in the teachings of Jesus Christ:

- **Discipline of loving God and others**. The discipline of loving God and others is a carryover from the Hebrew Scriptures. The disciplines of the word and of prayer are subsumed beneath the discipline of loving God.

    - **Discipline of the word**. The disciple's love for the word of God emanates from his love of God.

    - **Discipline of prayer**. In like manner, the disciple's love for communion with God through prayer emanates from his love of God.

- **Discipline of covenant-keeping**. This is another carryover from the Hebrew Scriptures.

- **Discipline of peace-making**. The disciple of Jesus Christ promotes peace as opposed to conflict, and he is skilled in resolving conflict whenever it occurs.

- **Discipline of truth-telling**. This is another carryover from the Hebrew Scriptures.

- **Discipline of money management**. Jesus had much to say about our attitude toward money and the things which money affords to us.

- **Discipline of following Jesus**. The disciples initially understood this in the rabbinical sense of literally following Jesus Christ and learning to walk in His way. Jesus added to that concept the need to follow Him to the cross.

- **Discipline of reproduction**. The discipline of reproduction emanates directly from the Great Commission mandate of Matthew 28:18-20.

Chapter 11. Household of the King. As we examine Scripture, the fact becomes evident that God has ordained that human societies be ordered in certain ways to reflect His nature and character and to mediate His authority to the world of mankind. In the first major section of this chapter, I derive from Scripture normative principles that govern the ordering of four spheres: the household or family, the covenant community of God's people, employment or vocational ministry, and civil government.

In the second major section of the chapter, I discuss how the church fathers adapted and extended the apostolic ordering of the church in order to accommodate a burgeoning number of disciples and churches toward the end of the 1st century and the beginning of the 2nd.

Chapter 12. Second Coming of the King. The whole motivation for diligence in the disciplines of the Christian life emanates from the teaching that one day Jesus Christ will return to gather His elect unto Himself and judge all mankind for the things done in this life. So important is this teaching that each of the three Synoptic Gospels includes a version of the Olivet Discourse, which was given by Jesus explicitly to answer the disciples' questions concerning the signs that would signal the imminence of His return and of the end of the age.

Part 3 – The Gospel of God

Part 3 of the WitW study consists of five chapters, which are summarized in the following paragraphs. SG booklets 13 through 17 correspond to the five chapters of Part 3.

Chapter 13. Introduction to the Gospel of God. The Gospel of John serves as an introduction to the gospel of God. It does this in two ways: first, by focusing attention on Jesus Christ as the one and only Son of God; and, second, by focusing attention on our proper response to His coming into the world, which is to believe into His name and receive Him as the One He claimed to be. The structure of the Fourth Gospel is built around seven **I AM** pronouncements of Jesus Christ and seven associated authenticating signs. By means of the seven **I AM** pronouncements, John places in evidence that Jesus clearly and repeatedly claimed to be the One who revealed Himself as Yahweh to Moses in the Burning Bush episode recorded in the 3rd chapter of Exodus. By means of the seven authenticating signs, John progressively builds a compelling body of evidence that Jesus was exactly who He claimed to be.

Chapter 14. Reason for the Gospel of God. The Apostle Paul devotes much of the first three chapters of the Epistle to the Romans to establishing a forensic or judicial case against the entire human race. In accordance with Paul's argument, God is not only the divine Judge, but also the offended party. God has revealed His righteous requirements for mankind by imbedding them into the human conscience and by codifying them in the Mosaic law. Not only are men guilty of transgressing these righteous requirements, but it is our nature to do so. In other words, we transgress because our nature is corrupt. By the conclusion of Paul's indictment in Romans 3:20, he has painted a picture of mankind in bondage to evil, sin, and death; a bondage so deep and pervasive that there is absolutely nothing we can do to release ourselves from it. If we are to be delivered, our deliverance must come from God.

Chapter 15. Content of the Gospel of God. I turn to Hebrews 4:2 to place in evidence the two-part structure of the gospel of God. [12] It consists of two complementary and interconnected components as follows: (1) deliverance from bondage to evil, sin, and death; and, (2) deliverance into an eternal Sabbath rest after a period of conflict and conquest.

This two-part gospel was richly enacted in the life of the nation of Israel in the Exodus and Conquest episodes. Through the plagues of Exodus and under the leadership of Moses, Yahweh powerfully delivered His people from bondage in Egypt. Later, under the leadership of Joshua, Yahweh delivered His people into rest in the promised land of Canaan. In the Epistle to the Romans, the Apostle Paul is occupied primarily with the exposition of the first aspect of the gospel of God.

Chapter 16. Perversions of the Christian Gospel. In the days of the Apostle Paul, there were two cardinal perversions of the Christian gospel; namely, **antinomianism** and **legalism**. In this chapter I discuss both the ancient and modern forms of these two perversions. Additionally, I discuss other heresies which have arisen over the course of the church age and have corrupted our understanding of the Christian gospel.

Chapter 17. Application of the Gospel of God. The 17th and concluding chapter consists of a survey of Paul's establishing priorities in his early epistles; that is, the teaching which the great apostle to the Gentiles considered as essential to establishing new disciples in the way of Christ and the apostles. By this means, I develop a profile of the lifestyle of a disciple of Jesus Christ according to the Apostle Paul.

Overview of the Appendices

Each of the ten appendices is briefly summarized in the following paragraphs:

> **Appendix A** presents a glossary of theological terms encountered in the WitW study.
>
> **Appendix B** summarizes the methods of biblical and exegetical theology.
>
> **Appendix C** describes the Socratic discussion method as applied throughout the WitW study.

Appendix D consists of a paper entitled *The Student, The Fish, and Agassiz*. It places in evidence the critical importance of careful observation, and it is presented in support of chapter 4, Discovering the Meaning of Biblical Books and Passages.

Appendix E presents two tools for analyzing the grammatical structure of didactic (i.e., teaching) passages of Scripture. They are **verbal purview** and **diagramming**. Both serve to focus the mind upon the literary clues embedded in the biblical text by which the author has conveyed his intended meaning.

Appendix F presents an analysis of the perplexing interaction between the sovereign grace of God and human responsibility.

Appendix G presents a model gospel proclamation which is consistent with the two-part Christian gospel presented and discussed in the WitW study.

Appendix H, entitled *A Testament of Devotion*, includes four components. First, it lists the twelve components of the manifold wisdom of God, thereby presenting an outline of the way of wisdom that leads to life. Second, it lists the seven components of the faith of Jesus Christ, which, according to the Apostle Paul, must abide in each disciple of Christ in order for us to be declared righteous and in order for us to successfully walk in the way of Christ and the apostles. Third, it summarizes the seven virtues of the Christian life according to the Apostle Peter in 2 Peter 1:3-15. Fourth, it presents a model prayer journal, including suggested Scriptures for memorization and recitation during your prayer time and a chronological listing of Scriptures for reading through the entire Bible in one year.

Appendix J, entitled *A Tale of Two Trees: From Defeat to Glorious Victory*, is a dramatic narrative which portrays the glorious plan of redemption for mankind.

Achieving the Overall Learning Objectives of the WitW Study

I stated at the outset that the preferred venue for teaching the WitW study is a church-based setting. In our experience, the optimum schedule for completing the 3-part study would be to complete each of the parts in a semester-length period of about 15 weeks, with each discussion session being at least two hours in length. Thus, the entire study could be completed in three semester-length periods and would involve about 90 hours of class time. The primary resource would be the 17 chapter-by-chapter SG booklets. However, the teacher / leader would need to study the four TR volumes, TR1 through TR4. Furthermore, the students should be encouraged to avail themselves of the TRs as well.

Following is a checklist for the teacher / leader:

- Before the first class meeting, the teacher / leader will assess the total number of SG sessions to be covered, and he will formulate a study plan that apportions these across the number of weeks that the class will meet. In our experience, covering one SG session in a 2-hour discussion is a pace that is appropriate for a typical church-based class.

- The teacher / leader will ensure that the students obtain the course materials well before the 1st class session. All students will need a copy of the SG, and some may desire a copy of the TR as well.

- The teacher / leader will issue the homework assignment for the 1st discussion session in time for the students to complete it before the session meets.

- The teacher / leader will prepare short lectures to introduce the overall WitW study, each of the three parts thereof, and each of the SG booklets that make up a given part of the study.

- At the beginning of the 1st discussion session for one of the parts of the WitW study, the teacher / leader will introduce himself to the class and elicit from each of the class members a brief introduction, including the student's expectations for the study.

- After the personal introductions, the teacher / leader will introduce the overall WitW study to the class, including overall learning objectives and a walkthrough of the course materials. He will then introduce the part of the study that is to be addressed, including learning objectives for that part. Finally, he will introduce the 1st SG booklet in the series for the part, including learning objectives for that booklet.

- As each SG booklet in the series is completed, the teacher / leader will introduce the next booklet, including its learning objectives. He will also encourage the class members to begin sharing what they have learned with family members and friends.

- At the conclusion of each discussion session, the teacher / leader will ensure that the students understand the homework assignment for the next discussion session.

- The teacher / leader will call attention to the life and ministry application project that each student needs to complete for each SG booklet.

- In connection with the life and ministry application projects, the teacher / leader will arrange to meet with each student, either individually or in small groups, in order to tailor a set of projects that correspond to the chapter-by-chapter learning objectives as well as to the student's ministry identity.

- In the case of a large class, the teacher / leader will facilitate the organization of the class into small groups for mutual encouragement and support in completing the homework assignments between the weekly class meetings.

Questions for Discussion

1. Having read this introductory chapter, thereby acquiring a sense of the contents of the WitW study, state in your own words your personal expectations and learning objectives for the WitW study.

2. The church needs to proactively do theology in community with respect to pressing cultural issues, such as recreational drug use and gay marriage. Select such a subject that is relevant to your cultural situation, and bring biblical teaching to bear upon it through group discussion.

Notes & Reflections

Use the space below to record additional insights and commentary resulting from your studies thus far.

Chapter 2.
Storyline of the Bible:
The Bible as True Narrative

A distinctive – perhaps even unique – feature of the WitW study is its focus on biblical narrative. In fact, a principal tenet of the entire WitW study is that we must always engage with the text of Scripture within the framework of the storyline of the Bible; that is, the overall message of what the Bible is about.

> *In other words, the storyline of the Bible defines the framework for doing theology.*

In this connection, we need to recognize that most of Scripture is narrative. In fact, I assert that the Bible is **true narrative**, and its property of being true narrative means that generalizations in the form of theological, moral, and ethical principles can be derived from it. If it were not true, then it could not support such generalizations. Therefore, the stature of the Bible as true narrative is crucial to our deriving from the text of Scripture valid, normative, and authoritative principles for guiding and directing life and ministry. This chapter includes Scripture quotations that support the proposed storyline formulation and provide the context for defining a number of important theological terms.

Learning Objective

The learning objective for this chapter is to come to grips with and internalize the principle that the storyline of the Bible defines the framework for doing theology. The storyline of the Bible corresponds to the overall message of what the Bible is about. After presenting a proposed formulation of the Bible's storyline, which has been derived through a lifetime of study of Scripture, I focus on a number of passages that serve as biblical pillars which support the formulation. This is not an exercise in proof-texting, for each of the passages is being read in a manner consistent with its literary context. Finally, I pose four questions that are motivated by the storyline of the Bible.

The Bible as a Representational System

Viewing the Bible as a **representational system** is a concept that is discussed at length in chapter 3. The Bible's stature as an authoritative representational system is the logically necessary consequence of its property of being **true narrative**. [13]

The Bible as True Narrative

According to the theory of true narratives propounded by John Oller, only a true narrative is capable of supporting and sustaining valid generalizations. Therefore, since a theological, moral, or ethical principle derived from Scripture is a form of generalization, its validity, normativeness, and authority depend on the biblical narrative being true. [14]

Hebraic View of History

Stanley Grenz and John Franke [15] address the unique understanding of history that the Jews introduced to the ancient world; that is, a **linear** as contrasted with a **cyclical** view. Referring to Figure 2-1, according to Jewish thought, history began at a definite point in time which I designate the **Alpha Event** – creation *ex nihilo* by Yahweh Elohim – and it will end at a definite future point in time, the **Omega Event** – the *telos* or the logical terminus or ending point – when Yahweh Elohim brings all things to their proper consummation according to His sovereign purpose and for His glory. Between these two events stretches the timeline of the biblical narrative. Intermediate between the Alpha and Omega Events is a pivotal event that occurred approximately 2,000 years ago, the **Chi Event** – the Christ event. Furthermore, very soon after the Alpha Event, the invasion

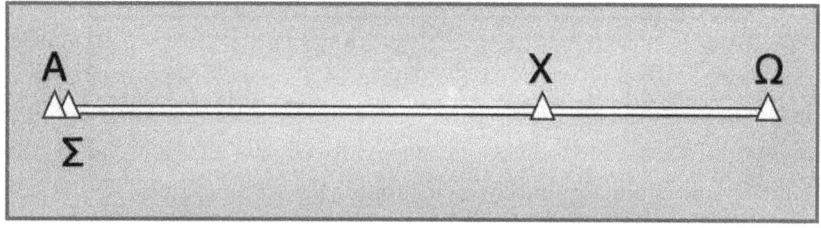

Figure 2-1. Time Line of the Biblical Narrative

of evil, sin, and death into the cosmos took place, which is designated the **Sigma Event**.

To **determine** is to authoritatively fix or specify; this is an important technical term in our discussion of the Bible as a representational system in chapter 3. However, in the present discussion I need to employ this term in regard to the four key events identified in Figure 2-1. And so here is my assertion:

> ***The biblical narrative which records these four events is determinative with respect to everything that is.*** [16]

Is this assertion true, and, if so, what is its significance?

In the case of each of the four key events, our modern culture has contrived and fabricated a narrative which opposes and contradicts the biblical narrative. By placing in evidence the vast difference between the implications of the biblical narrative and its contrary counterpart, I will endeavor to convince you of both the truthfulness and the importance of the assertion above. However, before I do, I need to present another, even more fundamental, assertion, which is this:

> ***All manner of material facts, including all scientific observations, are inherently indeterminate.***

This is another important axiom in the theory of true narratives propounded by John Oller. In other words, material facts themselves contain no declaration of their significance and relationship with other material facts. To interpret them requires that we bring a narrative to bear upon them. If the narrative is true, then our interpretation of the facts has the potential of being correct; however, if the narrative is false, then I can **guarantee** that our interpretation of the facts will be incorrect.

The Determinativeness of the Biblical Narrative of the Alpha Event

First, according to the record of the Alpha Event in the first two chapters of Genesis, God designed and shaped the entire cosmos, including all life forms. That is, the design, shape, makeup, significance, and interrelationship of everything in the cosmos was **determined** by Yahweh Elohim, the Infinite Personal God who is really there. Furthermore, according to a literal reading of the Genesis 1 narrative, He accomplished this feat in an incredibly short period of time.

Notice how modern science has contrived and fabricated an **opposing narrative of the Alpha Event**. In particular, it is postulated that an unguided, impersonal, random process operating over immense stretches of time has brought into being everything that is. In other words, according to this opposing narrative of the Alpha Event, the Infinite Personal God who is really there is replaced by what amounts to an **infinite time-plus-chance machine**.

The implications of choosing this alternative narrative of the Alpha Event are huge in regard to human personhood and significance. According to the infinite time-plus-chance machine explanation for the cosmos, I am **determined** to be nothing more than a **complex machine** as a matter of logical necessity, and those aspects of my makeup which distinguish me from others are entirely the result of an unguided, impersonal, random process. With this as the controlling narrative of the Alpha Event, I have no significance or purpose beyond that **which I may determine for myself**. When the machine which is me wears out, as it inevitably does, I cease to exist. On the other hand, in accordance with the biblical narrative of the Alpha Event, I am **determined** to be a **person**, specially created according to the image and likeness of my Infinite Personal Creator who is really there. I am crafted by Him to fulfill a specific purpose in this life and to realize an eternal destiny in the life to come.

In sum, for me to choose the infinite time-plus-chance narrative **is equivalent to suicide of my personhood**. In other words, by means of this choice, I transform myself into a **self-determined thing** rather than a person as a matter of logical necessity. On the other hand, in accordance with the biblical narrative of the Alpha Event, there is a cosmic significance and purpose for my being, which is determined by God and not by me.

I hope you are beginning to recognize the critical importance of the concept of determinativeness in relation to the Alpha Event. Let us now turn to the second key event identified in Figure 2-1, the Sigma Event.

The Determinativeness of the Biblical Narrative of the Sigma Event

On the basis of the biblical narrative of the Sigma Event, together with those of the divine judgments which resulted from that event, [17] I make the following assertion:

> *The Sigma Event, together with the divine judgments that resulted therefrom, are determinative with respect to all aspects of the physical, moral, and ethical landscape of the world in which we live.*

In other words, properly representing the world in which we live, including historical and current events, requires an understanding of the biblical narrative of the Sigma Event and the ensuing divine judgments, especially the Flood of Noah as recorded in Genesis 6 – 9.

Once again, notice how modern science has contrived and fabricated an alternative narrative of the Sigma Event. In fact, according to a Darwinian understanding of ancient human history, the Sigma Event recorded in the Bible never happened. Instead, man has evolved on a steadily upward trajectory over immense stretches of time from a primitive state to modern *homo sapiens*.

And so we have two competing narratives of the Sigma Event: the biblical narrative, which represents that mankind suffered a radical Fall, which was precipitated by the prideful rebellion of our first parents against the righteous rule of God; and the Darwinian narrative, which represents that the Fall never took place, but, instead, mankind has been on a steadily upward evolutionary trajectory over the course of immense stretches of time. In opposition to the Darwinian narrative, the biblical narrative of the Sigma Event teaches us that the impact of Adam's transgression has reverberated down through the millennia, such that all mankind effectively participated in Adam's disobedience. Moreover, according to the biblical narrative, mankind has been on a downward, rather than upward, trajectory ever since the Sigma Event.

How should we go about illustrating the vast difference between these two competing narratives of the Sigma Event? I have chosen the philosophy of civil government as the vehicle for representing the contrast between these two narratives. If the founders of a nation or the leaders of a people embrace the biblical narrative, what kind of government would they put in place and practice? And, in contrast, if the founders of a nation or the leaders of a people embrace the Darwinian narrative, what kind of government would they put in place and practice?

We can observe two modern case studies that provide answers to these questions. The first is the United States of America, whose founders deliberately designed a **constitutional republic** in accordance with the biblical narrative of the Sigma Event. In particular, they expressly put in place limitations, checks, and balances to restrain human iniquity, especially that within the hearts of the leaders of the nation. And the second is Nazi Germany under Adolf Hitler, who embraced the Darwinian narrative.

What are the enduring fruits of these two philosophies of government? The legacy of the fascist government of Adolf Hitler is the Holocaust; that is, the execution of millions of Jews and Christians, who were regarded as a threat to his rule and racially inferior to the Germans. In contrast, the legacy of the American constitutional republic is unparalleled blessing and prosperity, as symbolized by the Statue of Liberty standing at the entrance to New York's harbor.

The Determinativeness of the Biblical Narrative
of the Chi Event

There are a number of brief summations of the biblical narrative of the Chi Event to which we could turn. Of these, I have selected three: two biblical summations and the Nicene Creed.

First Biblical Summation: Titus 2:11-14. The first biblical summation of the Chi Event is found in the 2nd chapter of Paul's letter to Titus:

> For the grace of God has appeared, bringing salvation for all people, training us to renounce ungodliness and worldly passions, and to live self-controlled, upright, and godly lives in the present age, waiting for our blessed hope, the appearing of the glory of our great God and Savior Jesus Christ, who gave Himself for us to redeem us from all lawlessness and to purify for Himself a people for His own possession who are zealous for good works. [Titus 2:11–14, adapted from the ESV]

Second Biblical Summation: 1 John 5:9-12. The second biblical summation of the Chi Event is found in the 5th chapter of John's 1st epistle:

> If we receive the testimony of men, the testimony of God is greater, for this is the testimony of God that He has borne concerning His Son. Whoever believes into the Son of God has the testimony in himself. Whoever does not believe God has made Him a liar, because he has not believed into the testimony that God has borne concerning His Son. And this is the testimony, that God gave us eternal life, and this life is in His Son. Whoever has the Son has life; whoever does not have the Son of God does not have life. [1 John 5:9-12, adapted from the ESV]

The Nicene Creed. Following is the Nicene Creed, which was adopted in the 1st ecumenical council of the church in order to confront the heretical teaching of Arius. This council was held in Nicea in 325 AD:

> I believe in one God, the Father Almighty, Maker of heaven and earth, and of all things visible and invisible.
>
> And in one Lord Jesus Christ, the only-begotten Son of God, begotten of the Father before all worlds; God of God, Light of Light, very God of very God; begotten, not made,

being of one substance with the Father, by whom all things were made.

Who, for us men and for our salvation, came down from heaven, and was incarnate by the Holy Spirit of the virgin Mary, and was made man; and was crucified also for us under Pontius Pilate; He suffered and was buried; and the third day He rose again, according to the Scriptures; and ascended into heaven, and sits on the right hand of the Father; and He shall come again, with glory, to judge the quick and the dead; whose kingdom shall have no end.

And I believe in the Holy Ghost, the Lord and giver of life; who proceeds from the Father and the Son; who with the Father and the Son together is worshiped and glorified; who spoke by the prophets.

And I believe in one holy catholic and apostolic Church. I acknowledge one baptism for the remission of sins; and I look for the resurrection of the dead, and the life of the world to come. Amen.

In opposition to the biblical narrative of the Chi Event, the so-called Jesus Seminar was convened beginning in the 1980s to contrive and fabricate a contrary narrative that was the product of higher critical New Testament scholarship. The findings of the Jesus Seminar are codified by Funk, et al., in *The Five Gospels*, [18] but they can be briefly summarized as follows:

- All the miracle stories recorded in the canonical Gospels are not authentic. Instead, they are later additions which were fabricated by the Church Fathers in an endeavor to deify Jesus of Nazareth.

- In particular, this conclusion applies to the record of the death, burial, and resurrection of Jesus.

- Some of the sayings attributed to Jesus of Nazareth in the canonical Gospels are authentic, but many others are questionable in regard to authenticity. The lengthy discourses recorded especially in Matthew and John are almost certainly not authentic. Instead, they were added to the gospel accounts by the Church Fathers to promote their agenda to deify Jesus of Nazareth.

- In sum, the authentic record of the life and ministry of Jesus of Nazareth is totally devoid of all supernatural elements, according to the findings of the Jesus Seminar scholars. They represent Jesus of Nazareth as a thoroughly noncontroversial Jewish rabbi of the early 1st century AD who had no power whatsoever to save to the uttermost all that come unto God by Him (Hebrews 7:25).

Implications of the Two Opposing Narratives of the Chi Event. According to the Apostle John in the passage quoted above, only those who heartily embrace the biblical narrative of the Chi Event have life. Those who embrace the contrary narrative formulated by the Jesus Seminar scholars remain in their sins, they are spiritually dead while walking about in this life, and they are destined to...

> They will suffer the punishment of eternal destruction, away from the presence of the Lord and from the glory of His might, when He comes on that day to be glorified in His saints, and to be marveled at among all who have believed, because our testimony to you was believed. [2 Thessalonians 1:9-10, adapted from the ESV]

The Determinativeness of the Biblical Narrative of the Omega Event

The biblical narrative of the Omega Event is discussed in detail in chapter 12 of the WitW study. The passages from Titus, 1 John, and 2 Thessalonians quoted above, together with the Nicene Creed, all contain brief summaries of the biblical narrative of the Omega Event. The essence of that narrative is that Jesus Christ, the Son of God, will one day return to Planet Earth to judge the living and the dead and inaugurate His eternal kingdom. The contrary narrative put forth by the enemies of the Christian gospel is this: there is no Omega Event, because, for them, there is no God. Instead, they see a steadily upward evolutionary trajectory according to the Darwinian narrative, culminating in some utopian state that the mind of man can only imagine. As we did in the case of the

Sigma Event, let us examine the implications of these two competing narratives of the Omega Event in regard to the philosophy of civil government.

On the one hand, governmental leaders who embrace the biblical narrative of the Omega Event tremble at the thought that one day they will face the King of kings as their judge, and they exercise their governmental responsibilities as those who have a stewardship from God, and who will be held accountable by Him for the way in which they exercised their stewardship. If they exercise their stewardship in righteousness and truth, they will be rewarded; otherwise they will suffer loss.

On the other hand, governmental leaders who embrace the contrary narrative see themselves as agents who are helping to move mankind along the evolutionary trajectory toward a future utopian state. In fact, they see government as the agent to bring about that utopian state in the present to the maximum extent possible. This view gives rise to the progressive concept of social justice and redistribution of wealth, and it is the view which was being implemented in the US by the administration of President Barack Obama.

The Bible as True Meta-Narrative

In the foregoing discussion, we have seen that the biblical narratives associated with the four key events identified in Figure 2-1 uniquely do the following: they impart significance, purpose, and even nobility to humans; they enable us to correctly understand the physical, moral, and ethical landscape of our present world; they uniquely show the way of deliverance from evil, sin, and death; and, they enable humans to stand in the final judgment of mankind. Over against the biblical narratives, mankind has contrived and fabricated a false narrative associated with each of the four key events identified in Figure 2-1. They have done this in a futile endeavor to erect intellectual scaffolding to support their rejection of the Infinite Personal God who is really there. However, these false narratives deny man's personhood; they fail to create a framework for correctly understanding the physical, moral, and ethical landscape of our present world; they deny the way of deliverance through Jesus Christ, the Son of God; and they replace the eternal hope of the Christian with meaninglessness, hopelessness, abject despair, and, ultimately, eternal death.

On the basis of the foregoing discussion, you should be willing to at least consider, if not heartily embrace, the following assertion:

> *The biblical narrative is uniquely a true meta-narrative because it is determinative with respect to all other narratives and to all material facts. That is, it uniquely provides a representational framework through which all persons, events, circumstances, and things can be perceived and correctly comprehended.* [19]

The Storyline of the Bible: A Thematic Guide for Doing Theology

As we engage in a lifelong study of the Bible, we begin to gain a perspective as to what this book is about; to wit, that which God is endeavoring to communicate to us through the inspired text of Scripture. If we are able to correctly recognize and formulate the storyline of the Bible, then it becomes a thematic guide for reading Scripture and doing theology.

Following is my attempt to capture in a single sentence the storyline of the Bible:

> *The Bible is the story of the Infinite Personal God manifesting His glory through His lavishly gracious acts of creating, providentially caring for, calling out, and redeeming a community of saints – a family of servant kings – who are being conformed to the image of His Son.*

According to this formulation, God's purpose in creating, providentially caring for, and redeeming mankind **is to showcase His glorious grace**.

An alternative expression of what the Bible is about is presented by Robert Capon as follows:

> It is about the mystery by which the power of God works to form this world into the Holy City, the New Jerusalem that comes down out of heaven from God, prepared as a bride adorned for her husband. [20]

Yet another expression of the overall message of the Bible could be this: the Bible is about God establishing His kingdom on earth.

Each of these alternative expressions of what the Bible is about is an accurate representation of an important strand of biblical teaching. In chapter 5, where we discuss the Torah (i.e., the five books of Moses) as the fountainhead of wisdom, fourteen integrative motifs or themes are identified which surface in the Torah, which run through the entire Bible, and which provide a framework for addressing the thematic diversity of Scripture.

Returning to the first expression of the Bible's storyline, we need to unpack that expression to ensure that we really comprehend its significance.

The Glorious Grace of God

The **glory** of God is that divine attribute which is supremely precious and worthy of our adoring praise. In fact, according to John Piper, [21] there is nothing in all the cosmos that is more precious, and therefore more to be valued and enjoyed, than the glory of God. [22]

The Westminster Shorter Catechism states that "the chief end of man is to glorify God and enjoy Him forever." [23] Piper proposes that the following adjustment of the wording of this declaration would make it more accurate:

> ***The chief end of man is to glorify God by enjoying Him forever.*** [24]

Piper argues that Yahweh Himself rightfully takes delight in His own glory. In fact, because of the supreme worth of His glory, for Him to do otherwise would constitute an unthinkable act of idolatry on His part. Moreover, He has so constituted the personality of man that we find ultimate fulfillment and delight in glorifying God; that is, ascribing supreme worth to His glory through our way of life, our work, our words, our hymns of worship and songs of praise, and our tithes and offerings.

> ***Thus, every corpuscle of our beings should resonate and throb with the music of the unspeakable glory of God. In fact, for us to value anything more than the glory of God is tantamount to idolatry.***

The glory of God is a multifaceted and splendorous divine attribute. The particular facet of His glory that is the focus of the story of redemption is His **glorious grace**. [25]

Keynote Scripture Passages

In the following paragraphs I discuss a succession of keynote Scripture passages that support and motivate the formulation of the Bible's storyline presented above. The order in which they are discussed is in accordance with the logical flow of the storyline formulation. Theological terms and concepts that arise in the course of this discussion are defined in Appendix A.

Phrase 1 – "The Bible is the story..." (1 Corinthians 10:1-13)

> For I want you to know, brothers, that our fathers were all under the cloud, and all passed through the sea, and all were baptized into Moses in the cloud and in the sea, and all ate the same spiritual food, and all drank the same spiritual drink. For they drank from the spiritual Rock that followed them, and the Rock was Christ. Nevertheless, with most of them God was not pleased, for they were overthrown in the wilderness. **Now these things took place as examples for us,** that we might not desire evil as they did. Do not be idolaters as some of them were... We must not indulge in sexual immorality as some of them did... We must not put

Christ to the test, as some of them did... nor grumble, as some of them did... **Now these things happened to them as an example, but they were written down for our instruction,** on whom the end of the ages has come... [1 Corinthians 10:1-13, ESV, emphasis added]

In this passage, the Apostle Paul makes a most profound assertion concerning the true narrative of Scripture. As delineated in Figure 2-2, the events in the history of Israel **were so orchestrated by God** that they were pregnant with prophetic truth, and the events were recorded so as to be examples and lessons for us "on whom the end of the ages has come." While it is true that the particular focus of Paul's assertion in 1 Corinthians 10:1-13 is upon those paradigmatic [26] events which occurred in connection with the Exodus, we have biblical warrant to apply the assertion generally to the history of Israel. For example, the extended passage of Hebrews 3:7 – 4:13 provides warrant for applying Paul's assertion to the paradigmatic events that occurred in connection with the Conquest episode. Moreover, the manner in which the apostles refer to and quote from the Hebrew Scriptures to support their declarations in the Christian Scriptures means that we should regard the **entire story of Israel** as containing prophetic truth that is applicable to our lives and ministries in the 21st century.

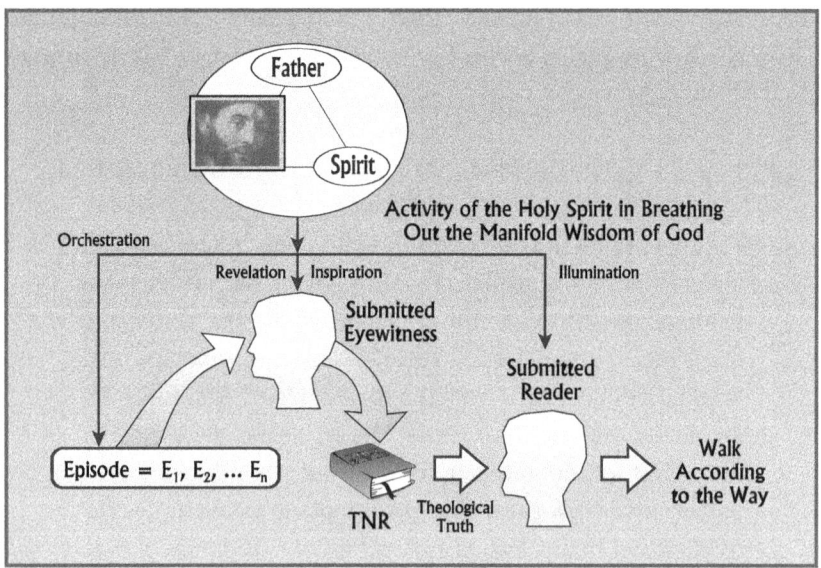

Figure 2-2. The Revelation of the Manifold Wisdom of God

Phrase 2 – "... of the Infinite Personal God..."
(Genesis 1 & 2, Exodus 3:13ff, 18:10-12 & 20:1ff, and Psalm 19:1-11)

This expression of God's name derives from *The God Who is There* by Francis Schaeffer. [27] The name of God employed with the greatest frequency in the Hebrew Scriptures is **Yahweh Elohim**, which is commonly rendered as "the LORD God" in our English translations. The divine name employed by Moses in the Genesis 1 narrative of the order of creation is Elohim, which is the plural form of the appellative divine name or title, El. [28] To be specific, El is the name of the highest deity in the Canaanite pantheon. Why did the Holy Spirit inspire Moses to employ the plural form of this appellative name? Some scholars suggest that Elohim is a primitive reflection of the Trinity. While this may be true, another explanation is that the plural form of the appellative name denotes **transcendence**. [29] It is noteworthy that David employs this appellative name in Psalm 19:1-6, which opens with the following declaration:

> The heavens declare the glory of Elohim, and the sky above proclaims His handiwork. [Psalm 19:1, adapted from the ESV]

The compound divine name employed by Moses in the 2nd chapter of Genesis is Yahweh Elohim. What meaning is contributed by the coupling of the personal or proper name, Yahweh, with the appellative name, Elohim? Yahweh formally introduces Himself to Moses in the Burning Bush episode recorded in the 3rd and 4th chapters of Exodus. In particular, note the following passage from the 3rd chapter:

> Then Moses said to Elohim, "If I come to the people of Israel and say to them, 'The Elohim of your fathers has sent me to you,' and they ask me, 'What is His name,' what shall I say to them?" Elohim said to Moses, "I AM who I AM." And He said, "Say this to the people of Israel, 'I AM has sent me to you.'" Elohim also said to Moses, "Say this to the people of Israel, 'Yahweh, the Elohim of your fathers, the Elohim of Abraham, the Elohim of Isaac, and the Elohim of Jacob, has sent me to you.' This is My name

forever, and thus I am to be remembered throughout all
generations." [Exodus 3:13-15, adapted from the ESV]

According to this passage, the absolute self-existence of God and His covenantal relationship with His people are both associated with and bound up in His proper or personal name, Yahweh. The fact that God has absolute self-existence means that His being is absolute; He, uniquely in all the cosmos, is the great uncaused Cause. All of God's creatures derive their existence from Yahweh Elohim. He, uniquely, is the source of all life, and apart from Him there is no life.

God's absolute self-existence also means that He is **absolutely self-sufficient**. His great works of creation, providence, and redemption, which are the focus of the Bible's storyline, were not motivated by any need that He has, such as for fellowship. Instead, as we shall see, they were motivated to showcase His glory – **especially His glorious grace**. While He does not need us, the reverse is not true; our need for Him is desperate. **In fact, we cannot exist apart from Him.**

It is noteworthy that in his testimony concerning the preciousness of the Torah in Psalm 19:7-11, David employs God's personal name, Yahweh. By this means, David brings to bear all the meaning and significance invested in God's personal name upon his testimony concerning the perfections of the Torah of Yahweh.

Thus, in summary, when Moses employs God's personal or proper name, Yahweh, he signifies the relational closeness or **immanence** of God. Therefore the compound name, Yahweh Elohim, signifies both the absolute immanence and absolute transcendence of God. He is, in fact, the **Infinite Personal God who is really there and who has created all things apart from Himself**.

Before turning to our next passage, note the manner in which Yahweh introduces the Ten Commandments in Exodus 20:1ff:

And Elohim spoke all these words, saying, "I am Yahweh
your Elohim... " [Exodus 20:1-2a, adapted from the ESV]

Moses employs the formula "Yahweh your Elohim" from this passage onward as he speaks to the people of Israel and endeavors to teach them to fear, love, obey, and serve Yahweh, and to carefully instruct their children in the way of Yahweh.

Concerning the transcendence of Yahweh, note the testimony of Jethro, Moses' father-in-law, in Exodus 18:10-12:

> Jethro said, "Blessed be Yahweh, who has delivered you out of the hand of the Egyptians and out of the hand of Pharaoh and has delivered the people from under the hand of the Egyptians. Now I know that Yahweh is greater than all elohim, because in this affair they dealt arrogantly with the people." [Exodus 18:10-11, adapted from the ESV]

In this statement Jethro reflects the ancient belief that one nation's defeat of another was not only a demonstration of superior military strength, but, more importantly, it was a demonstration of superior deities. Accordingly, through the plagues Yahweh inflicted upon the Egyptians, He demonstrated His transcendence with respect to all the gods of Egypt. Later, through the Conquest episode recorded in the Book of Joshua, He would demonstrate His transcendence with respect to all the gods of the Canaanites.

Phrase 3 – "... manifesting His glory through His lavishly gracious acts..." (Ephesians 1:3-14, 2:4-7 & 3:10-11)

Paul's epistle to the Ephesians sets forth the purpose of God in redemption as follows:

> But God, being rich in mercy, because of the great love with which He loved us, even when we were dead in our trespasses, made us alive together with Christ – by grace you have been saved – and raised us up with Him and seated us with Him in the heavenly places in Christ Jesus, so that in the coming ages **He might show the immeasurable riches of His grace** as expressed in His kindness toward us in Christ Jesus. [Ephesians 2:4-7, adapted from the ESV, emphasis added]

Note how this motivating purpose is also expressed in the following passage from the 1st chapter:

> Blessed be the God and Father of our Lord Jesus Christ, who has blessed us in Christ with every spiritual blessing in the heavenly places, even as He chose us in Him before the foundation of the world, that we should be holy and blameless before Him. In love He predestined us for adoption as sons through Jesus Christ, according to the purpose of His will, **to the praise of His glorious grace**, with which He has blessed us in the Beloved. [Ephesians 1:3-6, adapted from the ESV, emphasis added]

Accordingly, God's purpose in redemption is to **showcase His glorious grace** through the likes of us. And this showcasing of the glorious grace of God is not only for the eyes of our fellow sons of Adam, but also for "the rulers and authorities in heavenly places" in accordance with Ephesians 3:10-11. [30]

Phrase 4 – "... of creating, providentially caring for... "
(Acts 14:8-18 & 17:24-31)

The purpose of God in His work of creation and providence is most clearly set forth by Paul in his speech before the Areopagus recorded in the 17th chapter of Acts, of which our focal passage is the following:

> The God who made the world and everything in it, being Lord of heaven and earth, does not live in temples made by man, nor is He served by human hands, **as though He needed anything**, since He himself gives to all mankind life and breath and everything. And He made from one man every nation of mankind to live on all the face of the earth, having determined allotted periods and the boundaries of their dwelling place, that they should seek God, in the hope that they might feel their way toward Him and find Him. [Acts 17:23-27, adapted from the ESV, emphasis added]

In Paul's speech at Lystra, recorded in the 14th chapter of Acts, he states the following:

> ... We bring you good news, that you should turn from these vain things to a living God, who made the heaven and the earth and the sea and all that is in them. In past generations He allowed all the nations to walk in their own ways. Yet He did not leave himself without witness, for He did good by giving you rains from heaven and fruitful seasons, satisfying your hearts with food and gladness. [Acts 14:15-17, adapted from the ESV]

Accordingly, God's work of creation, providence, and redemption are links in an unbroken chain of redemptive purpose, all motivated by His desire to showcase His glorious grace through the elect. Note well from the Acts 17 passage that God does not need anything. That is, His works of creation and redemption were not done to fulfill a need that He had, such as for fellowship with beings like us. Our God possesses absolute being, which means that He is completely self-sufficient in Himself.

> *He created, providentially cared for, and redeemed mankind in order that we might eternally showcase and enjoy His glorious grace.*

Phrase 5 – "... calling out..." (Romans 8:29-30)

Paul offers a cosmic perspective on God's plan of redemption in the following passage in Romans:

> For those whom He foreknew He also predestined to be conformed to the image of His Son, in order that He might be the firstborn among many brothers. And those whom He predestined He also **called**, and those whom He **called** He also justified, and those whom He justified He also glorified. [Romans 8:29-30, ESV, emphasis added]

Taking into account the meanings of the Greek words translated "foreknew" and "predestined", we can paraphrase this passage as follows:

> For those whom He **knew beforehand** He also **marked out beforehand** to be conformed to the image of His Son, in

order that He might be the firstborn among many brothers. And those whom He marked out beforehand He also **called**, and those whom He **called** He also justified, and those whom He justified He also glorified. [Romans 8:29-30, adapted from the ESV, emphasis added]

At this point in the WitW study, it would not be appropriate for us to become embroiled in a debate concerning the theological concepts of God's foreknowledge and predestination. It is sufficient for us to assert that the whole plan of redemption emanates from the mind of God; that is, **He is the prime mover and active agent in redemption from start to finish.** [31]

I believe the best way to understand God's calling is to observe examples of it in the biblical narrative, as we do in much greater detail in chapter 8 entitled Called by the King. In particular, we should regard Jesus' calling of His disciples as being representative of the calling that each of us receives to become a disciple of Jesus Christ. Moreover, in chapter 5 as part of our discussion of The People of the New Way, we consider the amazing story of God's call to Abraham.

John 1:35ff records what appears to be the earliest contact between Jesus and some of the men who would become His disciples. This episode occurred while Jesus was in Judea near where John the Baptist was preaching and baptizing, perhaps shortly after Jesus Himself was baptized by John. The passage begins with two of the disciples of John the Baptist responding to John's testimony concerning Jesus by leaving John and following Jesus. One of those two was Andrew, and the other was very likely the Apostle John himself. This passage explicitly records Jesus' early conversations with Andrew, Peter, Philip, and Nathanael, and it includes His calling of Philip to follow Him as a disciple in the 43rd verse.

Jesus' formal calling of Peter, Andrew, James, and John is recorded in the 4th chapter of Matthew's gospel, and His calling of Matthew (i.e., Levi, the tax collector) is recorded in the 9th chapter.

Jesus' high priestly prayer in the 17th chapter of John's Gospel affords the greatest insight into the basis of Jesus' calling of the twelve men who would follow Him as disciples, eleven of whom would become His apostles. In John 17:6ff, Jesus states in His prayer that His disciples had been marked out beforehand (i.e., predestined) by God the Father, and then they had been given to Jesus Christ, the Son of God. Thus, the call issued by Jesus Christ was altogether intentional, and it logically followed the called individual having been known and marked out beforehand by God the Father. This is exactly the order stated by Paul in our focal passage, Romans 8:29-30.

Phrase 6 – "... And redeeming..." (Romans 3:23-24 and Titus 2:11-14)

To **redeem** is to buy back or out of. [32] The story of Yahweh's redeeming His people Israel out of bondage in Egypt is presented in the Book of Exodus. According to Paul's language in 1 Corinthians 10:1-13, the experience of Israel being redeemed out of bondage to the Egyptians serves as a prototype of our redemption from bondage to evil, sin, and death. Paul concisely represents the essence of redemption in our first focal passage, which states,

> ... For all have sinned and fall short of the glory of God, and are justified by His grace as a gift, through the **redemption that is in Christ Jesus**, whom God put forward as a propitiation by His blood, to be received by faith. [Romans 3:23-25, adapted from the ESV, emphasis added]

The word **propitiation** designates a theological concept that is related to redemption. To propitiate is to satisfy as by payment of a suitable consideration. [33]

Our second focal passage presents the Christian gospel in a manner that is both cogent and comprehensive as follows:

> For the grace of God has appeared, bringing salvation for all people, training us to renounce ungodliness and worldly passions, and to live self-controlled, upright, and godly lives in the present age, waiting for our blessed hope, the appearing of the glory of our great God and Savior Jesus Christ, who gave Himself for us to **redeem us from all**

lawlessness and to purify for Himself a people for His own possession who are zealous for good works. [Titus 2:11-14, ESV, emphasis added]

Reflecting more deeply on the prototypical experience of Israel in Egypt, the fact is evident that the Israelites were helpless to deliver themselves. Their state of enslavement and bondage to the Egyptian pharaoh was so absolute that deliverance had to come from a source external to themselves. While it is true that Moses became the human instrument whom Yahweh employed to bring about Israel's redemption and deliverance from bondage in Egypt, the narrative of Exodus clearly places in evidence the fact that it was Yahweh Elohim Himself who effected that redemption and deliverance. In like manner, our enslavement and bondage to evil, sin, and death was so absolute that we were impotent to effect our own deliverance. In fact, like the Israelites of antiquity, **we were disinclined to even seek deliverance**. Redemption and deliverance had to come from a source external to ourselves, even God Himself.

Phrase 7 – "... a community of saints, a family of servant kings..." (1 Peter 2:9-10 and Revelation 5:9-10 & 20:4)

Note the testimonies of the Apostle Peter and the Apostle John in the two Scripture passages identified above:

> But you are a **chosen race, a royal priesthood, a holy nation, a people for His own possession**, that you may proclaim the excellencies of Him who called you out of darkness into His marvelous light. Once you were not a people, but now you are God's people; once you had not received mercy, but now you have received mercy. [1 Peter 2:9-10, adapted from the ESV, emphasis added]

> And they sang a new song, saying, "Worthy are You to take the scroll and to open its seals, for You were slain, and by Your blood You ransomed people for God from every tribe and language and people and nation, and You have made them a **kingdom and priests** to our God, and **they shall reign** on the earth." [Revelation 5:9-10, ESV, emphasis added]

Peter's and John's testimony that we are a kingdom of priests is a reflection of what Yahweh announced to the nation of Israel through His servant Moses in Exodus 19:4-6, where we read,

> You yourselves have seen what I did to the Egyptians, and how I bore you on eagles' wings and brought you to Myself. Now therefore, if you will indeed obey My voice and keep My covenant, you shall be My treasured possession among all peoples, for all the earth is Mine; **and you shall be to Me a kingdom of priests and a holy nation**. These are the words that you shall speak to the people of Israel. [Exodus 19:4-6, ESV, emphasis added]

The people of Israel failed to fulfill this high calling, which is the overall thrust of the narrative of the Hebrew Scriptures. On account of their failure, Yahweh Elohim has brought into being a new covenant community which consists of both Jews and Gentiles, and He is making us into a new kingdom of priests under the terms of the new covenant announced in Jeremiah 31:31ff and confirmed by the Apostle Peter in 1 Peter 2:9-10.

The fact that we will reign with Christ is set forth in the following passage from the 20th chapter of Revelation:

> Then I saw thrones, and seated on them were those to whom the authority to judge was committed. Also I saw the souls of those who had been beheaded for the testimony of Jesus and for the word of God, and who had not worshiped the beast or its image and had not received its mark on their foreheads or their hands. They came to life and **reigned with Christ for a thousand years**. [Revelation 20:4, ESV, emphasis added] [34]

The concept of **servant king** comes across as an oxymoron. At the very least it is a paradoxical and counter-cultural concept. However, our Lord Christ modeled servant kingship for us, and He calls us, as His disciples, to learn to walk in His way:

"If anyone would be first, he must be last of all and servant of all." [Mark 9:35, ESV]

Phrase 8 – "... who are being conformed to the image of His Son." (Romans 8:29-30)

The fact that we are being conformed to the image of the Son is clearly set forth by the Apostle Paul in Romans 8:29:

> For those whom He foreknew He also **predestined to be conformed to the image of His Son**, in order that He might be the firstborn among many brothers. And those whom He predestined He also called, and those whom He called He also justified, and **those whom He justified He also glorified**. [Romans 8:29-30, adapted from the ESV, emphasis added]

As we walk through this present life, God commands us to "work out our salvation with fear and trembling; for it is God who is at work in us, both to will and to work for His good pleasure." [Philippians 2:12-13]. Our working out our salvation means that we actively cooperate with the Holy Spirit in the **lifelong project** of becoming conformed to the image of Jesus Christ in thought, word, and action.

We refer to the process of God conforming us to the image of his Son as **sanctification**, where sanctify means to consecrate or **to set apart as holy**. [35] The Apostle Peter represents sanctification as our becoming partakers of the divine nature in 2 Peter 1:4 by appropriating and practicing God's precious and magnificent promises. According to the Apostle Paul in 1 Corinthians 15:51ff and Colossians 3:4, and the Apostle John in 1 John 3:2, the process of sanctification will be consummated when Jesus returns. Then we will be changed in an instant, and what is mortal and perishable will be replaced by what is immortal and imperishable.

In chapter 3 I discuss the tabernacle in the wilderness as a rich biblical representation of the interrelated concepts of holiness, worship, and the life and ministry of Jesus Christ.

The Apostle Paul informs us in our focal passage that the ultimate goal of the process of sanctification, the consummation of our being conformed to the image of the Son, **is that we would be glorified**. [36] What language shall we employ to unpack this astonishing affirmation?

The glory of God combines the concepts of His sovereign majesty, His kingly splendor, His mighty power, and the unapproachable light that emanates from His countenance. Our sun is but a feeble representation of the glory of God, but it will serve as a model whereby we can approach the concept of our being glorified. Even as our moon reflects the brilliance of the sun, in like manner our glory will be a reflection of the glory of God. Whereas His glory is infinite, ours will be finite and a derivative of His. To be specific, to the extent that we now participate in the fellowship of the afflictions of Christ, in eternity there will be conferred upon us a participation in the glory of Christ.

> So we do not lose heart. Though our outer nature is wasting away, our inner nature is being renewed day by day. For this slight momentary affliction is preparing for us an eternal weight of glory beyond all comparison, as we look not to the things that are seen but to the things that are unseen. For the things that are seen are transient, but the things that are unseen are eternal. [2 Corinthians 4:16 – 5:1, ESV]

Questions Motivated by the Bible's Storyline

Our formulation of the storyline of the Bible is a very brief, and hopefully cogent, summary of the Bible's principal message. Therefore, it is inescapable that such a brief summary would motivate a number of questions. Following are four questions that come to mind:

1. Is there compelling evidence to support the assertion that the Bible is true narrative, and what is the significance of it being true narrative? [37]

2. What are the implications of the Bible being true narrative in regard to our reading and studying the Bible?

3. How should we represent the gospel or good news whereby mankind can be delivered from bondage to evil, sin, and death?

4. How should we represent the *Eschaton* – that is, the events and circumstances that are associated with the second coming of Jesus Christ – and how do those events and circumstances bear upon our life and ministry in the present?

Over the course of the WitW study, we will touch on answers to these four questions. A comprehensive study of Christian theology would seek answers to such questions and many others besides.

Questions for Discussion

1. In this chapter we have presented our formulation of the Bible's storyline. While we have devoted great care and reflection to this formulation, it is by no means engraved in granite. You should regard it as a point of departure for use in your own lifelong study of the Bible. For the time being, accepting it as a point of departure, we have parsed it into its eight constituent phrases, and have brought illumination from the Scriptures to bear upon each of the phrases. Reflecting upon the eight phrases which make up the storyline formulation, select the three that are most significant and meaningful to you. For each of the selected phrases, prepare a brief commentary on its significance to your own life and ministry.

2. Our proposed formulation of the Bible's storyline is based upon and built around the premise that the motivating purpose of God in His works of creation, providence, and redemption is to **showcase His glorious grace**. We have considered passages from the epistle to the Ephesians and elsewhere which state that this is, indeed, the case. Therefore, our purpose in being is to reflect the glorious grace of God, according to the measure of faith and the particular set of gifts and endowments He has allotted to us. Analyze and discuss each of three areas of your life and ministry in which you are challenged to better reflect the glorious grace of God.

Notes & Reflections

Use the space below to record additional insights and commentary resulting from your studies thus far.

Chapter 3.
The Bible as a Representational System

Chapter Overview

The concept of the Bible as a representational system was introduced in chapter 2 at the beginning of the discussion of the storyline of the Bible. In this chapter I thoroughly discuss the significance and importance of the Bible as a representational system. The thrust of the chapter is twofold:

- The Bible is a representational system that defines reality for the disciple of Christ.

- It is of life-critical importance for the disciple to embrace the Bible's representation of reality. In fact, to do so is the key to the **way of wisdom**; God bestows blessing upon those who walk in this way, and its end is eternal life. To do otherwise is the **way of folly**, and those who walk in that way are subject to the cursing of God. Moreover, the end of that way is ruination and death.

Learning Objectives

The learning objective for this chapter is twofold: first, to impart an appreciation for the Bible as a document which defines reality for the disciple of Christ; and, second, to enable the student to grasp the life-critical importance of his embracing and practicing that reality. The point of this chapter is that **the practice of the Christian life is radically counter-intuitive.** Therefore, it is necessary for the disciple to experience a transformation of his thinking process whereby he sees reality through the lens of Scripture rather than through the lens of his natural intuition and lived experiences apart from God.

In the Preface to the WitW study, I share how the insight that the Bible is a representational system was pivotal in my understanding of Scripture and my approach to Bible teaching. In this chapter, I will endeavor to share this insight with you so that you also may grasp its significance and importance, and that you may begin to apply it to your own life and ministry.

Some Definitions

In the following paragraphs I define some important terms that are necessary for understanding the subject matter of this chapter.

To represent is to bring clearly before the mind; to serve as a sign, symbol, model, or prototype; to describe an object as having a specified character or quality; or to act in place of in some respect. This multi-part definition is entirely consistent with the formal dictionary definition of **represent**.

To determine is to fix conclusively or authoritatively; that is, to specify, define, or establish the form, position, or character of an object; or to impart meaning, significance, and interrelationship with other objects.

A **biblical representation** is where the language of Scripture imparts the divine perspective on an aspect of reality. For example, in chapter 1 we noted seven representational statements in James 1:2-18. And, in the 8th chapter, we unpack the significance of the **calling of God** by studying the examples of Jesus' calling His disciples. A biblical representation which has been most perplexing to theologians and biblical scholars concerns the second coming of Christ. Jesus repeatedly represented His coming again as imminent, and yet His church has been anxiously awaiting His return for nearly 2,000 years.

While many biblical representations are bound to the particular historical and cultural context in which they were first presented, many others are normative; that is, they are applicable to all people, periods, and places. To distinguish between normative and non-normative biblical representations, we need to pay careful attention to the author's intention as revealed by the linguistic clues which he embedded into the text.

I speak of the Bible as being a **representational system** in the sense that the representations of reality that it sets forth are cohesive, harmonious, and logically consistent with the nature and character of God as opposed to being disjointed and heterogeneous, or even chaotic. In fact, the true narrative of Scripture creates the matrix which ties all the biblical representations into a logically consistent system.

Where might we turn to find representations of reality that are not cohesive, harmonious, and logically consistent? The sayings of Confucius in the *Lunyu* and the sayings of Muhammed in the *Quran* serve as examples. Both documents consist of disjointed statements or aphorisms that are disconnected from a true narrative, which would be required to impart determinativeness and generalizability. Therefore, in contrast to the Bible, the representations of reality formed by the *Lunyu* and the *Quran* are not cohesive, harmonious, and logically consistent. In other words, neither of them form a representational system.

I define **representational world** as a virtual world of the human mind which is made up of a whole constellation or network of individual representations. In other words,

Representational World = A Personal Virtual Reality

For any given disciple of Christ, some of the components of his representational world may be biblically based, while others may derive from his natural intuition and lived experiences apart from God. One of the objectives of this chapter is to demonstrate the life-critical importance of our replacing naturally intuitive representations with biblical ones. I submit that this is the principal purpose of the transformation of our thinking process of which Paul speaks in Romans 12:1-2. Moreover,

> *I assert that our thoroughly embracing a biblically-based representational world is an essential prerequisite for us to successfully walk in the way of Christ and the apostles.*

The *Mahal*. Lest you reject the concept of representational world as being too abstract and theoretical, a number of people groups in South Asia have a single word in their vocabulary whose meaning is equivalent to representational world. That word is ***mahal***. Not only do these people have an intuitive grasp of the meaning of the *mahal*, but they also grasp its significance as a determinant of behavior. Moreover, our friends in East Africa also manifest an intuitive grasp of the concept of representational world, as well as its importance with regard to walking in the way of Christ and the apostles.

Worldview. The concept signified by the term **worldview** is related to but different from that signified by representational world. Our worldview can be defined as the way we perceive the world around us. On the other hand, having defined representational world as the constellation or network of representations that we carry around with us as a virtual world of the human mind, the significance of our representational world is as follows:

- It determines how we **perceive** all the persons, events, circumstances, and things in our material time-space environment.

- It thereby determines how we **relate to and interact with** those persons, events, circumstances, and things.

- Accordingly, our representational world is more than the way we perceive the world around us; **it is a world in which we actually live**. The significance and power of the representational world as a determinant of behavior is strikingly portrayed in the movie *A Beautiful Mind*.

Two Ways of Representing Reality

In this section and the two which follow, I will endeavor to unfold the workings of two ways of representing reality: **a godly way versus a worldly way**. Our physical senses – sight, sound, smell, taste, and touch – are the sources of input information regarding persons, events, circumstances, and things in our material time-space environment. All of this raw input information is inherently indeterminant; in other words, it lacks the **power of self-determinativeness**. We process this input information in our brains through the **representational world (RW) mental filter**, which determines its meaning and significance, and thereby it determines how we relate to and interact with those persons, events, circumstances, and things. Because our RW mental filter is such a natural and intuitive part of our being, we may be unaware of the profound effect it exerts. And we also may be unaware of the basis of our RW mental filter, whether biblical or otherwise.

Because the RW mental filter determines how we respond to the information received from our physical senses, the pivotal question is this: What determines the RW mental filter? Is our cultural background, education, lived experiences, family heritage, media, and peer pressure the overriding determinant of the RW mental filter? Or, is the language of Scripture the overriding determinant of the RW mental filter?

- The overriding determinant of a **godly RW mental filter** is the language of Scripture as illuminated by the Holy Spirit. In other words, a godly RW mental filter corresponds to the spiritual mind and the mind of Christ in the language of 1 Corinthians 2:15-16.

- The overriding determinant of a **worldly RW mental filter** is a combination of cultural background, education, lived experiences, family heritage, media, and peer pressure. In other words, a worldly RW mental filter corresponds to the soulish mind of 1 Corinthians 2:14.

Before we proceed, what is the meaning of the biblical term **godly**? I once heard a certain preacher define godliness as taking God and His word seriously, and I would embrace this as a good, initial step toward a definition. A godly person is also one who fears, loves, and serves God, and who therefore walks in His way and keeps His commandments. In particular, a godly person endeavors to love God with all that he is and has.

> *In sum, a godly person represents God and reflects His glory; that is, he serves as a sign, symbol, or metaphor of what God is like, albeit imperfectly, but, nevertheless, substantially. The life of the godly person is occupied with the things of the Spirit; therefore he perceives persons, events, circumstances, and things in his material time-space environment through the eyes of Jesus Christ and according to His mind.*

In contrast, the life of a worldly person is absorbed with the things of the flesh – that is, material enjoyments, comforts, security, and prosperity. Despite the fact that the worldly person may be nice, fun to be with, and even religious, **he conducts his life as if God doesn't exist**.

> *The worldly person does not take God and His word seriously. He is, in fact, the opposite of a godly person. In other words, worldliness is equivalent to ungodliness. This is true despite the fact that the worldly person may display many positive attributes, and he may even be a religious person.*

Two Kinds of Faith

There are two kinds of faith which are associated with the two kinds of people identified above. The worldly person is able to exercise a **worldly faith** in persons and things with which he can interact physically. For example, the worldly person can comfortably board an airplane because he trusts that the airline company has maintained the aircraft to be airworthy and has assigned a competent air crew to that particular flight. Worldly faith is based entirely upon lived experiences.

In contrast, the godly person is able to exercise **godly faith** in the invisible things of God with which he cannot interact physically. Godly faith is based entirely upon what God has said in His word – that is, His precious and magnificent promises (2 Peter 1:4). It is by means of his godly faith that the godly person is justified, and it is by means of his godly faith that the godly person lives.

Godly faith is not an extension of worldly faith. Instead, the idea of godly faith is foolishness to the worldly person. As we will learn in Part 3 of the WitW study, godly faith is an alien faith that comes from a source outside the human personality, even Jesus Christ Himself. Godly faith is the result of the faith of Jesus being implanted and energized in the spirit of a person through the power-packed message about Christ in accordance with Romans 10:17.

The Workings of a Godly RW Mental Filter

Figure 3-1 illustrates the workings of a godly RW mental filter in terms of three lines as follows:

> **Line A**. By means of godly faith, the godly person conforms his RW mental filter to God's definition of reality as revealed in Scripture. He views persons, events, circumstances, and things

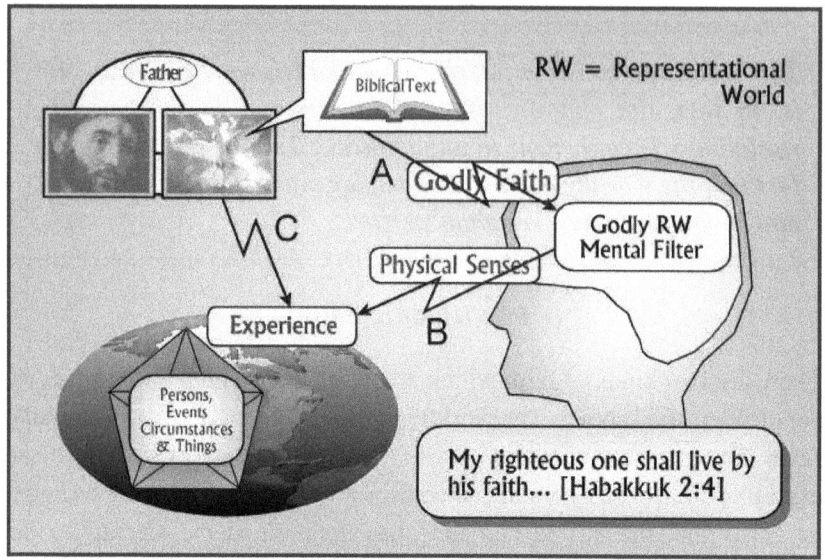

Figure 3-1. The Workings of a Godly RW Mental Filter

through the lens of Scripture – that is, through the eyes of Christ and according to the mind of Christ.

Line B. The godly person imposes his godly RW mental filter on the information received from his physical senses, thereby interpreting that information according to the mind of Christ instead of his natural intuition and lived experiences apart from God.

Lines A & B. In combination, these two lines represent the working of godly faith – the kind of faith that saves. Its object is the love, power, and promises of God.

Line C. God responds to godly faith by unleashing the power of His Spirit to cause circumstances to conform to His definition of reality. In fact, He may actually reorder the cosmos in response to the faith of His saints.

The Workings of a Worldly RW Mental Filter

In contrast to the godly RW mental filter, Figure 3-2 illustrates the workings of a worldly RW mental filter, which is based entirely upon worldly faith, natural intuition, and lived experiences apart from God.

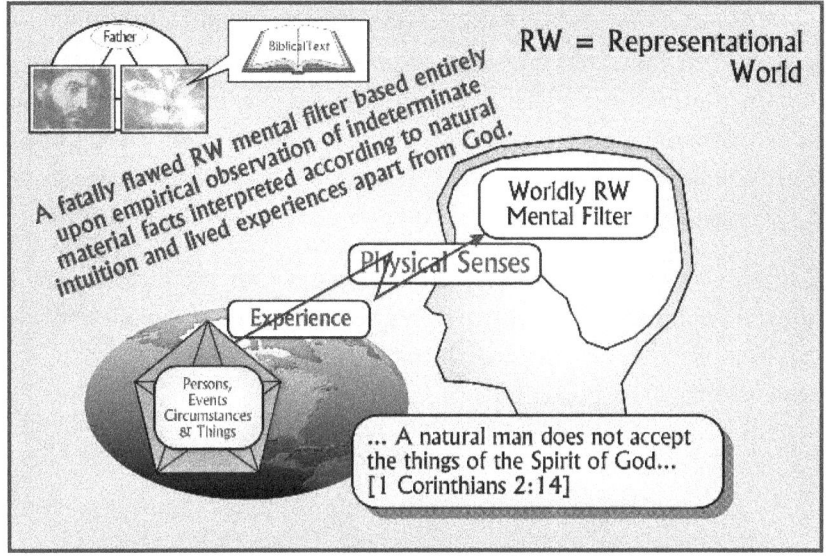

Figure 3-2. The Workings of a Worldly RW Mental Filter

As delineated in Figure 3-2, the worldly RW mental filter is ultimately derived from material facts which are inherently indeterminant. Thus, the worldly RW mental filter is fatally flawed by definition. Because the worldly person is repressing known truth concerning God, he is willfully living as if God doesn't exist. That is, he is living as a **functional atheist**.

Therefore, he is subject to the mental blindness and confusion described by the Apostle Paul in Romans 1:18ff, which we will address in detail in Part 3 of the WitW study.

What happens when a godly person chooses to operate with a worldly RW mental filter, at least temporarily? In effect, such a person is living as a **functional atheist** as is the case with the worldly person discussed above. In particular, he is, at least temporarily, rejecting God's definition of reality. As a result of God's withdrawing the power of His Spirit, the person actually experiences a reality without God, which is the reality he has chosen for himself.

On the other hand, the experience of the person who operates with a godly RW mental filter is in accord with God's definition of reality, which is the reality that he has appropriated by means of his godly faith.

As previously stated, Line C in Figure 3-1 signifies God's unleashing the power of His Spirit to reorder the cosmos in such a manner as to cause the experience of the godly person to correspond with God's definition of reality. In fact, His adjustment of the cosmos impacts not only the external circumstances of the godly person, but also the internal state of his personality through the sanctifying ministry of the Holy Spirit.

As we become increasingly habitual in our practice of a godly RW mental filter, even our intuition becomes progressively more and more godly – that is, it becomes aligned with the nature and character of God and His view of reality.

Proleptic Teaching

Often the invisible reality projected on our minds through Scripture takes the form of **prolepsis**; that is, a promised future state that is represented as if it were presently actualized. Proleptic teaching permeates Paul's epistles, especially in the case of the essential doctrines of salvation and sanctification. Consider, for example, the following passage that we have already had occasion to study in chapter 2:

> For those whom He **foreknew** He also **predestined** to be conformed to the image of His Son, in order that He might be the firstborn among many brothers. And those whom He **predestined** He also **called**, and those whom He **called** He also **justified**, and those whom He **justified** He also **glorified**. [Romans 8:29-30, adapted from the ESV, emphasis added]

Note the tense of the key verbs in this passage; in the English translation they are all expressed in the past tense. However, in the Greek, they are all expressed in the aorist active indicative tense, which designates an action accomplished at a point in past time which has timeless significance. How can Paul speak of our glorification in this way? From our vantage point on the treadmill of time, our glorification is a future reality for which we hope and toward which we press forward. **But God would have us lay hold of this future reality as if it were already actualized!** And, guess what! As delineated in Figure 3-1, to the extent we do, He unleashes the power of His Spirit to cause that promised future reality to become actualized in our present experience – perhaps not completely, but substantially. In fact, He fully intends and has made provision for our experiencing some of the glories of the age to come in this present life, but only to the extent that we are willing to lay hold of them through exercise of godly faith. The author of Hebrews cogently states this in the opening verse of the great chapter on the heroes of faith portrayed in the Hebrew Scriptures.

> Now faith is the assurance of things hoped for, the conviction of things not seen. [Hebrew 11:1, ESV]

And so proleptic teaching is similar to Moses' view of the promised land of Canaan from the summit of Mount Pisgah as recorded in Deuteronomy 34:1ff. For the nation of Israel, their entrance into the promised land was a future reality that was not yet actualized in experience. Although Moses would not lead the people across the Jordan into the land of Canaan, he was enabled by Yahweh to view the land from a distance and to visualize the tribes of Israel occupying their inheritances. However, in our case there is a difference. Through faith, we are enabled not only to **see** our inheritance from afar, but to **actually experience** some of its glories in this present life.

Crucifixion of the Flesh

Understanding the contrast between Figure 3-1 and Figure 3-2 and practicing the godly RW mental filter is essential to walking in the way of Christ and the apostles; this is the way of wisdom, and it is a way that is radically counter-intuitive. To perceive our material time-space reality through the godly RW mental filter of Figure 3-1 is a prerequisite to **walking in the Spirit**, but to perceive our material time-space reality through the worldly RW mental filter of Figure 3-2 guarantees that we are **walking in the flesh**. The teaching of Christ and the apostles is permeated by warnings that the way of the flesh is the way of fruitlessness and it leads to ruination and death. [38] In Galatians 5:24, Paul states the following:

> And those who belong to Christ Jesus have crucified the flesh with its passions and desires. [Galatians 5:24, ESV]

In other words, those who belong to Christ are constantly vigilant to discard the worldly RW mental filter of Figure 3-2, and they habitually embrace the godly RW mental filter of Figure 3-1. [39]

Life-Critical Importance of Embracing a Godly RW Mental Filter

There are two paradigmatic episodes in the Hebrew Scriptures which powerfully present the life-critical importance of embracing and practicing a godly RW mental filter. The first of these is the **Kadesh Barnea episode** recorded in the 13th and 14th chapters of Numbers, and the second is the **David and Goliath episode** recorded in the 17th chapter of 1 Samuel.

A third important biblical representation in the Hebrew Scriptures is the Tabernacle, which will be discussed after the two aforementioned episodes.

The Kadesh Barnea Episode Versus the Conquest of Jericho

The extended narrative of the Kadesh Barnea episode is recorded in the 13th and 14th chapters of Numbers, and an abbreviated summary is recorded in Deuteronomy 1:19-45. In contrast to the defeat at Kadesh Barnea, the 6th chapter of Joshua records the conquest of Jericho wrought by the hand of Yahweh, which was enabled by Israel's trust and obedience. In this discussion, I will endeavor to clearly place in evidence the representational issues that led to the apostasy and spiritual defeat which characterize the Kadesh Barnea episode versus the glorious victory that characterizes the conquest of Jericho.

According to Moses' narrative in Numbers, the Israelites had arrived at Kadesh Barnea, which is located near the southern boundary of the promised land. From Kadesh Barnea, Moses deployed and commissioned twelve spies to reconnoiter the land, one man from each of the twelve tribes of Israel. Of these twelve men, Caleb represented the tribe of Judah, and Joshua represented the tribe of Ephraim.

After traversing the land for 40 days, the spies returned to the Israelite encampment at Kadesh Barnea and presented their report to Moses. The following summarizes what they had observed:

- **Agricultural abundance**. The promised land did, indeed, flow with milk and honey.

- **Fortified cities**. The spies reported that a number of the Canaanite cities were heavily fortified.

- **Giants**. The spies also reported that they had seen men of great stature among the Canaanite population.

All twelve of the spies embraced these observations as being accurate. However, two of them – Caleb and Joshua – affirmed emphatically that the army of Israel should go in and take the land in spite of the apparent military superiority of the Canaanites. They did this on the basis of the following promises of Yahweh, the Elohim of Israel:

- **Land promise**. He promised to give the land of Canaan to Abraham and his descendants, which was confirmed and secured by a solemn blood covenant ceremony as recorded in the 15th chapter of Genesis.

- **Military force multiplication**. He promised repeatedly through Moses to give the Israelites victory over their enemies if only they remained true to His covenant. This promise is first stated in Exodus 23:20ff. It is then restated in Leviticus 26:1ff in terms of a one hundredfold military force multiplication. Finally it is confirmed at length and with great emphasis in Deuteronomy 28:1ff. [40]

In terms of military strength, Caleb and Joshua were absolutely convinced that if Israel remained faithful to their covenant with Yahweh, then He would cause their army to be an invincible force against the numerically superior armies of the Canaanites. In other words, Yahweh's blessing upon His chosen people would take the form of a 100-to-1 divine force multiplier in accordance with Leviticus 26:8. Accordingly, Caleb and Joshua **represented the armies of the Canaanites as being powerless to oppose Israel and as an already defeated enemy** in accordance with the love, power, and promises of Yahweh.

However, the other ten spies, **who had observed the very same material facts as Caleb and Joshua**, embraced a radically different representation. Their assessment of the military strength of the Canaanites in comparison with that of Israel was based entirely upon their natural intuition and lived experiences apart from God. Accordingly, they argued that Israel **should not** attempt to enter the land of Canaan in view of the apparent military superiority of the Canaanites. To argue this way, the ten spies had to willfully ignore Yahweh's land promise to Abraham recorded in Genesis 15, as well as the repeated assurances of His force-multiplying presence with the army of Israel, so long as they remained faithful to the terms of His covenant with them. Thus, based upon their observation of the same material facts as summarized above, the ten spies **represented Israel as powerless to defeat the armies of the Canaanites**.

In sum, Caleb and Joshua illustrate the operation of the godly RW mental filter delineated in Figure 3-1, and the other ten spies illustrate the operation of the worldly RW mental filter delineated in Figure 3-2. Unfortunately, the entire community of Israel refused the godly representation of the land reported by Caleb and Joshua, and instead they bought into and embraced the worldly representation reported by the other ten spies. The life-critical significance of their decision is placed in evidence by these facts: the ten spies who brought the bad report were struck down immediately by Yahweh Elohim, and the entire generation of fighting men who embraced the ungodly representation of those ten spies was condemned to perish outside of the land over the course of 38 years of fruitlessly wandering about in the Sinai desert.

The positive side of this story is the conquest narrative recorded in the Book of Joshua, according to which the new generation of fighting men under Joshua's leadership successfully defeated the Canaanites throughout the hill country of the land of Canaan as epitomized by the glorious conquest of Jericho. They accomplished this amazing feat because they trusted in the love, power, and promises of Yahweh, the Elohim of Israel. In other words, they embraced the godly RW mental filter of Caleb and Joshua, and they rejected the RW mental filter of the other ten spies. In response to their faith, the blessing of Yahweh took the form of the 100-to-1 divine force multiplier promised in Leviticus 26:8.

The David and Goliath Episode

The David and Goliath episode is recorded in the 17th chapter of 1 Samuel. The army of Israel under the personal command of King Saul was drawn up in battle formation against the army of the Philistines. Out from the ranks of the Philistines came forth the giant Goliath, who challenged the Israelites to choose a single champion who would engage him in one-on-one combat. The victor of this contest would decide the entire battle.

The entire Israelite army shrank away in mortal fear of Goliath, including their leader, King Saul. They represented him as invincible on account of his great stature and strength, his defensive armor, and his offensive weaponry. However, as it turned out, David had been sent by his father, Jesse, to encourage his brothers, and he arrived on the scene just as Goliath was shouting his daily challenge. As David listened to the giant, he exclaimed, "Who is this uncircumcised Philistine, that he should taunt the armies of the living God?"

When he was brought before King Saul, David stated that God had enabled him to successfully defend his father's flock against the attacks of lions and bears, "and this uncircumcised Philistine will be like one of them, since he has taunted the armies of the living God." Thus, David represented the Philistine, not as invincible, but as "dead meat" on account of the fact that he was blaspheming the name of Yahweh, the Elohim of Israel. As he ran to meet Goliath, he shouted that timeless and normative declaration, "Yahweh does not deliver by sword or by spear; for the battle is Yahweh's and He will give you into our hands." In response to David's declaration of faith, Yahweh enabled the stone slung by David to penetrate the giant's defenses, and "the stone sank into his forehead, so that he fell on his face to the ground. Thus David prevailed over the Philistine with a sling and a stone."

In sum, both David and the army of King Saul were presented with the identical material facts concerning Goliath's great stature and strength, his defensive armor, and his offensive weaponry. Whereas, Saul and all his men represented the giant as invincible in accordance with their natural intuition and lived experiences apart from God, David represented him as weak and vulnerable on account of the fact that he was taunting the army of Israel, and, thereby, he was blaspheming the name of Yahweh, the Elohim of Israel. Saul and all his men represented Goliath according to the worldly RW mental filter of Figure 3-2, but David represented him according to the godly RW mental filter of Figure 3-1. Had the worldly RW mental filter of Saul and his men prevailed, Israel would have been defeated by the Philistines. However, the godly RW mental filter of David prevailed, which brought about a glorious victory.

The stories of the Hebrew Scriptures are rich with theological, moral, and ethical teaching, as I will explain more fully in chapters 4 and 5. However, a factor which most, if not all, of them share is that they dramatize in real life experiences the radical difference between the operation of the godly RW mental filter delineated in Figure 3-1 versus the operation of the worldly RW mental filter delineated in Figure 3-2.

The Tabernacle in the Wilderness

We turn now to one of the richest biblical representations to be found in all of Scripture; namely, the **tabernacle in the wilderness**, which is illustrated in Figure 3-3. [41]

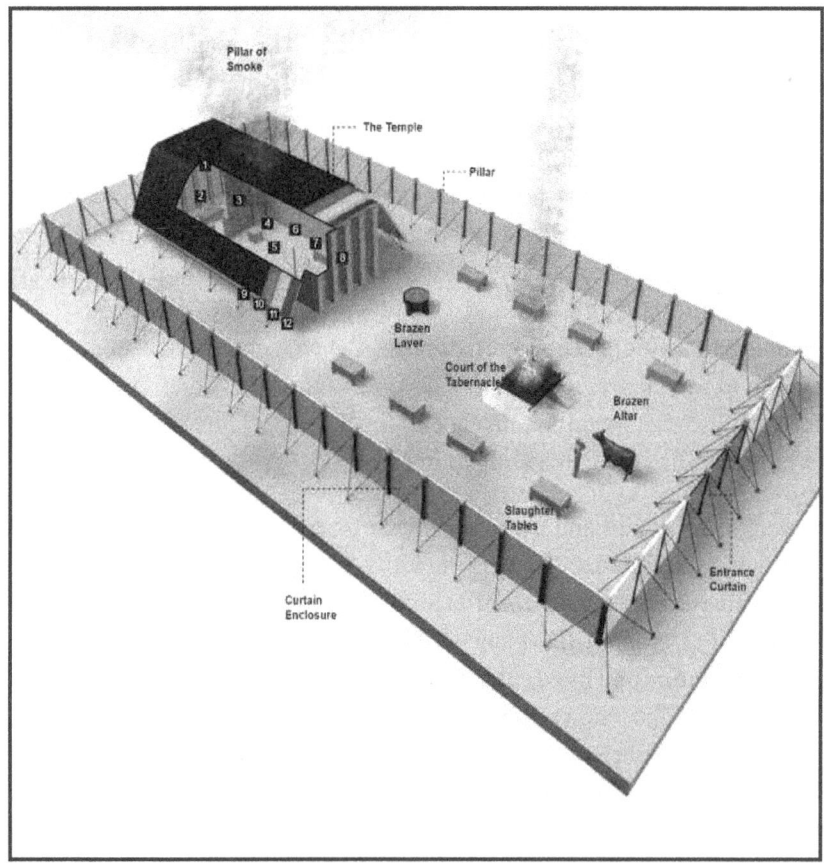

Figure 3-3. The Tabernacle in the Wilderness:
A Rich Biblical Representation

Yahweh's commands regarding the provision for and design of the tabernacle are recorded in Exodus 25 – 31, and its construction and erection are recorded in Exodus 35:4 – 40:38.

The tabernacle in the wilderness represents the holiness of God and how we, as sinful people, may suitably approach and worship Him. In fact, by means of the object lessons presented by the tabernacle and the associated Levitical worship system, Yahweh has powerfully and compellingly instructed us concerning the related concepts of holiness and sanctification. Moreover, the tabernacle and its furnishings richly represent the life and ministry of Jesus Christ.

The Tabernacle and Its Furnishings. First, the courtyard which surrounded the tabernacle marked the separation between the holy precinct inside the courtyard and that which was non-holy or common on the outside. Only the Aaronic priests – that is, the descendants of Aaron – could minister inside the courtyard. The tabernacle itself was divided into two rooms by the massive veil. The outer room was called the Holy Place, and in it were placed the table of showbread on the north side (to the right as one entered), the golden altar of incense on the west side immediately in front of the veil, and the lampstand on the south side. Any of the priests could minister in the Holy Place, which included replacing the loaves of showbread each morning, burning incense on the golden altar, and servicing the lampstand by trimming its wicks and replenishing its reservoirs of olive oil.

Correspondence With the Life and Ministry of Jesus Christ. Let us pause to reflect upon the correspondence between the tabernacle and its furnishings with aspects of the life and ministry of Jesus Christ.

- **The brazen altar** of burnt offering represents the fact that Jesus Christ gave Himself for us as a sin offering, as eloquently testified in Hebrews 13:10-13.

- **The table of showbread** represents the fact that Jesus Christ is the bread of life as testified in John 6:35-40.

- **The lampstand** represents the fact that Jesus Christ is the light of the world as testified in the 1st chapter of John's gospel and as exhibited through the miracle of restoring sight to the man born blind in the 9th chapter.

- **The golden altar of incense** reminds us that Jesus Christ is our Great High Priest, who intercedes for us from His heavenly throne. In Revelation 8:3ff we are told that incense serves as a metaphor for the prayers of the saints, and Romans 8:26-27 testifies concerning the intercessory ministry of the Holy Spirit, who interprets our prayers before the Father's Throne of Grace.

The Most Holy Place. Beyond the veil was the Most Holy Place, which contained the ark of the covenant, the holiest piece of furniture in the entire tabernacle complex – indeed, on the entire planet. The cover of the ark was called the mercy seat, and it was overshadowed by the wings of the golden cherubim. [42] Between the cherubim and above the mercy seat was the shekinah glory, the visible manifestation of the very presence of Yahweh, the Elohim of Israel. The words of the writer of Hebrews most cogently and eloquently represent the extreme sanctity of the Most Holy Place:

> These preparations having thus been made, the priests go regularly into the first section, performing their ritual duties, but into the second only the high priest goes, and he but once a year, and not without taking blood, which he offers for himself and for the unintentional sins of the people. [Hebrews 9:6-7, ESV]

Thus, as the worshiper of Yahweh imagined himself walking through the courtyard entrance, passing by the brazen altar of burnt offering and thence the bronze laver, then entering into the Holy Place, and finally entering the Most Holy Place, **he experienced an object lesson in holiness and worship.** [43] In other words, the tabernacle and its furnishings, together with the worship regulations associated therewith, objectified the concept of holiness and how a sinful man could suitably approach and worship an absolutely holy God.

The New and Living Way. To conclude our discussion of the representational richness of the tabernacle in the wilderness, let us reflect deeply upon the following exhortation in the 10th chapter of Hebrews:

> Therefore, brothers, since we have confidence to enter the Most Holy Place by the blood of Jesus, by the new and living way that He opened for us through the curtain, that is, through His flesh, and since we have a Great High Priest

over the household of God, let us draw near with a true heart in full assurance of faith, with our hearts sprinkled clean from a guilty conscience and our bodies washed with pure water. [Hebrews 10:19–22, adapted from the ESV]

From this passage we recognize that the massive veil that partitioned the Holy Place from the Most Holy Place served as a metaphor for the body of Jesus Christ. When He gave Himself for us, that veil was rent from top to bottom in accordance with Matthew 27:51 and Mark 15:38. Now, as a result of His atoning death, **the way into the Most Holy Place has been opened to each and every true disciple of Christ**. Any of us can appear before the Throne of Grace at any time with confidence and even boldness in accordance with Hebrews 4:14-16. Moreover, whereas only the high priest could enter the Most Holy Place once each year on the Day of Atonement under the terms of the old covenant, now, under the terms of the new covenant, we can all enter the Most Holy Place in heaven, the very throne room of God Himself!

Representations in the Christian Scriptures

Before turning from the subject of biblical representations, I want to draw your attention to some of the representations set forth in the Christian Scriptures. I encourage you to make this an adventure of discovery as you read or listen through the Bible. The teachings of Jesus Christ in the Sermon on the Mount and His parables are especially rich sources of biblical representations that are vitally important for the disciple of Christ. In the following paragraphs I will briefly discuss just three examples:

- Jesus' representation of the proper relationship of the disciple to Torah in Matthew 5:17-20.

- Jesus' representation of the life-critical importance of forgiveness in Matthew 18:21-35.

- Jesus' representation of the essence of salvation as restored fellowship with God in Luke 15:11-32.

Jesus' Representation of the Proper Relationship of the Disciple to Torah

From Jesus' teaching in the Sermon on the Mount concerning the Torah, there can be no doubt in the disciple's mind that the Torah of Moses continues as a timeless and normative representation of human righteousness, and it serves as the fountainhead of human wisdom, as is discussed at length in chapter 5. In fact, Jesus' statement concerning anyone who relaxes or diminishes the authority of Torah stimulates godly fear in the heart of the disciple.

> Therefore whoever relaxes one of the least of these commandments and teaches others to do the same will be called least in the kingdom of heaven, but whoever does them and teaches them will be called great in the kingdom of heaven. [Matthew 5:19, ESV]

Moreover, Jesus' statements near the conclusion of His Sermon on the Mount recorded in the 7th chapter of Matthew are absolutely frightening.

> On that day many will say to me, "Lord, Lord, did we not prophesy in your name, and cast out demons in your name, and do many mighty works in your name?" And then will I declare to them, "I never knew you; depart from me, you workers of lawlessness." [Matthew 7:22–23, ESV]

Thus, Torah continues in effect "until all is accomplished," in accordance with Matthew 5:18. But how does it continue in effect in view of the teachings of the Apostle Paul? He represents the disciple of Christ as having been delivered from the Law through the death of Jesus Christ. However, he also states,

> Do we then overthrow the law by this faith? By no means! On the contrary, we uphold the law. [Romans 3:31, ESV]

In my estimation, the key passage on the relationship between the disciple and the Torah of Moses is the following:

> ... For God has done what the law, weakened by the flesh, could not do. By sending His own Son in the likeness of sinful flesh and for sin, He condemned sin in the flesh, in order that the righteous requirement of the law might be

> fulfilled in us, who walk not according to the flesh but according to the Spirit. [Romans 8:3-4, adapted from the ESV]

The difference between the old covenant and new covenant arrangement is announced by the prophet Jeremiah.

> Behold, the days are coming, declares Yahweh, when I will make a new covenant with the house of Israel and the house of Judah, not like the covenant that I made with their fathers on the day when I took them by the hand to bring them out of the land of Egypt, My covenant that they broke, though I was their husband, declares Yahweh. But this is the covenant that I will make with the house of Israel after those days, declares Yahweh: **I will put My law within them, and I will write it on their hearts**. [Jeremiah 31:31-33, adapted from the ESV, emphasis added]

But, how does the new covenant announced by Jeremiah apply to Gentile disciples of Jesus Christ? It applies by virtue of our having been grafted into the community of Israel as taught by Paul through the olive tree metaphor in the 11th chapter of Romans and as stated directly in Ephesians 2:11-22. We conclude that the Torah of Moses does, in fact, remain as the timeless and normative representation of human righteousness; to wit, a pattern of human behavior that is consistent with the nature and character of Yahweh, and which therefore pleases Him. Such behavior flows from a heart that fears and loves Yahweh, and is therefore committed to walking in His way. However, **the dynamic of law-keeping has been radically altered** under the terms of the new covenant. Whereas under the old covenant men had to keep the Torah of Moses out from the energy of the flesh, under the new covenant we are enabled to behave righteously out from the energy of the indwelling Holy Spirit. In fact, according to Romans 8:3-4 quoted above, the reason for God "sending His own Son in the likeness of sinful flesh and for sin" was so "**that the righteous requirement of the law might be fulfilled in us, who walk not according to the flesh but according to the Spirit**." Under both covenants, however, the Torah of Moses serves as a representation of the lifestyle of the person who fears and loves Yahweh. In other words, **one logically necessary manifestation of the kind of faith that saves is a lifestyle that is righteous and holy**.

However, does the entire Mosaic law revealed in Exodus through Deuteronomy apply to the disciple of Christ as stated above? Or, are there portions of it that have found their fulfillment in Christ and are therefore no longer operative. For our purposes in this chapter, a convenient and appropriate way of representing the Mosaic law is in terms of three major components as follows:

1. The **moral law**, consisting of the Ten Commandments as set forth in Exodus 20:1-17 and repeated in Deuteronomy 5:5-21.

2. The **civil** or **case law**, which is distributed throughout Exodus, Leviticus, and Numbers, and repeated in a condensed form in Deuteronomy. This component of the Mosaic law sets forth the practical implications of the moral law in specific situations that could arise within the civil life of the Israelites.

3. The **religious** or **ceremonial law**, which is distributed throughout Exodus, Leviticus, and Numbers; a condensed summary is presented in Deuteronomy. This component of the law is especially the focus of Leviticus, where Moses sets forth the requirements for the religious life of the Israelites.

There is substantial agreement among biblical scholars that the only component of the Mosaic law that carries over and continues to be operative under the new covenant is the first: namely, the moral law. The civil law was instituted for the nation of Israel under the old covenant. While it now serves as a divinely inspired model for the ordering of a civil society, it is not mandatory. The religious law was instituted for the nation of Israel, and it is fulfilled through Jesus Christ's sacrifice of Himself for the sins of His people.

That said, the feasts and festivals of Israel form a far more comprehensive and articulate representational enactment of God's redemptive program than do the events of the Christian calendar.

Thus, in conclusion, the sense in which we are delivered from the Mosaic law through the death of Jesus Christ is this: we are no longer subject to it as an external, legalistic requirement. Instead, the inclination of our hearts is to keep it **as a matter of inner necessity** as prompted and energized by the Holy Spirit. Accordingly, Jesus' representation of Torah and its applicability to His disciples is seen to be rich, highly nuanced, and complex, especially when considered along with the teachings of the Apostle Paul.

Jesus' Representation of the Life-Critical Importance of Forgiveness

The Parable of the Unforgiving Servant recorded in Matthew 18:21ff presents a frightening truth concerning the doctrine of forgiveness.

Characters. Clearly, from the manner in which Jesus concludes the parable, the king represents God the Father. The 1st servant represents any of us in regard to our moral indebtedness to God the Father. The 2nd servant represents any of us in regard to our moral indebtedness to one another.

Money. To appreciate this parable, the amounts of money mentioned in it must be translated into modern equivalents. The 10,000 talents owed by the 1st servant to the king was equivalent to a billion days' worth of wages for a field laborer of the 1st century AD according to the HCSB Study Bible.[44] In our day, a laborer who is paid $10 per hour could earn about $120 per day, assuming a 12-hour workday as in the 1st century. Thus, a billion days' worth of earnings would be $120B. If the laborer in question worked 6 days per week and 50 weeks per year, his annual wage would be $36,000. Accordingly, to retire a debt of $120B would require 3.333 million years or 66,666 lifetimes, assuming 50 years of labor per lifetime. In comparison, the debt of 100 denarii owed by the 2nd servant to the 1st would be equivalent to 100 days' worth of wages for a field laborer. With the same assumptions as above, the modern equivalent of 100 denarii would therefore be $12,000, requiring 4 months of wages for repayment.

Biblical Representations in the Parable of the Unforgiving Servant. With the modern equivalent of the amounts of money understood, there are four profound truths to be derived from this parable, which are set forth in the paragraphs which follow.

1. **Representation of sin.** All human sin effectively creates a moral liability or debt that is owed by an offender to the offended party. The debt that each of us owes to God the Father on account of our sin is astronomical. In comparison, the debt owed to us on account of an offense by a brother or sister in Christ is infinitesimal.

2. **Representation of God's forgiveness**. The essence of forgiveness is an act of the will by which the offended part removes or wipes away the moral debt owed to him by the offender. Because human sin is a capital offense before God, death is the only consideration that can settle the moral debt that each of us owes to God on account of our sin. However, Jesus Christ as the God-Man has stepped forward. As a representative of all mankind, He has paid our debt so that God the Father is able to remain absolutely just and righteous in His act of extending forgiveness to each of us. Such forgiveness is like the wiping away of the astronomical debt which the 1st servant owed to the king.

3. **Representation of our forgiveness of one another**. Acts of forgiving one another for offenses is the **logically necessary result** of our having been forgiven by God. In other words, God's graciously forgiving our astronomical debt should stir in us **an irrepressible desire** to forgive others for whatever offenses they may commit against us.

The connection between our having received forgiveness from God and our extending forgiveness to others is so strong that an unforgiving spirit on our part is a sure indication that we have never really embraced and internalized God's forgiveness of us!

4. **Representation of the ultimate moral state of one who has an unforgiving spirit**. The state of the unforgiving servant at the conclusion of the parable is most noteworthy. Not only is the astronomical debt reinstated, but the king sends the servant off to prison until the debt is repaid. And Jesus concludes the parable by stating, "So also my heavenly Father will do to every one of you, if you do not forgive your brother from your heart." [Matthew 18:35, ESV] Accordingly, the final state of the unforgiving servant is analogous to eternal death, which is the only way we can repay God for the infinite moral debt we owe to Him on account of our sin, **if we refuse to accept and embrace His forgiveness of us through the atoning death of Jesus Christ our Lord.**

The following question arises: does Jesus' teaching on forgiveness apply only within the covenant community, or does it apply more generally? It is noteworthy that the parable was given by Jesus in response to Peter's question, "Lord, how often will my brother (= *adelphos*) sin against me, and I forgive him? As many as seven times?" By employing *adelphos* = brother, Peter probably had in mind a fellow Jew rather than a fellow human being. Moreover, in the parable, the two servants were related by living in the court of and being subject to the same king. Therefore, it seems to me that the immediate application of Jesus' teaching is to the covenant community. However, should we withhold forgiveness from a neighbor who is not a believer? I would answer no, even as Jesus, as He was dying on the Cross, implored the Father to forgive His executioners. [45] In like manner, as Stephen was being stoned to death, he implored God to forgive those who were killing him. [46]

One final comment is in order regarding the unforgiving servant. He did not lose his salvation on account of his unforgiving spirit. Because he never truly internalized the king's forgiveness of his astronomical debt, he was never truly justified and regenerated. He places this fact into evidence by his refusal to forgive his fellow servant.

Jesus' Representation of the Essence of Salvation as Restored Fellowship With God

In the Parable of the Prodigal Son recorded in Luke 15:11-32, Jesus represents the essence of salvation as restoration of fellowship with God the Father. There are at least two biblical representations in this parable, which are essential to our understanding the true nature of salvation as restored fellowship with God:

1. **<u>Scandalous attitude of the younger son</u>**. By requesting that his father distribute to him a share of the estate, the younger son is effectively saying to his father, "I wish you were dead right now." He thereby manifests his prideful rebellion against the rule of his father as patriarch of the household. It is noteworthy that such prideful rebellion on the part of the younger son is a capital offense in accordance with Deuteronomy 21:18-20.

    Since, in the world of the 1st century AD, an estate consisted largely of illiquid assets such as land and livestock, the father was forced to actually liquidate assets in order to comply with his younger son's request.

The younger son severs relationship with his father as he takes his money and departs to a country far away. Instead of protecting what his father has given him as a precious asset, he wastes it through riotous living. When the country where he is living is afflicted by a severe famine, he is forced to indenture himself to a citizen of that country, who sends him into the field to care for pigs. Feeding pigs represents a thoroughly despicable occupation for a young Jewish man.

2. **Repentance and faith**. In his state of absolute destitution and degradation, the younger son comes to his senses as he recognizes that even his father's servants are better off than he. And so picks himself up and returns to his father, trusting in the father's mercy and forgiveness.

This affords a picture of the kind of repentance and faith that saves. The essence of repentance is a profound recognition of the degraded state into which the sinner has fallen, an abhorrence of that state, and a turning from it. The essence of saving faith is a profound trust in and a casting of oneself upon the mercy and forgiveness of God. In combination, repentance and faith are not theoretical or abstract attitudes of the mind, but rather they result in action being taken, as exemplified by the prodigal's traveling back to his father.

Not only does the father extend mercy and forgiveness to his wayward son, but he joyfully celebrates his return to the household by putting on a feast. To place the father's treatment of his prodigal son in its cultural context, the accepted norm for this situation would be at least that the father would disown and cast out his son. In fact, according to Deuteronomy 21:18-21, the younger son was guilty of a capital offense and was liable to death by stoning. However, by running to meet his son, kissing and embracing him, commanding that he be clothed with the best robe and shoes, placing a ring on his finger, and putting on a feast to celebrate his safe return, the father made a public display of the fact that the prodigal was completely forgiven.

Summary: Evidence of the Kind of Faith That Saves

In the parables of Jesus Christ that we have examined, the fact is evident that the kind of faith that saves is manifested by righteous living in accordance with the Torah of Moses, by graciously and unconditionally forgiving brothers and sisters within the community of faith for any and all offenses that they may commit, and by being careful to remain in the Father's household, abiding by the rules of that household and thereby conducting oneself within the sphere of the Father's blessing. Indeed, the disciple's fellowship with his heavenly Father is the essence of blessing, and to be removed from that fellowship is the essence of cursing. This is in accordance with the **covenant of conditional blessing** integrative motif, to which we turn in chapter 5.

Guarding the Heart

In this section I address one of the most important applications of the concepts put forth in this chapter. In the 4th chapter of Proverbs we find the following wise counsel concerning the guarding of our hearts:

> Watch over your heart with all diligence, for from it flow the springs of life. Turn your back on the mouth that misleads, and keep your distance from lips that deceive. Let your eyes look straight ahead, and let your gaze be directly in front of you. Watch the path of your feet, and all your ways will be established. Turn neither to the right nor to the left; keep your foot clear of evil. [Proverbs 4:23-27, personal translation adapted from the New Jerusalem Bible]

Accepting the ascription to Solomon expressed in the 1st verse of Proverbs, we have, in the passage quoted above, Solomon's instruction to his son regarding an important aspect of the way of wisdom; namely, **guarding the heart with all diligence**. While this is, indeed, wise counsel that every disciple of Christ should carefully heed, its authoritative force would have been strengthened had Solomon's own life exhibited this aspect of the way of wisdom. What was Solomon's downfall in regard to his own admonition to guard the heart with all diligence? He failed to guard his heart in the sphere of sexual desire. As a result, his harem grew to the enormous size of some 1,000 women. And his many wives drew his heart away from Yahweh, the Elohim of Israel, and he began to join his wives in worship of their various deities. And so Solomon's life actually affords to us a powerful counter-example of **how not to guard one's heart**.

Identifying and Characterizing the Heart According to Scripture

Before moving forward in our discussion of guarding the heart, we need to pose this question: what did Solomon mean by "heart"? According to the way in which the term is employed in the Hebrew Scriptures, what aspect of the human personality does the term **heart** designate? The lexical form of the Hebrew word which is translated "heart" is *leb*, which designates the inner man, the mind, the will, or the heart. In the 17th chapter of his prophecy, Jeremiah makes the following assertion:

> The heart (= *leb*) is more deceitful than anything else, and incurable – who can understand it? I, Yahweh, examine the mind, I test the heart (= *leb*) to give to each according to his way, according to what his actions deserve. [Jeremiah 17:9-10, adapted from the HCSB]

In his prophecy of the new covenant in the 31st chapter, Jeremiah states,

> Instead, this is the covenant I will make with the house of Israel after those days," says Yahweh. "I will put My teaching within them and write it on their hearts (= *leb*). I will be their Elohim, and they will be My people. [Jeremiah 31:33, adapted from the HCSB]

Assuming Jesus employed the term "heart" in His teaching in a manner consistent with the ancient Hebraic understanding of the human personality, consider what He asserted according to 15th chapter of Matthew: [47]

> But what comes out of the mouth comes from the heart, and this defiles a man. For from the heart come evil thoughts, murders, adulteries, sexual immoralities, thefts, false testimonies, blasphemies. These are the things that defile a man, but eating with un-washed hands does not defile a man. [Matthew 15:18-20, HCSB]

Jesus' list of the evil things which proceed from the heart and Paul's list of the "deeds of the flesh" in Galatians 5:19ff, gives rise to the unmistakable impression that what Jesus meant by "heart" in the 15th chapter of Matthew corresponds to what Paul meant by "flesh" in the 5th chapter of Galatians. Moreover, Paul discusses the manner in which the flesh deceives and overpowers the mind in the 7th chapter of Romans.

And so let us assemble a list of the functions and attributes of the heart as revealed through the teaching of Solomon, Jeremiah, Jesus, and Paul:

- The heart is like a spring, and a person's way is like the stream that flows from the spring. Therefore, the heart is the seat of all desire, whether good or bad. Everything we say or do – our entire way of life – is the result of what is in the heart.

- On account of the Invasion of Evil, Sin, and Death – that is, the Sigma Event of Figure 2-1 – the impulses of the heart are naturally inclined toward evil.

- Prideful rebellion against the righteous rule of God is an attribute of the human heart, which means that the heart naturally responds to the commands of God with an **impulse toward disobedience** rather than an **impulse toward obedience**, as Paul explains in the 7th chapter of Romans.

- When a person responds to the Christian gospel by repenting of his prideful rebellion, choosing to submit to God's righteous rule, and receiving by faith the salvation that Jesus Christ purchased through His death, the Holy Spirit comes to abide within him as a **Paraclete** – one who is called alongside to render aid. [48] We designate this event **Christian conversion**.

- After conversion, the person discovers that the old desires and motivating impulses of his heart remain, but now he has a new set of desires and motivating impulses which compete for his attention – in fact, **the desires and motivating impulses of the heart of Jesus** – which are imparted by the Holy Spirit.

The last point above introduces the **flesh versus Spirit** conflict that the Apostle Paul discusses in the 5th chapter of Galatians. Following is the cardinal passage on this subject:

> Now the works of the flesh are obvious: sexual immorality, moral impurity, promiscuity, idolatry, sorcery, hatreds, strife, jealousy, outbursts of anger, selfish ambitions,

> dissensions, factions, envy, drunkenness, carousing, and anything similar. I tell you about these things in advance – as I told you before – that those who practice such things will not inherit the kingdom of God. But the fruit of the Spirit is love, joy, peace, patience, kindness, goodness, faith, gentleness, self-control. Against such things there is no law. [Galatians 5:19 -23, HCSB]

Thus, that aspect or component of the human personality that is the "heart" before conversion is transmuted into the "flesh"' after conversion. According to Paul's terminology, the **flesh** (= *sarx* in the Greek) is a technical term which designates the entire set of old desires and motivating impulses that determined my way prior to my conversion. Another term for the flesh is "our old self" as in Romans 6:6. In contrast, a new set of desires and motivating impulses are imparted by the indwelling Holy Spirit, and the essence of these is captured by Paul's **fruit of the Spirit** in Galatians 5:22-23 and Peter's **seven virtues of the Christian life** presented in 2 Peter 1:3-11. This new set of desires and motivating impulses correspond to **the heart of Jesus Christ being reproduced in my personality** by the Holy Spirit. Moreover, they also correspond to the Torah of Yahweh being written on my heart in accordance with Jeremiah's New Covenant Prophecy in Jeremiah 31:31ff.

Reformation or Resurrection

There is one more essential point that I need to assert before turning to what is entailed in guarding the heart. Given the conflict between the flesh (= old set of desires and motivating impulses = old self) and the Spirit (= new set of desires and motivating impulses = the heart of Jesus), the strategy for conquering the flesh that would make sense to us is **reformation**, such as by consistent, even habitual, engagement in religious practices. This is the method taught by traditional Roman Catholicism, which springs from their having embraced semi-Pelagianism during the Council of Trent in the 16th century AD. [49]

However, this is not the method taught by the Apostle Paul in his epistles. Instead, God's solution to the problem of the flesh is our union with Christ in His **death, burial, and resurrection**. According to Paul's teaching in the 6th chapter of Romans, all that I am by virtue of genetics, training, and lived experiences prior to conversion (= old self in Romans 6:6) – the good along with the bad and the ugly – has been joined with

Christ in His death and burial so that the resurrection life of Christ might become mine through the ministry of the indwelling Holy Spirit.

> *The flesh, according to the Apostle Paul's argument in the 7th chapter of Romans, is unreformable. I cannot tame or domesticate it, regardless of how hard I try. If I struggle against it with all the force of my own will, it will win. The only solution to the problem of the flesh is death by crucifixion and burial – that is, participation in the death and burial of Jesus Christ.*

This is an important example of proleptic teaching by Paul in which he presents a future reality as being actualized in the present. Recalling our discussion earlier in this chapter in connection with Figure 3-1, as we appropriate, lay hold of, and cling to the reality of our union with Christ in His death, burial, and resurrection, God unleashes the power of His Spirit to actualize this reality in our experience, as indicated by Line C in Figure 3-1. We will not experience the **complete fulfillment** of our union with Christ in His death, burial, and resurrection until the Omega Event of Figure 2-1 in chapter 2, but we can experience a **substantial actualization** through our exercise of faith in God's precious and magnificent promises as we endeavor to walk in His way in this present life. In fact, as I practice the discipline of heeding and obeying the new impulses and motivating desires imparted by the Holy Spirit, the old ones progressively lose their hold on me, and I am increasingly conformed to the nature and character of Jesus Christ. I will have more to share on this vital subject in the section entitled Walking in the Spirit in chapter 10.

The Key to Guarding the Heart

Let us now return to our focal passage in the 4th chapter of Proverbs. In connection with this passage, we noted that King Solomon failed to guard his heart toward the end of his life. Moreover, his father, King David, failed to guard his heart at a key juncture in his life. The key to knowing how to guard the heart so as to avoid experiencing a moral downfall like David and Solomon experienced is to understand the way in which **the heart is able to deceptively play upon the mind to bring about adjustments to the person's representational world**. This can take place in at least two ways:

- The lusting heart deceptively plays upon the mind to adjust the person's representational world so as to rationalize or even justify the desired sinful action.

- The heart seeks to protect itself from conviction by deceptively playing upon the mind to adjust the person's representational world so as to project and impute its own sin to other persons.

In the 5th chapter of *Taste and See*, [50] John Piper identifies an example of the first deception in the 22nd chapter of Proverbs, where we read,

> The slacker says, "There's a lion outside! I'll be killed in the public square!" [Proverbs 22:13, HCSB]

The heart of the slacker is inclined toward laziness, but how can he rationalize his desire to stay inside and not work? As an artifice, the lazy heart of the slacker plays upon the mind to adjust his representational world so as to put a ravenous lion in the street. Whereas no one would stand with the slacker if he appealed directly to his impulse toward laziness as the reason for his staying inside and not working, anyone would stand with him if there were a ravenous lion in the street.

Piper's insight opens to our view the fact that there is an interplay between the heart and the mind which can bring about a change in the person's representational world. Let's see if we can identify biblical examples of each of the two ways this can occur. As we engage in this exercise, we must be careful to keep in mind that the heart of which we are speaking corresponds to the flesh in accordance with Paul's terminology.

Example of the Lusting Heart

The first way that the heart deceptively plays upon the mind to adjust the person's representational world is to rationalize or even justify gratification of a sinful lust. The cardinal example of a godly man giving way to the lust of his heart is recorded in the 11th chapter of 2 Samuel – namely, King David's sin in the matter of Uriah the Hittite. [51] According to the narrative in that chapter, David remained behind in Jerusalem when he probably should have been with his troops in the battle against the Ammonites. Moreover, he had been taking a nap in his personal chamber while it was still day when he should have been with his court attending to the affairs of state. Having arisen from his rest, he strolled about on the roof of his palace. From this vantage point he spied a beautiful woman taking a bath.

We could argue that David's decisions to remain behind in Jerusalem and take an afternoon nap had placed him in a state in which there was the potential for moral compromise. However, David had not disobeyed the commandments of Yahweh up to and including his observing Bathsheba in her bathtub. Moreover, while we could justifiably accuse Bathsheba of indiscretion in taking her bath on the rooftop of her home in plain view of David's palace, her action was not immoral. The tipping point occurred when David began to process the visual information of a beautiful woman bathing.

Following is the text that we need to analyze to understand the moral tipping point when observation became lust, and lust precipitated David's moral downfall:

> One evening David got up from his bed and strolled around on the roof of the palace. From the roof he saw a woman bathing – a very beautiful woman. [2 Samuel 11:2, HCSB]

Let us focus on the period at the end of the 2nd verse. This marks the point at which David should have represented the beautiful woman who had entered his gaze as **Yahweh's gift to another man**. However, instead he represented her as a woman **he wanted to embrace himself**. This representational sin on David's part was **the moral tipping point**, at which mere observation of a beautiful woman morphed into overpowering lust to caress and embrace her body. The sinful desire that was lurking in David's heart played upon his mind to alter his representational world so as to rationalize his acting on that desire.

What actions then ensued on David's part? Having gone beyond the moral tipping point of misrepresenting the beautiful woman in her bathtub, he called one of his attendants to join him on the roof of his palace. "Who is that woman down there? Go find out for me." The attendant reported back to David, "This is Bathsheba, daughter of Eliam and wife of Uriah the Hittite."

> David sent messengers to get her, and when she came to him, he slept with her. Now she had just been purifying herself from her uncleanness. Afterward, she returned

home. The woman conceived and sent word to inform David: "I am pregnant." [2 Samuel 11:4-5, HCSB]

The Way of Escape. I am convinced that the promise stated by the Apostle Paul in the 10th chapter of 1 Corinthians is timeless and normative:

> No temptation has overtaken you except what is common to humanity. God is faithful, and He will not allow you to be tempted beyond what you are able, but with the temptation He will also provide a way of escape so that you are able to bear it. [1 Corinthians 10:13, HCSB]

So, what was the way of escape for David? What was the off-ramp that would have avoided the road to moral calamity that he was about to traverse? The way of escape occurred at the period that ended the 2nd verse in our focal passage. It was to say "no" to the deceptive impulse of his heart to play upon his mind and alter his representation of the beautiful woman in her bathtub. "This woman, whoever she may be, is Yahweh's gift to some other man; she is not for me to gaze upon, to caress, and to embrace." Had David availed himself of this way of escape, he would have bounced his gaze away from the woman, put the visual impression of her out of his mind, gone back inside his palace, and focused his attention back on the affairs of state, from which he should not have wandered in the first place. Had he done this, the entire trajectory of his kingship would have been radically altered for the better, and he would have spared himself and his household much heartache and bloodshed.

Example of the Heart Seeking to Protect Itself from Conviction

The second way that the heart deceptively plays upon the mind in order to bring about an adjustment to the person's representational world is to protect itself from conviction in regard to a sinful attitude. The biblical example of this is King Saul after the David and Goliath episode recorded in the 17th chapter of 1 Samuel. In order for us to appreciate the representational sin to which Saul fell prey, we need to briefly summarize the trajectory of his 42-year reign.

The Trajectory of Saul's Kingship: Two Fatal Lapses. The record of Saul becoming the first king of Israel is presented in 1 Samuel beginning in the 10th chapter. While Saul unified the twelve tribes of Israel under himself as head, and he conducted successful military campaigns against Israel's enemies, his kingship is forever defined by two fatal lapses and by his relentless pursuit of David in order to destroy him.

The first lapse episode is recorded in 1 Samuel 13:7ff. According to 1 Samuel 10:8, Samuel had instructed Saul to meet him at Gilgal. Saul was to wait for seven days until Samuel arrived to give him further instructions from Yahweh, the Elohim of Israel. Moving to 1 Samuel 13:7, we find Saul at Gilgal waiting for Samuel. However, the Israelites are under threat of attack by the Philistines, and Saul's men are deserting him in droves. As a means to rally his troops, Saul offered burnt offerings and fellowship offerings himself, which was a function strictly reserved for the Levitical priests. As it turned out, Samuel arrived just as Saul was performing this forbidden function. We find Samuel's stern rebuke of Saul in the following passage:

> As soon as he had finished offering the burnt offering, behold, Samuel came. And Saul went out to meet him and greet him. Samuel said, "What have you done?" And Saul said, "When I saw that the people were scattering from me, and that you did not come within the days appointed, and that the Philistines had mustered at Michmash, I said, 'Now the Philistines will come down against me at Gilgal, and I have not sought the favor of Yahweh. So I forced myself, and offered the burnt offering." And Samuel said to Saul, "You have done foolishly. You have not kept the command of Yahweh your Elohim, with which he commanded you. For then Yahweh would have established your kingdom over Israel forever. But now your kingdom shall not continue. Yahweh has sought out a man after His own heart, and Yahweh has commanded him to be prince over His people, because you have not kept what Yahweh commanded you." [1Samuel 13:10-14, adapted from the ESV]

Saul's second lapse was in not fully obeying the command of Yahweh to annihilate the Amalekites. The record of the Amalekite campaign is found in the 15th chapter of 1 Samuel. In particular, Samuel's commission to Saul to completely annihilate the Amalekites is recorded in 1 Samuel 15:1-3. Saul was not to spare anything that breathed; he was to destroy men, women, children, and livestock. Saul's incomplete obedience is recorded in 1 Samuel 15:7-9; he spared Agag, the king, and the most desirable animals of the livestock. His purpose was, allegedly, to present these as a burnt offering to Yahweh. The record of Samuel's confronting Saul is presented in 1 Samuel 15:12-35, of which the following two passages are most noteworthy:

> And Samuel said, "Has Yahweh as great delight in burnt offerings and sacrifices, as in obeying the voice of Yahweh? Behold, to obey is better than sacrifice, and to listen than the fat of rams. For rebellion is as the sin of divination, and presumption is as iniquity and idolatry. Because you have rejected the word of Yahweh, He has also rejected you from being king." [1Samuel 15:22-23, adapted from the ESV]

> As Samuel turned to go away, Saul seized the skirt of his robe, and it tore. And Samuel said to him, "Yahweh has torn the kingdom of Israel from you this day and has given it to a neighbor of yours, who is better than you. And also the Glory of Israel will not lie or have regret, for He is not a man, that He should have regret." [1Samuel 15:27-29, adapted from the ESV]

Notice in 1 Samuel 15:10ff that Saul insisted that he had carried out Yahweh's commission against the Amalekites. It is only after Samuel sternly rebukes him that he sees his error, as recorded in 1 Samuel 15:24ff.

From the Amalekite episode onward, Saul's kingship was on a serious downward trajectory, which was characterized by Yahweh's abandoning him to his own devices and no longer giving him guidance. As indicated in the second passage quoted above, Samuel had placed Saul on notice that Yahweh would appoint another man to be king over Israel.

The anointing of David by Samuel is recorded in the 16th chapter of 1 Samuel, and the David and Goliath episode is recorded in the 17th chapter. The 18th chapter opens with a record of the covenantal relationship that developed between David and Jonathan, Saul's oldest son. [52] Then in 1 Samuel 18:6ff we are told how Saul became furiously jealous of David on account of the song which was sung by the women in celebration of the glorious defeat of the Philistines:

> And the women sang to one another as they celebrated, "Saul has struck down his thousands, and David his ten thousands." And Saul was very angry, and this saying displeased him. He said, "They have ascribed to David ten thousands, and to me they have ascribed thousands, and what more can he have but the kingdom?" And Saul eyed David with jealousy from that day on. [1Samuel 18:7-9, adapted from the ESV]

Saul's Fierce Hostility Toward David. From this point onward, an uncontrollable jealousy and attending hostility toward David began to take control of Saul's life, for he had come to recognize that David was the one whom Yahweh had chosen to replace him as Israel's king.

The custom of kings in antiquity was to annihilate the members of the previous dynasty when a new king acceded to the throne. As we read the unfolding record of Saul's kingship from the 18th chapter until his death, the fact becomes evident that Saul persisted in imputing to David a malevolent spirit in accordance with this ancient custom, and he apparently did this as a means to provide cover for his own malicious hostility toward David. Even though David had demonstrated nothing but unfailing loyalty to Saul, as Jonathan repeatedly reminded his father, he is eventually forced to flee for his life and take up refuge in wilderness strongholds. I designate this **the wilderness period** of David's career.

The 22nd chapter of 1 Samuel records a number of statements by Saul which place in evidence the manner in which he had fabricated in his mind a false virtual reality with regard to David, Jonathan, and even the members of his court. The following passage is especially noteworthy in this regard:

> Saul heard that David and his men had been discovered. At that time Saul was in Gibeah, sitting under the tamarisk tree at the high place. His spear was in his hand, and all his servants were standing around him. Saul said to his servants, "Listen, men of Benjamin: Is Jesse's son going to give all of you fields and vineyards? Do you think he'll make all of you commanders of thousands and commanders

of hundreds? That's why all of you have conspired against me! Nobody tells me when my own son makes a covenant with Jesse's son. None of you cares about me or tells me that my son has stirred up my own servant to wait in ambush for me, as is the case today." [1 Samuel 22:6-8, HCSB]

Notice how Saul falsely represents all his servants, who are standing in his presence, as conspiring against him in order to gain the favor of David. He falsely represents his own son, Jonathan, as the ringleader of this conspiracy, and as one who is actively inciting David "to wait in ambush for me, as is the case today." Accordingly, in the false virtual reality of Saul's mind, David is transformed from a loyal servant and military commander into a mortal enemy who is seeking to destroy Saul.

David's Unswerving Loyalty to Saul. During the wilderness period of David's career, which is recorded in 1 Samuel 21 – 31, there are two episodes in which David demonstrates his unswerving loyalty to Saul. The first of these is recorded in the 24th chapter of 1 Samuel. Saul is on one of his campaigns to destroy David when he enters a cave to relieve himself. As it turns out, David and his men are hiding in that very same cave. During this moment of vulnerability, David has the opportunity to kill Saul, but he refuses to lay a hand on Yahweh's anointed. Instead, he cuts off a piece of Saul's robe, with which he confronts Saul as he is leaving the cave. In 1 Samuel 24:16ff, Saul weeps over his own unwarranted and malicious hostility toward David, and then he states the following:

> And now, behold, I know that you shall surely be king, and that the kingdom of Israel shall be established in your hand. Swear to me therefore by Yahweh that you will not cut off my offspring after me, and that you will not destroy my name out of my father's house." And David swore this to Saul. Then Saul went home, but David and his men went up to the stronghold. [1 Samuel 24:20-22, adapted from the ESV]

The second episode is recorded in the 26th chapter of 1 Samuel. Saul again gives way to a spirit of malicious hostility toward David, and he leads his men in pursuit of David in order to destroy him. There comes a point that Saul and his men are encamped in the valley, fast asleep, and

David and one of his men stealthily make their way into the camp. Rather than thrusting Saul through with his own spear, they take the spear and Saul's water jug to the top of the hill overlooking the encampment. From this vantage point, David accosts Saul and points out that he has taken the king's spear and water jug, thereby establishing beyond doubt that he had been in a position to thrust Saul through with his own spear. Once again, Saul recognizes his sin and apologizes to David. The concluding speeches in this episode are as follows:

> And David answered and said, "Here is the spear, O king! Let one of the young men come over and take it. Yahweh rewards every man for his righteousness and his faithfulness, for Yahweh gave you into my hand today, and I would not put out my hand against Yahweh's anointed. Behold, as your life was precious this day in my sight, so may my life be precious in the sight of Yahweh, and may He deliver me out of all tribulation." Then Saul said to David, "Blessed be you, my son David! You will do many things and will succeed in them." So David went his way, and Saul returned to his place. [1 Samuel 26:22-25, adapted from the ESV]

Harmful Spirit From Yahweh. Returning to the point just after the Amalekite campaign, we find the following noteworthy statement in the 16th chapter of 1 Samuel:

> Now the Spirit of Yahweh departed from Saul, and a harmful spirit from Yahweh tormented him. [1 Samuel 16:14, adapted from the ESV]

What is the meaning of this statement? So long as Saul heeded the prompting of the Spirit of Yahweh, He would continue to be the source of wisdom and the motivator of righteous behavior for the king. However, Saul had disobeyed the Spirit of Yahweh twice, and had thereby grieved Him. As a result, Yahweh withdrew His Spirit from the king. Moreover, He commissioned a demonic spirit to torment Saul. As a result, from this point onward Saul repeatedly fell prey to a spirit of hostility toward David which was both malicious and fierce. Contrary to David's demonstration of unswerving loyalty to Saul, the king represented David as a mortal threat which had to be destroyed. According to Saul's tortured logic, his representing David as a mortal threat provided cover for his malicious hostility toward his servant, and for his persistent campaign to destroy David from that point onward. It is noteworthy that, whereas Saul intended evil against David, Yahweh employed the tribulation brought about by Saul as a means of refining David's character and teaching him vital lessons of trust and obedience in accordance with His timeless and normative promise in Romans 8:28.

Ministry of the Spirit of Yahweh. I need to comment briefly on the ministry of the Spirit of Yahweh during the period of history covered by the Hebrew Scriptures, which is different from His ministry during the present dispensation. Prior to the Day of Pentecost, which occurred ca. 31 AD, the Spirit of Yahweh (= Holy Spirit) **came upon** and was **with** the servants of Yahweh to empower them for specific ministries and functions. Consider the following:

- As recorded in the 31st chapter of Exodus, the Spirit of Yahweh endowed Bezalel, Oholiab, and others with knowledge, wisdom, and technical skills needed to fabricate the tabernacle and all of its furnishings.

- After Samuel anointed Saul as the first king of Israel, as recorded in 1 Samuel 10:1ff, the Spirit of Yahweh came upon Saul. The first instance of this is recorded in 1 Samuel 10:6 & 10. A second instance is recorded in 1 Samuel 11:6.

- After Samuel anointed David as the second king of Israel according to 1 Samuel 16:13, the Spirit of Yahweh came upon David.

- Beginning with Elijah, the Spirit of Yahweh came upon and was with the prophets of Israel to empower their prophetic ministry, including the performance of marvelous signs and miracles.

- In his prayer of contrition and repentance after the Uriah episode, David pleaded with Yahweh not to remove His Spirit as recorded in Psalm 51:11.

- Just prior to His death, Jesus assured His disciples that the Holy Spirit "dwells with you and will be in you." (John 14:17)

Having summarized the trajectory of Saul's kingship, we are now in a position to answer this question: based upon the narrative of 1 Samuel, how should Saul have gone about guarding his heart against the spirit of self-deception, to which he eventually fell prey? The answer provided by the narrative is this: **by not grieving the Spirit of Yahweh**, which would have entailed the maintenance of a course of unswerving obedience to His promptings.

While the dynamics of the Holy Spirit's presence in the life of the Christian disciple is different from His presence in the lives of the saints of the Hebrew Scriptures – He is in us, not just with us – we are commanded to neither **grieve** nor **quench** the Holy Spirit in Ephesians 4:30 and 1 Thessalonians 5:19, respectively. We grieve the Spirit by refusing to obey Him, and we quench the Spirit by refusing to allow Him to fill us. An especially critical form of disobedience is to give in to the deceptions of the flesh and allow our representational world to deviate from Scripture in order to act on some carnal lust or protect ourselves from conviction.

> *Accordingly, we guard our hearts during this present dispensation by being careful to obey the Spirit's promptings in everything, and, should we disobey, being quick to confess our sin and restore our fellowship with the living God.*

Questions for Discussion

1. This chapter has presented some concepts which are probably new to you, and you may have struggled to make sense of them. To help with this process, define the following concepts using your own words and in a way that is meaningful to you:

    - Represent
    - Determine
    - Biblical representation
    - Representational system
    - Representational world (RW)
    - Godly RW mental filter

- Worldly RW mental filter

2. Discuss the concepts of the godly and worldly RW mental filters in reference to your own thinking process. Which one comes naturally, and which one requires mental effort? Why is it important to discard the worldly RW mental filter and practice the godly RW mental filter? Is this accomplished all at once or piece by piece? *Hint*: Relate the project of godly representational world construction to the process of sanctification; that is, the process by which we become conformed to the image of Jesus Christ.

3. Select two biblical representations other than those discussed in this chapter. In particular, select one from the Hebrew Scriptures and one from the Christian Scriptures. They can be drawn from any literary genre – narrative, poetry, didactic or teaching literature, or apocalyptic literature. Analyze and discuss the significance of each. What indications do you see that the author of the passage in question intended that you embrace the representation as normative? What lessons do you derive from each passage?

4. Our representational world impacts our emotions, will, and behavior. Identify and discuss a specific arena of life and ministry in which you have practiced a worldly RW mental filter. What fruit or outcome was produced by this? If, in your selected arena of life and ministry, you had practiced a godly RW mental filter instead, what different fruit or outcome would have been produced?

5. Identify and discuss an arena of your own life and ministry which is being impacted significantly by the insights gained from this chapter. Discuss the ways in which your life and ministry in that arena will be altered in the future as a result of your practicing the insights gained from this chapter.

6. We have associated our natural intuition and lived experiences apart from God with a worldly RW mental filter. What happens to our intuition as a result of the sanctification process whereby our personalities are progressively conformed to the image of Jesus Christ? A related question is this: what happens to our intuition as

we learn to practice a godly RW mental filter with increasing consistency?

7. In the concluding section of this chapter, entitled Guarding the Heart, two ways were identified in which the heart may deceptively play upon the mind to bring about an adjustment to the person's representational world, either to rationalize a sinful desire of the heart, or to protect the heart from conviction. From your own life and ministry, have you observed either or both of these taking place, either in yourself or someone close to you? Carefully describe the manner in which the heart deceptively played upon the mind to bring about the desired adjustment to the person's representational world.

Notes & Reflections

Use the space below to record additional insights and commentary resulting from your studies thus far.

Chapter 4.
Discovering the Meaning of Biblical Books and Passages

The Importance of Rightly Handling the Word of Truth

In the previous chapter, I have endeavored to persuade you that rightly handling the word of truth in order to derive from it the normative principles that determine a godly representational world is a life-critical matter. That is, the representational world which we construct and inhabit determines all aspects of life and ministry. To operate out from a godly representational world is the way of wisdom that results in the blessing of God and leads to life; and to operate out from an worldly representational world is the way of folly that results in the cursing of God and leads to ruination and death.

If our constructing a godly representational world is life-critical, and if the Bible is the primary source of godly representations, then our rightly handling of the biblical text as disciples of Christ is also life-critical. In this chapter I will summarize the principles of rightly handling the biblical text with a view toward deriving from it normative theological, moral, and ethical principles to govern life and ministry.

Learning Objective

The learning objective for this chapter is that the student would grasp and internalize the importance of rightly handling the word of truth, and that he would learn and begin to practice the elements of the science and art of biblical interpretation for the four principal literary genres found in Scripture.

Structure of the Canon of Scripture

Before turning to the biblical principles of biblical interpretation, I need to define the **canonical structure of the Bible**.[53] **Canon** is a technical term that derives from the Greek *kanon*, which designates a measuring rod or standard. The **Canon of Scripture** is a technical term which designates the collection of books **recognized** by the community of faith as divinely inspired down through the centuries.

The Bible is divided into two major sections. The first of these consists of the collection of 39 books revered by the Jewish community, which is customarily designated the Old Testament. The second consists of the collection of 27 additional books revered by the Christian community, which is customarily designated the New Testament. However, in all my work I prefer to designate the Old Testament as the **Hebrew Scriptures** and the New Testament as the **Christian Scriptures** for the following three reasons:

1. While it is true that the Middle English word "testament" can serve as a synonym for "covenant," the word is not employed in any modern English translation of the Bible. In fact, "testament" is employed in the King James Version (KJV) of the Bible instead of "covenant," and the word "testator" is employed in the KJV rendering of Hebrews 9:15-16 in reference to God. However, the word does not accurately represent the character of the Bible to the typical modern reader.

2. In my view, the designation "Old Testament" diminishes the importance and relevance of the first section of 39 books in comparison with the second section of 27 books in the mind of the modern reader. This is due to the fact that the evolutionary worldview has so permeated modern culture that "old" means worn out, decrepit, no longer useful, or no longer relevant.

3. The terminology "Old Testament" and "New Testament" suggests a distinct partition between the first section of 39 books and the second section of 27 books. In contrast, the language of Scripture emphasizes a substantial continuity from the first section into the second.

Accordingly, in the WitW study, I designate the first section of 39 books revered by the Jewish community as the Hebrew Scriptures or the **Hebrew Canon**, and the second section of 27 additional books revered by the Christian community as the Christian Scriptures or the **Christian Canon**. I designate the entire Bible revered by Christians as simply the **Bible**.

Four-Part Structure of the Hebrew Canon

I embrace the four-part structure of the Hebrew Canon as follows:

- The Torah, consisting of the five books of Moses, often designated the Pentateuch.

- The Early Prophets, consisting of Joshua through 2 Kings.

- The Latter Prophets, consisting of Isaiah through Malachi, but excluding Daniel.

- The Writings, consisting of all the remaining books of the Hebrew Canon.

The literary genre of narrative dominates the Torah, the Early Prophets, and a number of the books in the Writings section of the Hebrew Canon. Referring to Figure 4-1, the storyline through the narrative sections of the Hebrew Canon supports and sustains all of the theological, moral, and ethical principles derivable from the Hebrew Scriptures. In other words, the normativeness of the doctrine derivable from the Hebrew Scriptures is a result of the trueness and integrity of the story set forth in the narrative sections of the Hebrew Canon. In fact, all the key doctrines of the Hebrew Scriptures originate in the Torah. That is why I refer to the Torah as the fountainhead of wisdom.

> *The other three sections of the Hebrew Canon can thus be represented as commentary on the theological, moral, and ethical applications and implications of the governing principles set forth in the Torah.*

Four-Part Structure of the Christian Canon

The Christian Canon is also divided into four sections as follows:

- The four Gospels and the Book of Acts.

- The Pauline Epistles.

- The General Epistles.

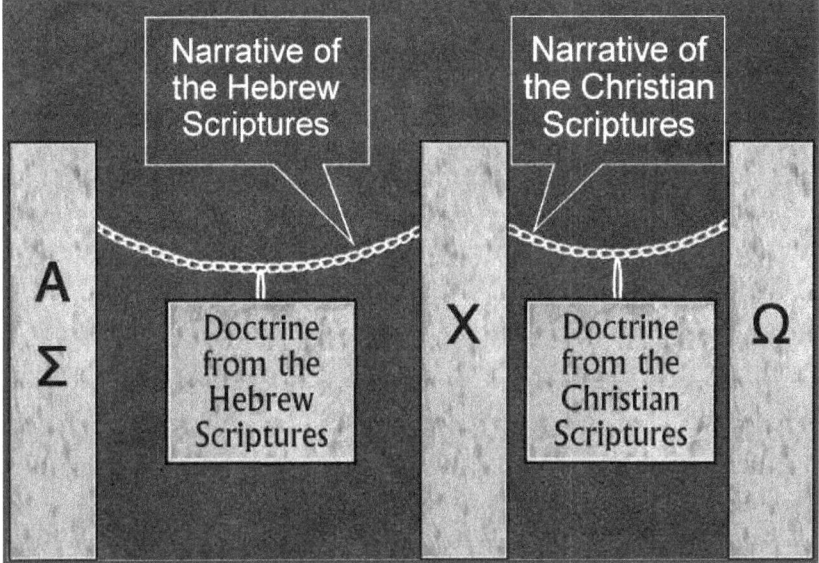

Figure 4-1. True Narrative Supports Doctrine

- The Johannine Literature, consisting of the three Epistles of John and the Book of Revelation.

Referring again to Figure 4-1, the narrative sections of the Christian Canon are almost entirely contained in the first canonical section consisting of the four Gospels and the Book of Acts. As illustrated in Figure 4-1, the storyline through the narrative sections of the Christian Canon supports and sustains all of the theological, moral, and ethical principles derivable from the Christian Scriptures. In other words, the normativeness of the doctrine derivable from the Christian Scriptures is a result of the trueness and integrity of the story set forth in the narrative sections of the Christian Canon.

The Pauline Epistles, the General Epistles, and the Johannine Literature can be accurately represented as commentary on the theological, moral, and ethical applications and implications of the story set forth in the four Gospels and the Book of Acts.

The Primacy of the Bible's Story

The point of our study in chapter 2 is this: because the story of the Bible is true, it can support and sustain generalizations in terms of theological, moral, and ethical principles. In fact, the approach to biblical interpretation presented in the WitW study is distinctive in that it is based upon the firm conviction that the story of the Bible is primary, and that principles derived from the text of Scripture – that is, doctrine – are secondary. By stating this, I am in nowise suggesting that doctrine is unimportant.

> *What I am asserting is simply that the normativeness of the doctrine derives from and depends upon the trueness and integrity of the story.*

Normativeness of the Doctrine Depends Upon the Trueness and Integrity of the Story

This assertion is illustrated in Figure 4-1. The storyline of the Bible is represented by a chain that is supported by three great pillars. The pillar on the left is labeled **A** and **Σ**; it represents the **Alpha Event** and the **Sigma Event** identified in Figure 2-1 and defined in the associated discussion in the 2nd chapter as follows:

Alpha Event　　=　　the creation of the cosmos by Yahweh Elohim, the Infinite Personal God who is truly there.

Sigma Event　　=　　the invasion of evil, sin, and death into the cosmos.

The pillar on the right represents the **Omega Event** identified in Figure 2-1 and defined in the associated discussion in the 2nd chapter as follows:

Omega Event　　=　　the event when Yahweh Elohim brings all things to a consummation according to His sovereign will and to display His glory.

The middle pillar represents the **Chi Event** identified in Figure 2-1 and defined in the associated discussion in the 2nd chapter as follows:

Chi Event = the Christ Event; that is, the life, ministry, death, burial, and resurrection of Jesus Christ.

I have asserted that these four events, **Alpha**, **Sigma**, **Omega**, and **Chi**, are **determinative with respect to all reality**. In other words, these four events impart meaning and significance to everything else, including all persons, events, circumstances, and things. In particular, the meaning and significance of our individual lives and ministries are entirely defined in relation to these four events.

In the 1st chapter, I defined **doing theology** as the act of deriving from Scripture normative theological, moral, and ethical principles to govern life and ministry. In Figure 4-1, all such principles that are derived from the Hebrew Scriptures are represented by the tablet on the left that is suspended from the chain. In like manner, the principles derived from the Christian Scriptures are represented by the tablet on the right.

> *If we define doctrine as the entire set of principles derived from Scripture for governing life and ministry, the normativeness of the doctrine depends upon the trueness and integrity of the Bible's story.*

Our approach to biblical interpretation, which gives primacy to the Bible's story, is in contrast to that of the systematic theologian, who gives primacy to doctrine. For him, the story of the Bible is only secondary; it exists as background for propositional truth or doctrine. As a result of the systematic approach to theology, doctrine is no longer rooted in the story, but rather it exists as an entity that is separated from the story. Thus, the systematic approach to theology tends also to disconnect doctrine from the lives of the people of God down through the ages. To the extent this is true, systematic theology is disconnected from experience and practice. **It defines belief but not behavior**. In fact, the doctrinal system formulated by the theologian tends also to become a lens or grid through which Scripture is read, thereby impeding the recognition of the biblical author's intended meaning. In fact, a dogmatic system is tantamount to an idol that stands between the mind of the disciple and the knowledge of God. In this regard, the following instruction of the Apostle Paul is most noteworthy:

> For the weapons of our warfare are not of the flesh but have divine power to destroy strongholds. We destroy arguments and every lofty opinion raised against the knowledge of God, and take every thought captive to obey Christ, being ready to punish every disobedience, when your obedience is complete. [2 Corinthians 10:4-6, ESV]

Biblical Principles of Biblical Interpretation

I begin our discussion of the science and art of biblical interpretation by first considering what the Bible itself has to say on this vital subject.

Embracing the Bible as the Word of God

First, according to Scripture, which is also confirmed by experience, the factor which most clearly distinguishes between those who are truly disciples of Christ and those who are not is the **recognition** that the Bible is God's written word. According to the teachings of Jesus in the 10th chapter of John's Gospel, His sheep know and listen to His voice. According to the teaching of the Apostle Paul in the 2nd chapter of 1 Corinthians,

> The natural person (= *psychikos* = soulish person) does not accept the things of the Spirit of God, for they are folly to him, and he is not able to understand them because they are spiritually discerned. The spiritual person (= *pneumatikos*) judges all things, but is himself to be judged by no one. For who has understood the mind of the Lord so as to instruct Him? But we have the mind of Christ. [1 Corinthians 2:14-16, adapted from the ESV]

It is noteworthy that the phrase "natural person" translates the Greek *psychikos*, which literally means one who is dominated by the things of the soul. The opposing concept is conveyed by the Greek word *pneumatikos*, which means one who is dominated by the things of the human spirit. Referring back to our discussion in the 3rd chapter, Figure 3-1 illustrates the operation of the mind of the man who is dominated by the **things of the spirit**, and Figure 3-2 illustrates the operation of the mind of the man who is dominated by the **things of the soul**.

The disciple of Christ is one who has been born again and born from above in accordance with the 3rd chapter of John's Gospel. As a result, the disciple has been spiritually quickened and enabled to perceive and understand the wisdom of God which is imparted by the word of God. The non-disciple has not been thus quickened and enabled, and therefore he cannot perceive and understand the wisdom of God. In fact, he regards it as foolishness.

In sum, the new birth causes a person not only to recognize but also to embrace the Bible as God's word, and it enables that person to begin the lifelong project of deriving from Scripture the manifold wisdom of God to rightly govern life and ministry.

Summary of Biblical Principles

The subject of biblical interpretation or **hermeneutics** is often approached theoretically and scientifically. However, the biblical text itself provides clear direction as to how we should study it, and thereby draw meaning from it. In particular, I shall discuss the implications of the following six biblical principles:

1. The biblical text is God-breathed in accordance with 2 Timothy 3:16-17.

2. The biblical text is exceedingly precious in accordance with Psalm 19:7-11.

3. The biblical text is authoritative in accordance with Matthew 5:17-20, Matthew 24:35, Matthew 28:18-20, and John 16:12-16.

4. The author's intended meaning is determinative in accordance with 2 Peter 1:19-21.

5. The biblical text is understandable in accordance with Deuteronomy 29:29, Psalm 19:7, Proverbs 8:1-9, John 7:17, and James 1:5.

6. The biblical text deserves intensive, lifelong devotion in accordance with Joshua 1:8.

The Biblical Text is God-Breathed. In 2 Timothy 3:16-17 the Apostle Paul states,

> All Scripture (= *pas graphe*) is breathed out by God (= *theopneustos*) and is profitable for teaching, for reproof, for correction, and for training in righteousness, that the man of God may be competent, equipped for every good work. [2 Timothy 3:16-17, adapted from the ESV]

The phrase "all Scripture" translates *pas graphe*, which literally means "every writing," When Paul penned these words, he was referring to the Hebrew Scriptures. However, there is biblical warrant, as we will see momentarily, for asserting that God continued to breathe out His word through the authors of the Christian Scriptures, each of whom was either an apostle of Jesus Christ himself, or he was closely associated with one of the apostles. The fact that God has graciously given us His written word should excite within us an awe and a reverence for the Bible as the word of God. This, in turn, should motivate a lifelong devotion to the careful study of it. According to our focal passage, because all Scripture is breathed out by God it is "profitable for teaching, for reproof, for correction, and for training in righteousness, that the man (or woman) of God may be competent, equipped for every good work."

The Biblical Text is Precious and Delightful. In Psalm 19:7-11 King David states,

> The Torah of Yahweh is perfect, reviving the soul;
> > the testimony of Yahweh is trustworthy, making wise the simple;
> > the precepts of Yahweh are right, rejoicing the heart;
> > the commandment of Yahweh is radiant, enlightening the eyes;
> > the fear of Yahweh is pure, enduring forever;
> > the judgments of Yahweh are sure, and altogether righteous.
> More to be desired are they than gold, even much fine gold;
> > sweeter also than honey and drippings of the honeycomb.
> Moreover, by them is your servant warned;
> > and in keeping them there is great reward.
> [Psalm 19:7-11, adapted from the ESV]

Why did King David consider the Torah of Yahweh so precious and delightful? I can identify five reasons, as follows:

1. Because it was breathed out by Yahweh Himself, the creator, providential sustainer, and sovereign ruler over the entire cosmos;

2. Because it records the history of Yahweh fastening His love upon Abraham and his descendants;

3. Because it embodies the covenant relationship between Yahweh and the people of Israel;

4. Because it marks out the way of wisdom that leads to life – even eternal life; this is in contrast to the way of folly that leads to ruination and death; and,

5. Because it accurately represents the lifestyle which emanates from a heart that is fully devoted to Yahweh.

> *In particular, regarding the Torah as precious and delightful, it accurately represents the lifestyle of Jesus Christ, who stands as the ultimate and perfect model of a person who is fully devoted to Yahweh.*

There can be no reasonable doubt that the five books of Moses were commonly recognized by the Jews as inspired writings in the time of David, ca. 1000 BC. However, the formal recognition of the Early Prophets (Joshua through 2 Kings) as part of the Hebrew Canon did not occur until well after David's time. If David were to be living today, would he declare the entire Bible to be precious and delightful? I am convinced that the answer to this question is yes, for Jesus Christ, the son of David, embraced the entirety of the Hebrew Scriptures as authoritative. He then provided for the inspirational ministry of the Holy Spirit whereby the breathing out of the word of God would continue through the apostles and their associates. And so we should embrace and extol the entire Bible as the instruction of Yahweh, which is perfect for the saving and reviving of our souls.

The Biblical Text is Authoritative. In Matthew 5:17-20, Jesus Christ confirms the continuing authority of the Torah of Yahweh. In Matthew 24:35, He claims eternal authority for His words. In Matthew 28:18-20, Jesus claims universal authority for Himself, and He commands His disciples to "make disciples of all nations... teaching them to observe all that I have commanded you." [Matthew 28:19-20, ESV] In John 16:12-16, Jesus provides for the continuing ministry of the Holy Spirit, who "will guide you into all the truth, for He will not speak on His own authority, but whatever He hears He will speak, and He will declare to you the things that are to come." [John 16:13, adapted from the ESV] Accordingly, Jesus Christ, the Son of God, confers His divine and universal authority upon the entire Bible.

The Author's Intended Meaning is Determinative. What I mean by the author's intended meaning being determinative is this: the author of a text is sovereign over the meaning of the text, and not the reading subject. In 2 Peter 1:19-21 the Apostle Peter states,

> And we have something more sure, the prophetic word, to which **you will do well to pay attention** as to a lamp shining in a dark place, until the day dawns and the morning star rises in your hearts, knowing this first of all, that **no prophecy of Scripture comes from one's own interpretation**. For no prophecy was ever produced by the will of man, but men spoke from God as they were carried along by the Holy Spirit. [2 Peter 1:19-21, adapted from the ESV, emphasis added]

These verses come from a section of Peter's letter in which he is addressing the trustworthiness of the prophetic word of God. This section begins at 2 Peter 1:16 and continues through the 21st verse. Thus, in the literary context of the passage, the trustworthiness of the prophetic word of God is contrasted with "cleverly devised myths." [2 Peter 1:16, ESV] Moreover, in 2 Peter 2:1, the Apostle addresses the ministry of false prophets. Thus, because the prophetic word of God is true and trustworthy, having been breathed out from the mind of God through the ministry of the Holy Spirit, **and because it is not subject to private interpretation**, we should pay careful attention to it. In particular, it is our place to discover the meaning intended by the authors of Scripture, and we should carefully and constantly avoid reading into the text of Scripture a meaning that emanates from our own minds.

The Biblical Text is Understandable. In Deuteronomy 29:29 Moses states,

> The secret things belong to Yahweh our Elohim, but the things that are revealed belong to us and to our children forever, that we may do all the words of this law. [Deuteronomy 29:29, adapted from the ESV]

This verse concludes a section of the 29th chapter in which Moses is affirming the tragic consequences that will befall the people of Israel should they fail to keep the covenant with Yahweh. Moses' point is this: Yahweh has been very clear and articulate in His statement of the terms of His covenant with Israel. And should Israel choose to rebel, it would not be due to any lack of clarity on Yahweh's part.

I am convinced that we now have biblical warrant to extend "the things that are revealed" to the entire Bible. Thus, the things that Yahweh has revealed by breathing out His word through the human authors of Scripture have been given to us for the purpose that we would not only know them, but also that we would practice them. By implication, this means that "the things that are revealed" are clear and understandable, not remote and obscure.

We have already noted that in Psalm 19:7 David states, "the testimony of Yahweh is trustworthy, making wise the simple." In this verse, "simple" translates the Hebrew *pethi*. In the literary context of this passage, the meaning of *pethi* is best approximated by "inexperienced" or "unschooled." Thus, our understanding the instruction of Yahweh and practicing it as the way of wisdom does not require an advanced degree, or even many years of study. The instruction of Yahweh is accessible to the inexperienced and unschooled person as well as to the biblical scholar.

The clarity and accessibility of the biblical text is confirmed by Solomon in Proverbs 8:1-9. In particular, the 8th and 9th verses state,

> All the words of My mouth are righteous... They are all clear to the one who is perceptive, and right to those who discover knowledge. [Proverbs 8:9, adapted from the ESV]

In John 7:17, the Apostle John quotes Jesus making the following statement:

> If anyone wants to do God's will, he will know whether the teaching is from God or whether I am speaking on My own authority. [John 7:17, adapted from the ESV]

The implication of this statement by Christ is that **the gatekeeper to understanding Scripture is the will to obey what it says.** John Piper

sheds additional light on this issue in the 60ᵗʰ chapter of *Taste and See*.
[^54]

Finally, we have the declaration in James 1:5 that if we lack wisdom, such as in understanding a deep truth in Scripture, we should ask God, "who gives generously to all without reproach, and it will be given him." [James 1:5, ESV]

In conclusion, we have no excuse for failing to understand the word of God. If we are experiencing difficulty with a passage, then we should ask God to help us. The help may not come through a dream or vision, but it will come.

The Biblical Text Deserves Intensive Lifelong Devotion. Consider Yahweh's instruction to Joshua as He commissioned him to assume leadership of Israel.

> This Book of the Torah shall not depart from your mouth, but you shall meditate and audibly recite it day and night, so that you may be careful to practice all that is written in it. For then you will make your way prosperous, and then you will have good success. [Joshua 1:8, adapted from the ESV]

In the ESV translation of this verse, "meditate" translates the Hebrew *hagah*, which signifies more than silent meditation. In my memorization of Scripture, I recite it aloud as an act of worship to Yahweh, and I return it to Him as a prayer that He would enable me to actually practice and experience the precious and magnificent promises of His word, that I might increasingly reflect and become a partaker of His nature in accordance with 2 Peter 1:4.

Implications of Biblical Principles

In the following paragraphs, I will state the implications of the biblical principles examined above by way of providing a bridge between them and my discussion of the science and art of biblical interpretation.

Doctor and Patient Relationship

I believe we can cogently summarize the biblical teaching we have just examined through the metaphor of the doctor / patient relationship.

> **For the disciple of Christ, the word of God is the doctor, and the mind of the disciple is the patient.**

In other words, the disciple voluntarily submits his mind to the authority of the biblical text, and he allows the biblical text, in the hands of the illuminating Spirit of God, to operate upon his mind. This proper relationship is powerfully represented by the following Scripture:

> For the word of God is living and active, sharper than any two-edged sword, piercing to the division of soul and of spirit, of joints and of marrow, and discerning the thoughts and intentions of the heart. And no creature is hidden from His sight, but all are naked and exposed to the eyes of Him to Whom we must give account. [Hebrews 4:12-13, adapted from the ESV]

I want to draw a sharp contrast between the **proper orientation** of the disciple's mind to the Bible as God's word with **the improper orientation** of the mind of the critical scholar. In fact, the critical scholar assumes the role of doctor, and he effectively represents the biblical text as his patient.

> **In accordance with this improper orientation, the critical scholar dissects the text and subjects it to critical scrutiny as if it were a dead animal.**

Discovering the Author's Intended Meaning

The disciple of Christ should approach the biblical text with...

- A mind that is submissive and open to the authoritative text.

- Confidence that the Holy Spirit will illuminate and enable an adequate understanding of the text for the needs of the disciple at that particular point in his development.

- An inquisitive mind which is committed to discovering the author's intended meaning as understood by his original audience.

- A profound recognition of the vast gulf that exists between the linguistic and cultural context of the disciple and that of the ancient Near East in which the word of God was revealed and written down.

Regarding the last point, the disciple of Christ needs to avail himself of resources to at least partially bridge the linguistic and cultural gulf, and thereby approximate the meaning of a given passage as intended by the author and as understood by his original audience. I will suggest some appropriate Bible study resources later in this chapter.

Reading the Bible as a Cohesive Literary Work

A first approximation to the author's intended meaning of a given passage is achieved by reading the passage in context as part of a cohesive literary work. The Bible incorporates a variety of literary genres, each of which must be interpreted according to a set of rules specific to that genre. The four most important genres represented in the biblical literature are narrative or story, Hebrew poetry, didactic or teaching literature, and apocalyptic literature – prophecy that is dominated by the use of dramatic word pictures and symbols. Later in this section, the interpretation principles and procedures that apply to each of these literary genres are summarized. [55]

General Principles of Biblical Interpretation

Before turning to the specific principles of interpretation applicable to each of the four main literary genres found in Scripture, I need to present a few principles that are generally applicable to the entire Bible.

The Critical Importance of Context

The first such principle is the **critical importance of context**. We must always read Scripture as a **cohesive literary work**, which means that we must be sensitive to the context of the passage under study. Recognizing and understanding the context of a biblical passage is the prerequisite to understanding the meaning of the passage. There are five dimensions of context, which are theological, historical, cultural, canonical, and linguistic.

Theological Context. We get at the **theological context** of a biblical passage by answering the following question: **What theological pre-**

understanding did the author assume on the part of his intended audience? Theological context is therefore a function of the unfolding self-disclosure of God up to that point in revelatory history. However, a complicating factor enters in regard to theological context. In the case of prophetic writings, the intended audience may not have been limited to the contemporary audience; instead, it may have included a future audience. The Apostle Peter testifies to this fact in 1 Peter 1:10-12. In other words, the human authors of prophetic Scripture may not have fully understood the theological significance of their own writings.

Historical Context. The **historical context** of a biblical passage is determined by researching the geo-political situation that existed at the time of its writing; that is, when was the book written, what was going on in the world at that time, and what was the significance of that geo-political situation to the unfolding of biblical history?

An example of the importance of historical context concerns the timing of the Exodus and Conquest episodes in relation to the rise and fall of empires in the ancient Near East. Due to the devastation of Lower Egypt caused by the plagues of the Exodus, the military and political hegemony exercised by Egypt throughout Canaan began to wane after the death of Thutmosis IV, ca. 1406 BC. [56] In fact, by the time the people of Israel were ready to enter Canaan, ca. 1366 BC, there was no Egyptian military and political presence remaining in Canaan. This explains why the Conquest episode in the Book of Joshua does not mention any encounters with Egyptians. Had the Conquest of Canaan been attempted earlier than this, Joshua and the Israelites would have been confronted by the army of Egypt. In fact, the rise of the nation of Israel as an important political and military power in the eastern Mediterranean region occurred entirely during the hiatus between the waning of Egypt beginning in the 14th century BC and the rise of Assyria in the 8th century BC.

Cultural Context. All Scripture was written within the ancient Near Eastern **cultural context**. However, because revelatory history spans a period of several millennia, the cultural context of the patriarchal narratives in Genesis is vastly different from that of the four Gospels and the Book of Acts. While it is impossible to completely bridge the divide that exists between the cultural context of the human author of a book of the Bible and that of a modern reader, at least we must be sensitive to the existence of the divide and bridge it to the best of our ability.

Two examples of cultural context that help to illuminate the biblical text are, first, the betrothal and marriage custom of the ancient Near East, and, second, the four-room house configuration that was in use from the time the people of Israel became established in Canaan until the 1st century AD. The betrothal and marriage custom of the ancient Near East is summarized later in this chapter in the section entitled Interpreting Didactic Literature. The four-room house configuration featured a central courtyard in which most of the life of the household took place; stalls for animals and rooms for storage of food and sleeping surrounded the courtyard.

Canonical Context. The canonical structure of the Bible has already been addressed. It is important to read each biblical passage with a sensitivity to its **canonical context**. That is, each book of the Bible is part of a canonical collection of books which are linked together by an integrative theological and literary purpose.

Linguistic Context. The **linguistic context** of a biblical passage includes the literary genre of the passage. Is it narrative, Hebrew poetry, didactic, or apocalyptic literature? The distinctive principles and procedures for interpretation that apply to the various literary genres in the Bible must be respected, and these will be discussed later in this chapter.

Moreover, linguistic context includes the meanings of ancient words and figures of speech that were commonly understood at the time of the writing of the book, but whose meaning may have become obscured by the passage of time. Most of us must rely upon the skill of translators to capture such ancient meanings in modern language. However, all of us should be sensitive to the fact that the Bible we hold in our hands is actually a very ancient book, the earliest sections of which were written in languages and scripts far removed from contemporary languages and scripts. Therefore, we need to recognize the vast linguistic divide that actually exists between the author of a book of Scripture and ourselves.

Discovering the Author's Intended Meaning

What are the implications of this principle of interpretation? First, an important component of our study of Scripture should entail either listening to the text being read or reciting it aloud to ourselves. Second, we should process Scripture in units of thought rather than fragmenting the text into verses, phrases, and words. This in nowise implies that words and phrases are unimportant. The point is that the meaning of words and phrases is largely determined by the linguistic context in which they occur.

To place in evidence the importance of context as a determinant of meaning, consider the fact that in Strong's Exhaustive Concordance the Hebrew lexicon contains less than 9,000 words, and the Greek lexicon contains less than 6,000 words. In contrast, even an abridged English dictionary contains upwards of 100,000 words. Thus, the range of possible meanings for a given word in the Hebrew or Greek text is an order of magnitude greater than the average word in English.

Embedded Genres. Before launching into a discussion of each of the principal literary genres found in Scripture, I need to comment on the fact that most of the books of the Bible contain multiple genres. For example, while the books of the Torah are dominated by narrative, they contain embedded covenants, treaties, law codes, and poetry. Likewise, the books of the Early Prophets are dominated by narrative, but they contain significant passages of embedded poetry. Thus, the reader needs to switch gears as he studies a given book or passage, interpreting each of the various genres that he encounters in the manner appropriate to that genre.

Having defined the objective of all biblical interpretation as the discovery of the author's intended meaning, I now consider each of the four principal literary genres found in Scripture; namely, narrative, Hebrew poetry, didactic literature, and apocalyptic literature.

Interpreting Biblical Narrative

My discussion of biblical narrative is focused primarily upon the narrative of the Hebrew Scriptures, since that is where most of the narrative literature of the Bible is located. Generally, the same principles of interpretation apply by extension to the narrative sections of the Christian Scriptures.

Not only did the ancient Israelites innovate a linear concept of time and history as delineated in Figure 2-1 and discussed in the associated text of the 2nd chapter, but they innovated **prose narration** as the means to record their history. [57] The ancient Near Eastern cultures surrounding

Israel were all polytheistic, embraced an endlessly cyclical view of history, and they generally employed epic poetry as the preferred genre in which to represent their historical roots. [58]

Evolutionary Concept of History

Before proceeding to a discussion of the interpretation of biblical narrative, I must comment on the **evolutionary concept of history** that was introduced by G. W. F. Hegel (ca. 1770-1831) and then became established dogma after the work of Charles Darwin (ca. 1809-1882). The inevitable result of embracing an evolutionary concept of history is the depreciation of the value of history and traditions handed down from past generations, even to the point of abject neglect. When combined with the **new hermeneutic**, which depreciates the weight of authorial intent and makes the reading subject sovereign over the meaning of a text, there has emerged a propensity to actually reconstruct history to support the postmodern political and philosophical agenda. These two aspects of postmodernism seriously imperil the interpretation of ancient documents, such as the historical sections of the Hebrew Scriptures.

> *These aspects of postmodernism have so permeated popular culture, at least in Europe and the United States, that they must be deliberately and forcefully confronted in any discussion of biblical interpretation.*

Summary of Important Resources

To correctly handle biblical narrative with a view toward deriving from it normative theological, moral, and ethical principles, we must be acutely sensitive to the author's intention. On the one hand, we must avoid overstepping the author's intention by finding a normative principle under every rock, as it were; on the other hand, we must not fail to recognize a normative principle that is brought to the fore by clear textual clues.

I have found the following resources to be especially helpful in regard to the science and art of interpreting biblical narrative.

Alter (1981) Robert Alter in *The Art of Biblical Narrative* treats the complexity and aesthetic quality of biblical narrative. He does this in spite of embracing the higher critical view of Scripture, according to which he represents the ancient narratives of the Hebrew Scriptures to be "historicized fiction." [59]

Kass (2003) Leon Kass in *The Beginning of Wisdom: Reading Genesis* provides a worthy model of carefully reading the narrative of Genesis in order to recognize the theological, moral, and ethical principles the author intended to convey. I must hasten to add that I do not agree entirely with Kass, such as his over-critical handling of the Joseph story. However, to the extent we learn to apply his method, we are well positioned to read biblical narrative theologically, morally, and ethically.

Sailhamer (1992) John Sailhamer in *The Pentateuch as Narrative* asserts that essential aspects of the storyline through the five books of Moses are lost if we fail to consider the Pentateuch as a cohesive literary work. He points out that the entire Pentateuch is consistently designated in Scripture as the "book of the law," such as in Joshua 1:8. Thus, Sailhamer encourages us to adopt a holistic view of the Pentateuch. Similar considerations would apply to the Early Prophets, in which 1 & 2 Samuel and 1 & 2 Kings were each single, integrated books in the ancient Hebrew Canon. Accordingly, as we approach any canonical section of the Bible, we should strive to recognize the important integrative strands that run through the entire section.

Wenham (2000) Gordan Wenham in *Story as Torah: Reading Old Testament Narrative Ethically* models the careful reading of the narrative in Genesis and Judges so as to recognize the author's theological, moral, and ethical stance. As with Kass, to the extent we grasp Wenham's method, we prepare ourselves to derive normative principles from biblical narrative in general.

Aesthetic Quality of Biblical Narrative

Whereas Alter embraces the higher critical view of the Hebrew Scriptures and characterizes the ancient narratives contained therein as "historicized fiction," we embrace as true Paul's statement in 2 Timothy 3:16 that every writing is God-breathed. Accordingly, the insights that Alter presents regarding the aesthetic quality of the narratives of the Hebrew Scriptures actually inspire wonder and awe, not only due to the manifest literary skill of the human authors of the text, but, more importantly, the manner in which the Holy Spirit has superintended its production so that the result is not only rich with theological, moral, and ethical significance, but it is truly elegant as a cohesive literary work. Thus, contrary to the Darwinian evolutionary hypothesis, the authors of the ancient biblical narrative were highly sophisticated in regard to the efficient transmission of complex and normative theological, moral, and ethical principles through the medium of prose narration.

Important Attributes of Biblical Narrative

The principal attributes of the ancient narratives of the Bible, to which the reader should be sensitive and which should guide interpretation, are identified in the paragraphs which follow. [60]

Characterization. The attribute of characterization refers to the manner in which the narrator in a given text shapes and represents the characters in the story. This is seldom done directly by means of narrator declarations. Instead, characterization is accomplished indirectly through the actions of the characters, through the speeches they utter and dialogue in which they participate, and through the dynamics of the unfolding story.

Consider, for example, the story of the deception of Isaac by Jacob at the direction of his mother, Rebekah, which is recorded in the 27th chapter of Genesis. In this story, the narrator offers no direct assessment of the morality or ethics of Jacob's action by which he wrests the blessing of the firstborn from his older brother, Esau. The reader is forced to carefully read the text in this chapter, together with those which precede and follow it, in order to determine Yahweh's role in and assessment of the deception episode.

According to Leon Kass, [61] Yahweh orchestrated the deception episode through Rebekah in order to ensure the transmission of the blessing of the firstborn to Jacob instead of Esau. Isaac favored his older son for a thoroughly carnal reason – he liked the taste of Esau's game – and he was intent on conferring the blessing of the firstborn upon Esau. However, Yahweh had explicitly revealed to Rebekah that Jacob was to inherit the blessing according to Genesis 25:23. She undoubtedly shared this information with her husband, but Isaac rejected it and embraced Esau as the favored son. Given this history, Rebekah resorted to the only method available to her – guile – to cause her husband to do the right thing. From Genesis 27:33 it appears that Isaac finally comprehended the significance of what had just taken place, and how close he had come to defying Yahweh's expressed elective choice. And so the episode concludes with Isaac conferring upon Jacob the blessing of the firstborn and the covenant of Abraham. Moreover, Isaac sends Jacob off to the north country near the city of Haran to take a wife from the family of his mother. Esau, on the other hand, consoles himself by nursing a grudge against his younger brother and taking another wife from the family of Ishmael. And poor Rebekah is destined to die before ever seeing Jacob again. Accordingly, she enacts through her experience the biblical principle that life is begotten by the act of dying.

Type-Scenes. Before leaving the subject of characterization, I need to deal briefly with the subject of **type-scenes**. [62] Robert Alter suggests that type-scenes are part of the narrative convention that was commonly understood by author and audience. He employs the example of the **betrothal episode** that repeatedly occurs in the narratives of Genesis and Exodus. The elements of the betrothal convention that the audience would have expected to see are as follows:

- The man (or his representative) arrives at a well where he meets, apparently by accident, the young woman who will become the bride.

- She excitedly runs back to her home and informs her family of the stranger who is waiting at the well.

- The head of the family (or his representative) invites the man to join the family in a meal.

- After the meal, the man states his errand, and the betrothal negotiations ensue.

The first instance of this type-scene is found in Genesis 24:10ff, which is the account of Abraham's servant seeking a wife for Isaac. The second is found in Genesis 29:1ff, which is the story of Jacob's encounter with Rachel, the daughter of his uncle Laban. The third instance is found in Exodus 2:11ff, which is the story of Moses' encounter with Zipporah, the daughter of Reuel, the priest of Midian. The distinctive features of each of these stories – that is, the manner in which they depart from the convention – contribute to the author's skillful representation of the characters in the story as follows:

- Rebekah dominates the story of her betrothal to Isaac, which is recorded in the 24th chapter of Genesis. In fact, Isaac is altogether absent, and a representative acts in his behalf. This contributes to the characterization of Rebekah as the strong matriarch who acts decisively, and Isaac as the most passive of the patriarchs.

- In Jacob's encounter with Rachel, which is recorded in the 29th chapter of Genesis, he has to remove the stone which covers the well, which contributes to the representation of Jacob as one who has to struggle against adversity, including his own nature.

- In Moses' encounter with Zipporah, which is recorded in Exodus 2:11ff, he is called upon to rescue the seven sisters from hostile shepherds, after which he helps them water the flocks. This contributes to the representation of Moses as the one called by Yahweh to rescue the people of Israel from bondage in Egypt.

Whereas Alter assumes that the biblical authors employed type-scenes in the same way a fictional author would, I am convinced that Yahweh orchestrated the actual events in question so that, when written down, the account contained exactly those elements which were theologically, morally, or ethically significant. The concept of Yahweh's orchestration of events is delineated in Figure 2-2, and it is discussed in the associated text in chapter 2.

Repetition. The art of **repetition** for emphasis applies to key words and phrases, which serve to tie the segments of a story together. Moreover, they often point to a transcendent theological, moral, or ethical idea that is in play.

Consider, for example, the story of Judah that is interposed between Joseph's brothers selling him to the Ishmaelites according to Genesis 37:28 and the Ishmaelites selling Joseph to Potiphar according to Genesis 39:1ff. [63] The key word sequence, "Please identify... identified...", that bookends the story of Judah in the 38th chapter, occurs in Genesis 37:32-33 and Genesis 38:25-26. In the first passage, Joseph's brothers ask their father, Jacob, to identify the blood-stained garment, and Jacob identifies it as being Joseph's. In the second passage, Tamar asks her father-in-law, Judah, to identify the signet, cord, and staff which she had retained as security, and he identifies them as his. Moreover, the brothers employ the blood of a slaughtered goat to deceive their father according to Genesis 37:31, and Judah sends a young goat by means of his friend, Shua the Adullamite, in order to redeem his signet, cord, and staff.

Thus, the author employs subtle word play to link the Judah story on both ends into the larger narrative concerning Jacob's sons. By means of this artifice, he places in evidence the fact that the Judah story in the 38th chapter is not a disconnected parenthesis or interpolation, but rather an important element of the narrative flow that eventuates in the emergence of Judah and Joseph as joint bearers of the covenant and leaders among the twelve patriarchs of Israel.

Narrative Analogy. This attribute designates the artifice of the author's employing one passage of text to provide an oblique commentary on another passage. For example, as we have already seen, Yahweh's statement to Rebekah in Genesis 25:23 informs and illuminates the significance of the deception episode in Genesis 27.

Syntax. This attribute designates the precise way in which the author arranges words into phrases and sentences. The "Please identify... identified" construction cited above as an example of repetition is also an example of syntax that is important in the Judah story.

Speeches and Dialogue. This attribute refers to statements made by the characters in a story. Consider, for example, the first recorded speech by Adam in the 2nd chapter of Genesis, which occurs in the 23rd verse. This statement is important for two reasons:

1. It is expressed in the form of poetry, by which the author emphasizes its theological, moral, and ethical importance.

2. It is explicitly quoted by Jesus in His teaching on marriage and divorce in the 19th chapter of Matthew and the 10th chapter of Mark, and it thereby serves as the theological basis for human marriage.

Thus, an author's use of speeches and dialogue is not merely the factual quotation of something said by one of the characters. Instead, it is a tool in the author's hands by means of which he represents the characters in the story and highlights important theological, moral, or ethical ideas.

Another example is the manner in which legal code is embedded into the narrative of Exodus, Leviticus, and Numbers; namely, as dialogue between Yahweh and Moses. This exemplifies the preference of biblical authors for dialogue as compared with direct narration. Repeatedly, they place the important elements of the story on the lips of the characters rather than simply recounting what happened. [64]

Concluding Comments Regarding Biblical Narrative

By way of conclusion to this discussion of narrative, I quote from Robert Alter as follows:

> I would prefer to insist on a complete interfusion of literary art with theological, moral, or historiosophical vision, the fullest perception of the latter dependent on the fullest grasp of the former.

In other words, to successfully and accurately glean theological, moral, or ethical principles from biblical narrative requires that the reader be sensitive to the author's highly sophisticated and elegant use of language. Through his skillful employment of literary art, the author has embedded such principles into the text so as to cause the reader to search for and dig them out by paying careful attention to his use of literary tools such as characterization, repetition, narrative analogy, syntax, speeches, and dialogue.

Interpreting Hebrew Poetry

The genre of poetry, especially Hebrew poetry, is a powerful and efficient means of communicating profound theological concepts. I believe the reason for this is twofold: first, poetry is powerful because it connects with the emotions in a way that didactic or teaching literature does not;

and, second, it employs, by design, highly figurative language which efficiently transmits complex ideas through word pictures and analogies.

The literary genre of Hebrew poetry dominates the Latter Prophets and the Writings sections of the Hebrew Canon. To properly interpret Hebrew poetry, it is essential that we understand and appreciate its structure. The foundational structural element in Hebrew poetry, as is the case with all poetry, is the **line**. A **strophe** or **strophic unit** consists of two or more lines. The lines within a strophic unit are related to one another in accordance with a concept called **parallelism**, of which there are six basic types as follows:

1. Synonymic

2. Antithetic

3. Synthetic

4. Repetitive-additive

5. Chiastic or introverted

6. Mixed

Modern biblical scholars have come to regard this six-fold categorization of parallelism in Hebrew poetry as simplistic and even misleading. [65] However, no replacement scheme has won a consensus. Therefore, for the purposes of the WitW study, we shall be content to work with the traditional categories of parallelism.

While Hebrew poetry includes rhyme – that is, rhythm of sounds – parallelism is **rhythm of thought**. The fact is evident that the preservation of rhyme in a translation of the Hebrew text is nearly impossible. However, parallelism can be preserved, and therefore appreciated, in a translation. The most effective way to introduce the student to the six kinds of parallelism is to identify examples, which is done in the paragraphs which follow. Most of the examples are drawn from the Book of Psalms.

Synonymic Parallelism

Even as synonyms are words that mean the same thing, in like manner, synonymic parallelism designates the case wherein the succeeding lines of a strophic unit restate the thought expressed by the first line. An example is found in the 1st Psalm as follows:

> But his delight is in the Torah of Yahweh,
>   and on his Torah he meditates day and night.
> [Psalm 1:2, adapted from the ESV]

This example actually illustrates the subtle difference between synonymic and synthetic parallelism, to which we presently turn. In the example cited above, the second line of the strophe explains the meaning of delighting in the Torah of Yahweh. The Hebrew word translated "meditates" is *hagah* which means to audibly muse or recite as well as to silently meditate. Therefore, the emotion of delighting in the Torah of Yahweh motivates continual meditation and audible recitation, presumably toward the objective of memorization. In sum, delighting in the Torah of Yahweh entails obedience to Yahweh's instruction to Joshua in Joshua 1:8.

The prophets like Isaiah and Jeremiah employed synonymic parallelism frequently in their writings. Consider the following example from Isaiah:

> Why do you spend your money for that which is not bread,
>   and your labor for that which does not satisfy?
> Listen diligently to Me, and eat what is good,
>   and delight yourselves in rich food.
> Incline your ear, and come to Me;
>   hear, that your soul may live;
>   and I will make with you an everlasting covenant,
>   My steadfast, sure love for David.
> Behold, I made him a witness to the peoples,
>   a leader and commander for the peoples.
> Behold, you shall call a nation that you do not know,
>   and a nation that did not know you shall run to you...
> [Isaiah 55:2-5, ESV]

There are five strophic units in this passage, of which the 1st, 2nd, 4th, and 5th each consist of two lines that display synonymic parallelism; the 3rd, or middle, strophe consists of four lines and displays synthetic parallelism. From these examples, the fact is evident that in synonymic parallelism the second line restates the idea of the first, but with different words so as to clarify, explain, and emphasize the essential element of truth being expressed.

Antithetic Parallelism

Even as an antithesis presents an opposing idea to that expressed by a thesis, antithetic parallelism designates the case wherein the second line of a strophic unit expresses a thought which is opposite to that expressed by the first line. An example is found in the 1st Psalm as follows:

> For Yahweh knows the way of the righteous,
>   but the way of the wicked will perish.
> [Psalm 1:6, adapted from the ESV]

The lexical form of the Hebrew word translated "knows" is *yada*, which means to know relationally, intimately, and with approval. Thus, by means of this antithetical construction, the psalmist places in evidence the marked contrast that exists between the **two ways** – that of the righteous versus that of the wicked. The first way leads to eternal life in fellowship with Yahweh, whereas the second leads to ruination and eternal death as affirmed by the Apostle Paul in the following passage:

> They will suffer the punishment of eternal destruction, away from the presence of Yahweh and from the glory of His might... [2 Thessalonians 1:9, adapted from the ESV]

Synthetic Parallelism

Synthetic parallelism designates the case wherein the succeeding lines of a strophic unit develop or enlarge upon the thought expressed in the first line. An example is found in the 42nd Psalm as follows:

> As a deer pants for flowing streams,
>   so pants my soul for you, O Elohim. [66]
> My soul thirsts for Elohim, for the living El.
>   When shall I come and appear before Elohim?
> [Psalm 42:1-2, adapted from the ESV]

These four lines are all concerned with desiring fellowship with God, and are therefore considered to be a single strophe. The synthetic parallelism in the 1st and 2nd lines employs a comparison to represent the intensity with which our souls should desire fellowship with God. The 3rd and 4th lines further develop the concept of thirsting for God and longing to be in His presence.

It is true that the single category of synthetic parallelism fails to do justice to the richness of Hebrew poetry. Consider the opening verses of the 19th Psalm, a beautiful psalm of David:

> The heavens declare the glory of Elohim,
>   and the sky above proclaims the work of His fingers.
> Day after day pours out speech,
>   and night after night reveals knowledge.
> While there is no speech nor language,
>   and their voice is not heard,
>   their message goes out through all the earth,
>   and their words to the end of the world.
> In them He has set a tabernacle for the sun,
>   which comes forth like a bridegroom leaving his chamber,
>   or a champion who rejoices to run his course.
> Its rising is from one end of the heavens,
>   and its circuit to the other end thereof,
>   and there is nothing hidden from its heat.
> [Psalm 19:1-6, adapted from the ESV]

This passage is replete with a rich variety of synthetic parallelism. For example, the strophic unit concerning the sun, which includes the 5th verse, consists of three lines, of which the 2nd and 3rd lines employ a figure of speech called **simile** to describe what the sun is like. This strophic unit is actually the easiest to categorize. In the first three strophic units, David skillfully employs synthetic parallelism to represent clearly to our minds the mute but articulate testimony of the cosmos concerning the infinite power and majesty of God. In sum, Hebrew poetry in general, and synthetic parallelism in particular, is like a rare and exquisite wine – it must be tasted to be appreciated; and language about it can only go so far in describing it.

Repetitive-Additive Parallelism

Repetitive-additive parallelism, otherwise known as staircase parallelism, designates the case wherein the succeeding lines of a strophic unit combine the features of synonymic and synthetic parallelism as exemplified by the following passage from the 29th Psalm:

> Ascribe to Yahweh, O heavenly beings, [67]
>> ascribe to Yahweh glory and strength.
> Ascribe to Yahweh the glory due His name;
>> worship Yahweh in the splendor of holiness.
> [Psalm 29:1-2, adapted from the ESV]

We see this passage as consisting of a single strophe which is concerned with the proper worship of Yahweh. The synonymic aspect of the passage is the repetition of the phrase, "Ascribe to Yahweh." The synthetic aspect of the passage is the progressive development of the meaning of true worship. In fact, the departure from the repeated pattern in the 4th line places emphasis upon the verb "worship." It is noteworthy that the lexical form of the Hebrew word translated "glory" is *kabod*, which literally means weight or worth. The lexical form of the Hebrew word translated "worship" is *shachah*, which means to bow down.

Thus, in this strophe of four lines, David articulates the essential meaning of worship as an act of ascription or **representation**, through language, of the worth or merit of Yahweh.

> *External acts of bowing down, raising the hands, singing hymns, or presenting offerings which do not emanate from a heart attitude of representing God as glorious and majestic lack the essential ingredient of true worship.*

Introverted or Chiasmic Parallelism

The most effective approach to succinctly defining introverted or chiasmic parallelism is to first define **chiasm**. A chiasmic structure is delineated in Figure 4-2.

The designation of this structure is inspired by the Greek letter *chi*, or **X**. In the delineation of Figure 4-2, the element **C** is a point of symmetry, or a hinge point, whereby the element **A** corresponds to **A'** and the element **B** corresponds to **B'**.

Thus, the logical progression from **A** to **B** to **C** is reversed or inverted in **C** to **B'** to **A'**. Chiasm can be employed in a pericope [68] or passage consisting of multiple strophic units, or within a single strophic unit.

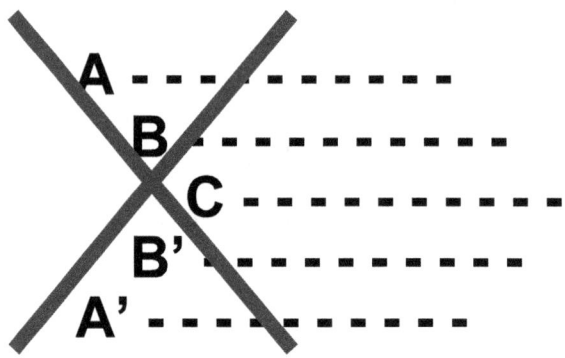

Figure 4-2. Delineation of a Chiasmic Structure

Inverted or chiasmic parallelism refers to the second case. An example of such parallelism is found in Psalm 58:6 as follows:

> O Elohim,
> > break the teeth in their mouths;
> > tear out the fangs of the young lions,
> O Yahweh!
> [Psalm 58:6, adapted from the ESV]

In this case, the logical progression of thought is **A B B' A'**. It is noteworthy that in **A** David employs the appellative divine name or title, Elohim, whereas in **A'** he employs the personal divine name, Yahweh. He thereby incorporates into this single strophic unit both the transcendence of God, signified by Elohim, and the immanence of God, signified by Yahweh.

Another example of a chiasmic structure is found in Isaiah 55:8-9 as follows:

> For My thoughts are not your thoughts,
> > neither are your ways My ways, declares Yahweh.
> > > For as the heavens are higher than the earth,
> > so are My ways higher than your ways
> and My thoughts than your thoughts.
> [Isaiah 55:8-9, adapted from the ESV]

This strophic unit, consisting of five lines, displays the progression **A B C B' A'**. Moreover, the "my... your" order in **A** is reversed in **B**. The pivot element, **C**, employs the seemingly infinite elevation of the vault of the heavens above the earth to signify the infinite moral elevation of God's ways above our ways, and His thoughts above ours. In other words, when we lift our eyes to gaze into the night sky, we should not only recognize a testimony as to the glory of Elohim, as stated by David in Psalm 19:1ff, but we should also recognize a testimony as to His infinitely exalted nature and character.

Mixed Parallelism

Mixed parallelism designates the case in which a strophic unit displays two of the above forms of parallelism. An example is found in Psalm 27:1 as follows:

> Yahweh is my light and my salvation;
>   whom shall I fear?
> Yahweh is the stronghold of my life;
>   of whom shall I be afraid?
> [Psalm 27:1, adapted from the ESV]

This strophic unit consists of four lines, designated **A B A' B'**. **B** and **B'** display synonymic parallelism, and **A** and **A'** display synthetic parallelism. In fact, **A'** represents an essential dimension of Yahweh's being David's light and salvation; to wit, Yahweh is like an invincible mountain stronghold where David could take refuge and be protected from his enemies. It is noteworthy that during the wilderness period of David's career, when he was forced to hide from Saul in wilderness strongholds, he learned experientially the significance of Yahweh's being the stronghold of his life.

Poetry affords a highly efficient and affective means of communication. It is efficient because it permits the communication of profound theological concepts and principles with few words. It is affective in that its language can powerfully impact our emotions through the use of figures of speech.

For an example of poetry as power-packed communication, study the 18th Psalm in its entirety, noting not only the various kinds of parallelism employed, but also the rich use of figures of speech, including hyperbole.

While a hyperbolic statement can be defined as a deliberate exaggeration to emphasize a point, in Psalm 18 David's use of hyperbole in describing his plight and Yahweh's response to it more accurately represent the theological concepts and principles being conveyed, as compared with straightforward, non-figurative language.

Concluding Comments Regarding Hebrew Poetry

By way of conclusion of this brief exposition of representative passages of Hebrew poetry, the following facts are evident:

- Hebrew poetry must be tasted with the palate of the mind. Having sensitized the student to the variegated richness of Hebrew poetry in terms of the kinds of parallelism or thought rhythms to be observed, there is no substitute for actually reading it and deeply reflecting on its message.

- Many of the psalms – especially those of David – emerged from a particular historical situation as documented in 1 and 2 Samuel. Understanding the historical situation illuminates the message of the psalm.

Interpreting Didactic Literature

The descriptive label **didactic** derives from the Greek word *didache*, which means teaching or instruction. Thus, the **didactic literature** in the Bible consists of those books and passages that are devoted to teaching theological, moral, or ethical principles directly through persuasive discourse, as compared with indirectly, such as through stories or poetry. The epistles of the Christian Scriptures, written by Paul, Peter, John, and others to address specific issues arising in the churches of the 1st century, are all didactic. Moreover, the major discourses of Jesus Christ contained in the Gospels of Matthew and John fall into this category as well.

Interpretation of didactic passages requires that the student address the following four essential factors:

- Literary context.

- Historical and cultural context.

- Grammatical structure.

- Word meanings.

Didactic literature is different from narrative, poetic, and apocalyptic literature in that the author makes his teaching points directly through persuasive discourse and logical argumentation. Thus, even though these four factors apply to all biblical passages, the manner in which they apply to didactic passages is distinctive. In the paragraphs which follow, the manner in which each of these four factors affects interpretation is explained.

Literary Context

> *One of the most basic principles of biblical interpretation is that the intended meaning of any passage is the meaning that is consistent with the sense of the literary context in which it occurs.*

A proposed interpretation of a word, phrase, sentence, or paragraph that is inconsistent with the author's main point in the context in which it is found is not likely to be a correct interpretation.

Literary context defines overall flow of thought and thus also the relationship between units of thought. Even word meanings are defined by their literary context. The danger in focusing too narrowly on a verse-by-verse interpretation of Scripture is that it tends to divert attention from the literary context. Individual verses should never be considered in isolation, but always in their immediate and larger contexts. Like any piece of great literature, each book of the Bible was written in units of thought, not in isolated phrases or sentences. Therefore, to interpret a biblical passage properly, we must pay attention to its literary context.

The immediate literary context is defined as the portion of Scripture that precedes and follows the passage under study. Since units of thought correspond to paragraphs in didactic literature, the immediate context of a paragraph would be defined by the paragraphs which precede and follow it. But we must pay attention to larger units of thought as well. Some recently published English Bibles offer section and subsection headings which help the reader sense the flow of thought and the boundaries of the successive units of thought. Thus, for a given passage, we can visualize concentric circles of literary context, beginning with the immediate, then progressing outward to the subsection and section, and thence to the entire book. In the case of an author who has produced a collection of books, the other books in the collection help define the literary context of a given passage. The outermost circles of literary context correspond to the canonical section in which the passage is located, and thence to the entire Bible.

To illustrate the importance of literary context as a determinant of meaning, consider the following familiar verse:

> I can do all things through Him who strengthens me.
> [Philippians 4:13, ESV]

Perhaps you have heard this verse quoted as a basis for believing that God will impart to His saints invincible strength to surmount every adversity. However, the literary context of the verse suggests a different meaning. The entire Epistle to the Philippians reads very much like a letter from a missionary to one of his supporting churches. In particular, Philippians 4:10-20 is a section of the letter in which Paul is expressing gratitude for a financial gift recently received from the church at Philippi. In the paragraph which contains the 13th verse, Paul is emphasizing that he has learned to be content in all manner of material circumstances, ranging from deprivation to plenty. In the 13th verse, the lexical form of the main verb in the Greek is *ischuo*, which does not mean "can do" in the sense of implementing or performing. Instead, it means "able to prevail." Moreover, in the Greek there is no object corresponding to "all things" in the ESV translation. Thus, a more accurate translation would be as follows:

> In all (circumstances) I am able to prevail in the One empowering me.

Within the literary context, Christ enables Paul to prevail over his inner emotional state by remaining serenely content regardless of his material circumstances. This sense of Philippians 4:13 is decidedly different from that derived from a less careful reading of the verse.

By way of conclusion of the discussion of literary context, I need to comment further on two issues: first, the importance of the narrative context of a didactic passage; and, second, the importance of the Hebrew

Scriptures as part of the literary context for the didactic literature in the Christian Scriptures.

Narrative Context. The storyline that runs through the four Gospels and the Book of Acts contributes to the literary context of the rest of the Christian Scriptures by defining their narrative context. In particular, referring to Figure 4-1 again, the doctrinal content of Paul's epistles are suspended from the narrative of the four Gospels and the Book of Acts. Moreover, the didactic literature in the Christian Scriptures can be accurately represented as commentary on the practical implications of the narrative; that is, the story of Christ and His apostles.

Throughout the Christian Scriptures, the authors quote from, refer to, and allude to the Hebrew Scriptures. In the case of outright quotations, identification of the passage being quoted is usually clear. However, the theological meaning conferred upon the quoted passage by the literary context of the quotation is sometimes unexpected. For example, consider the collection of passages in the Hebrew Scriptures from which Paul quotes in Romans 3:9-18 in support of his argument that all men are guilty before the judgment bar of God. If we check the literary context of each of these quotations, we discover that in some instances Paul is conferring an additional theological meaning beyond that imparted by its literary context in the Hebrew Scriptures. In other instances, Paul expects his reader to import and keep hold of the theological context of the quoted passage.

While exhaustive treatment of this issue goes far beyond the bounds of the WitW study, suffice it to say that a thoroughgoing understanding of the Hebrew Scriptures is needed in order to properly interpret the didactic literature in the Christian Scriptures.

Historical and Cultural Context

I have already commented on the importance of historical and cultural context in the section entitled General Principles of Biblical Interpretation.

While the Book of Revelation is predominantly apocalyptic literature, to which we will turn next, the series of letters from Christ to the seven churches recorded in the 2nd and 3rd chapters take the form of embedded didactic literature. Two examples from these letters serve to illustrate the importance of historical and cultural context. First, in Revelation 3:2, Jesus commands the church at Sardis to wake up or become alert. The city of Sardis was situated on a seemingly impregnable cliff. However, it had twice been conquered by attacking armies who had scaled the walls at night while the city slept. Second, Jesus' words to the church at Laodicea include the following statement:

> ... You are neither cold nor hot. Would that you were either cold or hot! So, because you are lukewarm, and neither hot nor cold, I will spit you out of my mouth. [Revelation 3:15-16, ESV]

Laodicea lacked a good water supply. Hot water could be piped from hot springs at Hierapolis, and cold water could be brought from Colossae. However, by the time either stream reached Laodicea, the temperature had turned lukewarm – neither soothingly hot nor refreshingly cold.

Another aspect of historical and cultural context which we need to understand is the marriage customs of the ancient Near East. For example, understanding the Parable of the Wedding Banquet in Matthew 22:1-14, the Parable of the Ten Virgins in Matthew 25:1-13, and the significance of the church as the Bride of Christ all depend upon an appreciation for this aspect of cultural context. The ancient Near East marriage took place in the following four phases:

- **The betrothal**. The betrothal was arranged by the fathers of the bride and groom. The betrothal was usually a significant period of time, such as one year. During this period, the bride and groom were required to keep themselves sexually pure.

- **The wedding procession**. At the end of the betrothal period, when the wedding was to take place, the relatives and friends of the couple would gather. The groom would lead a procession to the home of his bride, and then he would bring her triumphantly to the home of his father for the wedding banquet.

- **The wedding banquet**. A wedding banquet is recorded in the 2nd chapter of John's Gospel. The family and friends of the bride and groom would gather to celebrate the joining together of the new couple as man and wife.

- **The consummation**. After the wedding banquet, the marriage would be consummated. The new couple would often establish their residence adjacent to the home of the groom's father.

With the church represented as the Bride of Christ, we are presently in the betrothal period. At the time of Christ's second coming, He will take His bride onto Himself, and after that the wedding banquet will take place in the home of His Father.

Grammatical Structure

For purposes of understanding how to interpret didactic passages, we can represent **grammatical structure** as consisting of two aspects: **morphology** and **syntax**. Morphology designates how words are formed to indicate their function in language. A term that is related to morphology is **inflection**; this term designates the variation of form that words undergo to mark distinctions of case, gender, number, tense, person, mood, voice, etc. Syntax designates how words are arranged in order to form a meaningful phrase, sentence, or larger unit of thought.

Grammatical structure is especially important in didactic literature because the author is striving to select words and arrange them grammatically to express with precision a certain theological, moral, or ethical idea. In regard to grammatical structure, we can state the following principle: **an accurate interpretation of a passage is one that is consistent with the grammatical structure of the passage**.

As Walter Kaiser points out in his text on exegetical theology, a careful analysis of grammatical structure requires understanding biblical Hebrew and Greek. [69] [70] In fact, Kaiser suggests two levels of biblical language study for the student of biblical exegesis. The first level would acquaint him with the morphology of Hebrew and Greek nouns and verbs and with language tools whereby he could discover the meaning of words actually used by a biblical author. The second level is far more rigorous and would equip the student with an understanding of the nuances of biblical Hebrew and Greek grammar and syntax and the ability to undertake translation himself. Clearly, for purposes of this course of study, only the first level can reasonably be assumed. Fortunately, the sophisticated and user-friendly computer-based tools that have become available over the past 30 years enable a student who is acquainted with biblical Hebrew and Greek grammar and syntax to safely and fruitfully navigate the waters of biblical exegesis.

Assuming the WitW student has, at most, a passing acquaintance with biblical Hebrew and Greek grammar and syntax, the fact is evident that our exegetical endeavors are heavily reliant upon good translations from the biblical languages, such as into English. In fact, we should carefully choose a translation that is both literal and understandable. As discussed by Leland Ryken in his little monograph on Bible translations, [71] there are two fundamentally different approaches to the translation of Scripture: **word-for-word** and **thought-for-thought**. A word-for-word translation is customarily designated as **literal**, and a thought-for-thought translation is designated as **dynamic equivalent**. In general, the more a given translation is weighted toward literal, the closer is the correspondence of grammatical structure in the target language, such as English, to the grammatical structure in Hebrew or Greek. However, highly literal translations tend to suffer from poor readability. On the other hand, the more a given translation is weighted toward dynamic equivalent, the more readable it is. However, the danger of dynamic equivalent or thought-for-thought translation is the intrusion of the translator's interpretation, and thereby his theological bias, into the translation.

I would recommend for serious consideration two recently released English translations, the English Standard Version (ESV) and the Holman Christian Standard Bible (HCSB). (Most of the Scripture quotations in this Theological Reader are derived or adapted from these two translations.) Both translation teams employed conservative evangelical scholars, and both teams have endeavored to achieve an optimized English translation that is strongly weighted toward literal, but not to the extent that readability and understandability are unduly compromised. Both translations offer a study Bible with copious notes, and both offer an on-line edition of their study Bibles. Of the two, I am inclined to favor the HCSB, for which the on-line Bible is accessible free of charge at http://mystudybible.com. The on-line HCSB study Bible includes an impressive and very useful tool for exegesis which is accessed by simply moving the mouse pointer to a word in the text. This action causes a window to appear with the transliterated form of the Hebrew or Greek word, its definition, and its morphology.

Analytical Methods. Appendix E summarizes two approaches to analyzing the grammatical structure of a didactic passage to determine the author's intended meaning with greater precision as compared with simply reading the passage. The two methods are **verbal purview** and **diagramming**.

Concluding Comments Regarding Grammatical Structure. By way of concluding this discussion of the importance of grammatical structure in the interpretation of didactic literature, we need to keep in mind the following three points:

- The author has embedded clues as to his intended meaning in the grammatical structure of the text. Therefore, we must pay careful attention to grammatical structure in order to arrive at an accurate understanding of his intended meaning.

- On account of limited understanding of biblical Hebrew and Greek grammar and syntax, most of us are forced to rely upon the translator's care and skill in mapping grammatical structure from the biblical Hebrew or Greek into a target language, such as English.

- Therefore, we need to carefully select the translation of the Bible that we will employ for study. In particular, we should choose a translation that is strongly weighted toward literal word-for-word as contrasted with thought-for-thought. Having done this, we can be reasonably confident that the grammatical structure in the Hebrew or Greek is closely approximated by that in our translation.

Word Meanings

Didactic literature is characterized by the author's endeavoring to clearly articulate theological, moral, or ethical meanings through the use of words and grammatical structure. Therefore, it is often the case that certain words acquire a precise, technical meaning in the vocabulary of a given author.

For example, in some Pauline contexts, **the flesh** (= *sarx* in the Greek) is invested with a theological meaning; to wit, it designates the unregenerate human personality which is in bondage to evil, sin, and death. In the case of a disciple of Christ, the flesh represents the residual corruption of the human personality; that is, it embodies "the law of sin and death" spoken of by Paul in Romans 8:2. This law is in opposition to the "the Spirit's law of life in Christ Jesus." The conflict between flesh and Spirit is the subject of Paul's argument in Galatians 5:16-24. However, in other Pauline contexts, flesh = *sarx* designates the physical human body; this is true in Galatians 2:20, for example.

The above discussion of flesh = *sarx* places in evidence an essential principle of biblical interpretation: **context always determines meaning**. Nevertheless, careful Bible study, such as to prepare a message for preaching or a lesson for teaching, often requires that we explore the meaning of words. In performing word studies, there are two important technical terms that we need to understand:

- **Semantic field**. This technical term designates a set of words that can be employed to represent a given concept, entity, state of being, etc. The words in a given semantic field are not synonymous, but they all can be used to represent the same segment of reality. For example, "field," "plot," and "acre" belong to a semantic field that designates a piece of real estate.

- **Range of meaning**. This technical term designates the set of meanings that can be invested in a given word. For example, "hand" can designate a part of our body or the act of giving applause.

Importance of Literary Context

The importance of literary context as a determinant of meaning has already been addressed in general terms. With respect to word meanings, literary context is critically important. Suppose, for example, that we are exploring the meaning of an important technical term in Romans 3:21-31; namely, "the righteousness of God" (= *dikaiosynē theou* in the Greek). We will have occasion to explore the theological meaning of this entire passage in chapter 14, Content of the Gospel of God. My purpose here is to define some parameters for exploring the meaning of this particular term. Where should we turn for this purpose? I suggest the following, listed in order of precedence:

- The lexical definition of *dikaiosynē*, which defines the range of meanings this word can assume, depending upon context.

- The immediate context of the paragraph in Romans, together with those which precede and follow.

- Investments of meaning derived from the Hebrew Scriptures to which Paul refers in Romans, especially in the 2nd, 3rd, and 4th chapters.

- Other contexts in the Epistle to the Romans.

- Contexts in the other early epistles of Paul; namely, Galatians, 1 & 2 Thessalonians, and 1 & 2 Corinthians.

- Contexts in the middle and late epistles of Paul.

- Contexts elsewhere in the Christian Scriptures.

- Ancient Christian commentaries on the passage in question from the Church Fathers.

- Modern Christian commentaries on the passage in question.

I have arranged this list according to a decreasing order of relevance to the passage in question. In general, the further one ranges afield from the immediate context, both in a literary sense and in a chronological or historical sense, the less relevant a given resource is likely to be. A general principle is this: **with regard to word meanings, Scripture should be used to interpret Scripture to the maximum extent possible**. Resources other than the Bible should be used with caution.

At the conclusion of this chapter, I will suggest a few resources to which the student can turn for help with word meanings.

Interpreting Apocalyptic Literature

Apocalyptic literature is dominated by the use of symbols, figures of speech, and word pictures. The vast majority of apocalyptic passages in the Bible are contained within the prophetic books of the Hebrew and Christian Scriptures.

The word "apocalyptic" derives from the Greek *apokalypsis*, which means a disclosure, revelation, or unveiling. In fact, this is the word which is translated "revelation" in Revelation 1:1, and apocalyptic language dominates the Book of Revelation. Other biblical books which are dominated by apocalyptic language are the prophecies of Ezekiel, Daniel, and Zechariah.

The Nature of Biblical Prophecy

A prophet is one who represents God to mankind. This is in contrast to a priest, who represents mankind to God. Thus, both prophets and priests serve as **mediatory agents** between God and mankind. While the Bible recognizes instances wherein men were appointed to be prophets and priests without the calling and anointing of God, the true prophet and the true priest are called, anointed, and empowered by God to serve in these special capacities.

Prophetical passages in Scripture can serve either of two purposes.

- **Prophecy as declaration.** Prophets were often called upon to declare to people on God's behalf the theological, moral, or ethical implications of present states of affairs or behaviors. This kind of prophecy can be described as **forth-telling**. In other words, the man of God is warning God's people of the end result of continuing along a given path. Much of Isaiah and Jeremiah are this form of prophecy.

- **Prophecy as prediction.** Prophets were also enabled by God to predict future events; in many cases, events that would take place in the distant future. This kind of prophecy can be described as **foretelling**. Predictive prophecy is a dominant component of Ezekiel, Daniel, and Zechariah in the Hebrew Scriptures and the Book of Revelation in the Christian Scriptures.

Apocalyptic language is occasionally employed in declarative prophecy, and it is frequently employed in predictive prophecy.

Before I turn to the principles governing the interpretation of apocalyptic literature, there are three specific aspects of prophecy in general that I need to define.

The Present Age and the Age to Come

Prophets generally segment time into the **present age** and the **age to come**. In particular, this kind of segmenting of time is observed in Revelation 1:19.

> Write therefore the things that you have seen, **those that are** and **those that are to take place after this**. [Revelation 1:19, ESV, emphasis added]

Multiple Fulfillments

The two tiers of Figures 4-3 illustrate the prophetic versus human viewpoints in regard to multiple fulfillments of predictive prophecy. Note that in the lower tier of this figure, the three events refer to the Alpha Event, the Chi Event, and the Omega Event of Figure 2-1.

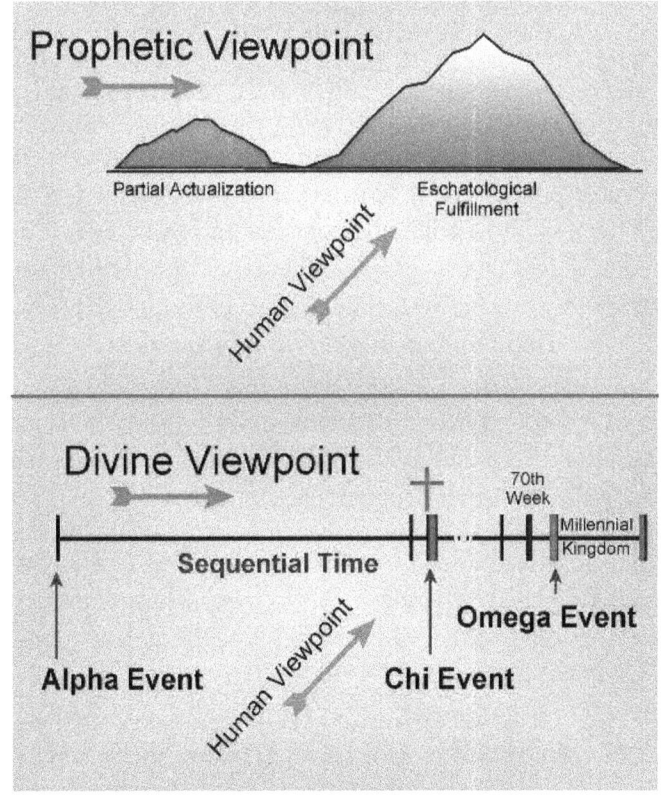

Figure 4-3. Multiple Fulfillments

For many prophetic passages, there is a **near-term, partial actualization** and a **long-term or eschatological fulfillment**. The first is a prototype or prefigurement of the second. These multiple fulfillments are illustrated in the upper tier of Figure 4-3 as two mountain ranges viewed from afar through a pair of binoculars or a telephoto camera lens. According to this perspective, the more distant and higher range is perceived as immediately behind the closer and lower range. In other words, according to the prophetic perspective, the possibly vast chronological separation between the two events, which is perceived according to our human perspective, is highly compressed.

A passage of Scripture which places this factor in evidence is Isaiah 61:1-4, a portion of which is read by Jesus in his message to the synagogue in Nazareth as recorded in Luke 4:16ff. It is noteworthy that Jesus' reading of the passage terminates with the phrase "to proclaim the year of Yahweh's favor." [Isaiah 61:2a, adapted from the ESV] This is because only the first part of Isaiah's vision would be fulfilled during Jesus' first coming; the rest of the vision would be fulfilled at His second coming.

Thus, according to the prophet's perspective, the two advents of Christ are seen as a single event, whereas from our perspective they are separated by nearly two millennia (and counting). Multiple fulfillments are also observed in Daniel's prophetic visions. Daniel's highly articulate visions extended from his own time, ca. 6th century BC, all the way to the Omega Event. In his interpretation of Nebuchadnezzar's dream in the 2nd chapter of Daniel, he sees a succession of four great world empires. The character of these are further articulated in the 7th and 8th chapters. The 9th chapter sets forth Daniel's vision of the 70 Weeks, which is summarily illustrated in the lower tier of Figure 4-3.

In this vision, each week represents a period of 7 prophetic years, with each prophetic year consisting of 360 days. Thus, a period of 490 prophetic years is projected, which begins with the decree "to restore and build Jerusalem." [Daniel 9:25, ESV] This event occurred "in the twentieth year of King Artaxerxes" in accordance with Nehemiah 2:1, the calendar date for which is 445 BC. A period of 69 weeks or 483 prophetic years would transpire from Artaxerxes' decree to the cutting off of the anointed one – that is, the Messiah – in accordance with Daniel 9:26.

Accordingly, there would be 1 week left over, which would occur sometime after the cutting off of the Messiah. As seen by Daniel, this leftover 70th week was contiguous with the 69th week; however, according to our perspective, there is an ellipsis of nearly 2 millennia (and counting) separating the end of the 69th week and the beginning of the 70th week, as delineated in the lower tier of Figure 4-3. I will have much more to say concerning Daniel's vision of the 70 Weeks in chapter 12, Second Coming of the King: the Last Days According to Jesus.

Conditionality

Prophecy may be either **conditional** or **unconditional**. That is, predicted outcomes or events may either be conditioned upon human responses or they may be unconditional. Consider the following examples of conditional prophecy:

- Moses' proclamation of blessings and cursings in Deuteronomy 28:1ff was conditioned upon whether Israel did or did not remain faithful to the covenant with Yahweh.

- In Jeremiah 18:5-11 and Ezekiel 33:1ff, the building up or tearing down of a nation or a kingdom is conditioned on whether or not that nation or kingdom repents of its evil ways in response to the proclamation of coming judgment.

- The Book of Jonah records just such an instance. Jonah proclaimed impending judgment of Nineveh, and the people all repented of their evil ways. As a consequence, Yahweh was merciful and relented from bringing judgment to bear at that time. It is noteworthy that the impending judgment proclaimed by Jonah was expressed as unconditional.

An instance of unconditional prophecy is the immutable covenant that Yahweh cut with Abraham as first stated in Genesis 12:1ff, and then confirmed by means of a solemn blood covenant ceremony in Genesis 15:1ff.

Principles of Interpretation

In relation to the storyline of the Bible, apocalyptic passages perform the function of linguistic illustrations. In other words, they portray through word pictures events that occur in the great meta-narrative that connects the Alpha Event and the Omega Event. This is especially true of events that will precede and accompany the Omega Event.

Let us consider the Book of Revelation. I would assert that this is the most important piece of apocalyptic biblical literature for us to understand, and yet most disciples of Christ find it to be confusing and difficult to understand. So, how should we unlock the mysteries of the word pictures that dominate the 1st chapter and the 4th through the 22nd chapters of this book? Fortunately, the Apostle John defines the word pictures of the 1st chapter in the immediate context. What about the four living creatures that appear in the worship scene of chapter 4? We encounter similar living creatures in the 1st chapter of Ezekiel, where they also appear in proximity to the vision of the glory of God. I suggest that the four faces – lion, ox, man, and eagle – signify the four aspects of Jesus Christ as the King of Israel (face of a lion), the suffering servant of Yahweh (face of an ox), the Son of Man (face of a man), and the Son of God (face of an eagle). [72]

The vision of the first beast with 7 heads and 10 horns in Revelation 13:1ff corresponds to the terrible beast of Daniel 7:7-8. From the context in Daniel, this beast is seen to represent the Roman Empire. However, based upon Nebuchadnezzar's dream, which is interpreted in Daniel 2:1ff, the Roman Empire of antiquity, represented by the legs of iron in the king's vision, will be reconstituted in the last days, as represented by the feet and toes of iron mixed with clay. Thus, the beast of Revelation 13:1ff represents a reconstituted form of the ancient Roman Empire, but it will not have the strength of that ancient empire.

Believe it or not, the principles of interpreting apocalyptic literature in the Bible are manifested in the preceding paragraph. Understanding the symbols and word pictures employed in apocalyptic passages requires a thoroughgoing familiarity with preceding revelation, especially preceding apocalyptic passages. This is certainly the case in the Book of Revelation, where the symbols and word pictures employed by the Apostle John are derived from those employed in the prophecies of Ezekiel, Daniel, and Zechariah in the Hebrew Scriptures.

Interpretation Tools

I want to avoid overwhelming the student with a prescription for a massive investment in a research library. For most students of the WitW study, such an investment is beyond reach and unnecessary. Fortunately, however, study resources have recently come online that satisfy most of the needs that have been identified in the foregoing discussion of biblical interpretation. They are as follows:

- **The English Standard Version (ESV) Study Bible**. In addition to the printed edition, this resource is accessible on line via a code that is provided with a printed copy. It contains copious notes and scholarly introductions to each canonical section and book.

- **The Holman Christian Standard (HCSB) Study Bible**. In addition to a printed edition, this resource is available online without restriction at www.MyStudyBible.com. The online version includes a handy tool for exegesis.

- **The Archaeological Study Bible**. Apparently this resource is only available as a printed edition. It contains a wealth of archaeological information that helps to inform and illuminate the historical and cultural context of biblical books and passages.

Beyond these, there is a wealth of informational and encyclopedic resources available via the internet that can be employed to illuminate and inform the biblical text.

Concluding Comments Regarding Biblical Interpretation

I conclude this lengthy chapter on discovering the meaning of biblical books and passages by emphasizing a set of takeaway concepts and principles.

- **Discovery of the singular meaning intended by the author**. First, I have emphasized that the **objective of biblical interpretation is always the discovery of the singular theological concept or principle that the author intended to communicate**. The fact that I represent that theological concept or principle as **singular** does not necessarily mean that it is **simple**. The singular meaning may have several, perhaps even many, layers and dimensions.

- **The singular meaning may engender manifold applications.** Second, while the author's intended meaning is singular, the **application** of that meaning may be manifold, as a function of the life situation and state of spiritual development of the reading subject. **Moreover, application always follows interpretation.** Whereas interpretation is the act of discovering the author's intended meaning, application is the act of discovering how that meaning impacts my life and ministry. Thus, it is essential that the disciple of Christ cultivate the discipline of reading or listening to Scripture prayerfully, asking the Holy Spirit to shine a light on how a given passage applies to him.

- **Importance for spiritual formation.** Third, **we need to regard our intake of Scripture as food for the human spirit.** Spiritual formation and development is promoted by participation in a whole set of spiritual disciplines, including:

  - Reading Scripture
  - Memorizing and audibly reciting Scripture
  - Prayer
  - Worship
  - Obedience and practice

  Scripture as food for the human spirit is the subject of chapter 65 of *Taste and See* by John Piper. [73]

Questions for Discussion

1. For each of the four principal literary genres in Scripture (i.e., narrative, Hebrew poetry, didactic, and apocalyptic) select a paragraph-length passage to analyze. For each selected passage, discuss both your method of interpretation and the results thereof. In terms of results, state in your own words a paraphrase of the passage which illuminates the author's intended meaning along with any theological, moral, or ethical principles derived from the passage.

2. For each of the four principal literary genres in Scripture, discuss how application of what you have learned from this chapter will help to shape and enrich your approach to studying the Bible. Also, discuss the impact of what you have learned upon your future life and ministry.

Notes & Reflections

Use the space below to record additional insights and commentary resulting from your studies thus far.

Chapter 5.
Torah: The Fountainhead of Wisdom

Chapter Overview

I embrace the Torah – that is, the five books of Moses – as the fountainhead of wisdom. In particular, as unfolded in this chapter, there are **fourteen integrative motifs** or themes that surface in the Torah and that run through all of Scripture. Even as the storyline formulation affords an overall interpretive framework for understanding the trajectory of biblical teaching, each of the integrative motifs affords an interpretive framework for tracing important strands of teaching from the Alpha Event to the Omega Event (see Figure 2-1 and associated discussion) in accordance with the biblical theology method.

Learning Objective

The learning objective for this chapter is twofold: first, to recognize, appreciate, and internalize the significance of the fourteen integrative motifs which surface in the Torah and which run through the entire Bible; and, second, to grasp and internalize how each of these motifs undergoes a transformation by the Chi Event – that is, by the life and ministry of Jesus Christ. Thus, each of the motifs take a form under the terms of the new covenant which Jesus Christ enacted by means of his death, burial, and resurrection which is different from its form under the old covenant which was enacted through the ministry of Moses.

Overview of the Fourteen Integrative Motifs

The fourteen integrative motifs are as follows:

1. **The name of God**, signifying all that He is according to His nature and character.

2. **The temple**, signifying the way in which fallen man can approach, worship, and enjoy fellowship with Yahweh, the God of Israel.

3. **The Sabbath**, being the one day in seven to be set apart for rest, reflection upon and worship of Yahweh, and fellowship with one another.

4. **The *Imago Dei***, being the Latin phrase that signifies the human personality created in the image of God.

5. **The marriage metaphor**, signifying the way in which human marriage represents the relationship between God and His people.

6. **The invasion of evil, sin, and death** into the terrestrial domain, which took place when the serpent's beguilement of Eve brought about Adam's intentional disobedience to the command of Yahweh.

7. **The seed of the woman**, signifying the way in which the promised Redeemer would be incarnated through a virginal conception and birth.

8. **The acceptable sacrifice**, signifying the bloody sacrifice pioneered by Yahweh Himself in providing garments to cover the nakedness of Adam and Eve after the Fall.

9. **The city of man versus the kingdom of God**, signifying the way in which the rule of man exists alongside of and often in opposition to the rule of God.

10. **The people of the new way**, signifying the manner in which Abraham and his descendants were called out and set apart by Yahweh to walk in His way that leads to life as contrasted with the way of human intuition apart from God which leads to ruination and death.

11. **The gospel**, by which men might be delivered from the power of darkness, evil, sin, and death and brought under the kingly rulership of God.

12. **Sovereign election and human responsibility**, according to which Yahweh has unconditionally chosen a people for His kingdom apart from any human merit, and yet He holds us accountable for our self-determined choices.

13. **The prototype**, signifying the ways in which the nation of Israel serves as a model of redemption and sanctification through the Exodus and Conquest episodes.

14. **The covenant of conditional blessing**, enacted through Moses and continuing to the present day according to which Yahweh promises to bless those who walk in His way and to curse those who refuse to do so.

In the following paragraphs, each of the motifs is briefly summarized.

The Name of God

We speak of the divine name in the singular because that is the way in which biblical characters always refer to it. In particular, Proverbs 18:10 states that the name of Yahweh is like a strong tower. Jesus refers to the Father's name by which we are kept safe and to the name the Father had given to Him. In Philippians 2:5-11, Paul speaks of the name which the Father conferred upon the Son, the name that is above every name.

However, on account of God's manifold nature and character and the infinite dimensionality of His person, Scripture reveals a multitude of divine names, many of which are compound names. It is only by this means that we can acquire a proper and comprehensive representation of God's nature, character, and personality.

The Temple

It is appropriate that we conceptually define the temple as that place or sphere in which man can approach, worship, and enjoy fellowship with God. Thus, the primordial temple was the Garden of Eden. In Genesis 1:26-28 God declared that the man whom He had created was to be fruitful and multiply so as to fill the entire earth, and he was to have dominion over the entire terrestrial creation. We believe this is a reflection of the fact that God intended from the beginning that His temple would encompass the entire earth, and that all peoples would worship Him and have access to fellowship with Him.

The paradigmatic post-Fall temple is the **tabernacle in the wilderness** depicted in Figure 3-3 and discussed in connection with that figure in chapter 3. The tabernacle in the wilderness is paradigmatic because it presents the first comprehensive biblical representation of the means by which fallen man could approach, worship, and enjoy fellowship with Yahweh, the absolutely holy God of Israel.

The Sabbath

According to Genesis 2:1-3, God blessed and consecrated the Sabbath as one day in seven in which man should rest from his labors, devote himself to reflection upon God and His ways, worship God, and enjoy fellowship with one another. In Exodus 31:12ff, God declares Himself to be Yahweh M'Qadash – the God who makes us holy – in connection with the faithful keeping of the Sabbath on the part of His people. In other words, Sabbath-keeping is linked with the process of sanctification. While there are certainly other tools which God employs to bring about sanctification of His people, such as affliction and suffering, our progress in sanctification will be limited if we refuse to set apart one day in seven for rest, reflection upon God, worship, and fellowship with one another. The weekly Sabbath is a microcosm of our eternal Sabbath, which will be devoted entirely to reflection upon and worship of Yahweh and fellowship with one another.

The *Imago Dei*

Imago Dei is the Latin phrase which means "the image of God." Genesis 1:26-28 declares that Yahweh created man in His own image and according to His likeness, and Genesis 2:7 declares that Yahweh created the personality of man by conjoining two substances: namely, a body formed from "the dust from the ground," and "the breath of life," which is a reference to the human spirit. The joining of these two substances resulted in a "living creature" or a conscious personality.

The Marriage Metaphor

Human marriage was instituted by God Himself according to Genesis 2:18-25. With the unfolding of revelation in the Hebrew Scriptures, the fact becomes evident that human marriage serves as a metaphor of God's relationship with His people, which is most clearly articulated by Paul in Ephesians 5:22-33. The three divinely ordained purposes of human marriage are as follows: first, to serve as a representation of God's covenantal relationship with His people; second, for the procreation and raising up of godly offspring; and, third, for human enjoyment. It is noteworthy how the invasion of evil, sin, and death, to which we turn next, brought about an overturning of these divine purposes for human marriage. [74]

The Invasion of Evil, Sin, and Death

The **invasion of evil, sin, and death** is the first motif to be discussed in detail later in this chapter.

The fall of the archangel Lucifer is described by Isaiah in the 14th chapter of his prophecy and by Ezekiel in the 28th chapter of his. As a result of his fall, Lucifer became the devil and Satan – "the prince of the power of the air, the spirit that is now at work in the sons of disobedience." [Ephesians 2:2, ESV] In the Garden of Eden, he disguised himself as a talking serpent, and he successfully beguiled Eve to partake of the forbidden fruit by asserting that she would become like God. When Eve offered some of the fruit to her husband, he too ate. While Eve was deceived into partaking of the fruit, Adam did so in open and prideful rebellion against the command of God. And so when he ate of the fruit, **and only then**, the impact of his disobedience was felt; Adam and his wife became ashamed of their nakedness. Because Adam stood as federal head of the entire human race, in the eyes of God we all sinned at the point of time when Adam sinned. On account of the Fall as recorded in the 3rd chapter of Genesis, evil, sin, and death invaded the terrestrial domain. Moreover, the entire race of Adam became subject to divine judgment.

Divine Judgment and the Fear of Yahweh. This is an important corollary motif which is subsumed beneath the invasion of evil, sin, and death. Taking the genealogical progression in the narrative of Genesis at face value, that narrative covers a period of nearly four millennia. During that time, Yahweh brought to bear two cataclysmic judgments upon mankind; that is, judgments that were both sudden and terrifying in their devastation. The two judgments to which I refer are the Flood of Noah as recorded in Genesis 6:1ff, and the destruction of the cities of the plain as recorded in the 19th chapter of Genesis. These two judgments were not only warranted by the extreme moral depravity to which mankind had fallen, but they were designed and intended to inspire the fear of Yahweh, which is the beginning of wisdom. Thus, they were to serve as a deterrent against sin for all generations to follow.

The Seed of the Woman

The seed of the woman motif is announced by Yahweh Elohim in the *protoevangelium* of Genesis 3:15. The lexical form of the Hebrew word which is translated "seed" in this verse is זֶרַע. By replacing the Hebrew consonants and vowel pointings with their English equivalents, the transliteration of this word is *zera*.

From the *protoevangelium* passage, the Genesis narrative traces this mysterious strand of DNA through the patriarchal genealogies to Abraham. In Genesis 15:5, God promises to give Abraham a great multitude of seed or descendants. In fact, the Hebrew word translated "offspring" in this verse is זֶרַע = *zera* as in Genesis 3:15.

In Galatians 3:16, Paul identifies the singular Descendant of Abraham through whom this promise is fulfilled – namely, Jeshua Ha Mashiach or Jesus the Messiah. It is noteworthy that God's promise of descendants to Abraham was the particular focus of Abraham's faith response, on which basis God imputed righteousness to him in accordance with Genesis 15:6.

The Acceptable Sacrifice

According to Genesis 3:21, Yahweh replaced the garments of fig leaves that Adam and Eve had fabricated for themselves with garments of animal skins. By this act, Yahweh initiated a sacrificial trajectory that runs through the entire Bible. To provide those skins, animals were slaughtered by the hand of Yahweh Himself. Because man's sin is a capital offense against an absolutely holy and righteous God, it is only through the shedding of blood that a covering for sin can be provided.

The City of Man Versus the Kingdom of God

The paradigmatic **city of man** throughout Scripture is **Babylon**. According to Genesis 10:10, the ancient city of Babylon was founded by Nimrod. It is noteworthy that the lexical form of the Hebrew name for this city is בָּבֶל, which is translated as "Babylon" in Genesis 10:10. By replacing the Hebrew consonants and vowel pointings with their English equivalents, בָּבֶל can be transliterated as *Babel*.

This same city surfaces again in Genesis 11:9, where the HCSB correctly translates בָּבֶל as "Babylon." Unfortunately, except for the HCSB, most English translations employ the transliteration of this Hebrew word in the 11th chapter of Genesis, creating the impression that a different place is being referred to than Babylon. I embrace the HCSB rendering such that בָּבֶל = Babylon wherever it appears. Thus, the tower in the 11th chapter of Genesis is designated **the tower of Babylon**.

The last appearance of Babylon in Scripture is in the 17th and 18th chapters of Revelation. The apocalyptic language of the Apostle John clearly portrays the abominable character of Babylon in the 17th chapter, and the final destruction and downfall of this paradigmatic city of man is portrayed in the 18th chapter.

As a segue into our discussion of the people of the new way, we cannot help but note the stark contrast drawn in the Genesis narrative between the foolish rebellion of mankind as revealed in the tower of Babylon episode of the 11th chapter and the introduction of the people of the new way in the 12th chapter. [75]

The People of the New Way

The **people of the new way** is the second motif to be discussed in detail later in this chapter.

Yahweh called out and set apart Abraham as the pioneer and progenitor of a new way. In Genesis 18:19 this **new way** is represented for the first time in Scripture as the "way of Yahweh."

The Gospel

The **gospel** is the third motif to be discussed in detail later in this chapter.

The *protoevangelium*, or proto-gospel, is first announced in Genesis 3:15. It is then expanded in Yahweh's covenant with Abraham that he would be blessed in order to become a blessing to all nations and peoples. It would be through Abraham that the promised seed of the woman would ultimately emerge. Through that promised seed, the head of the serpent would be crushed, and all the effects of the invasion of evil, sin, and death would be obliterated.

Sovereign Election and Human Responsibility

Sovereign election and human responsibility is the fourth motif to be discussed in detail later in this chapter.

A noteworthy pattern that we observe throughout the Book of Genesis is Yahweh's choosing the younger instead of the older to be the bearer of the covenant. Abel and then Seth are chosen instead of Cain; Isaac is chosen instead of Ishmael; Jacob is chosen instead of Esau; and Judah and Joseph are chosen instead of Reuben. When Jacob blessed the two sons of Joseph, he elevated Ephraim, the younger, above his older brother, Manasseh. Continuing into the Book of Exodus, Moses is chosen to be the deliverer of Israel instead of his older brother, Aaron. And the people of Israel are chosen to be God's special people instead of any of the other nations of the world. And then much later in biblical history, David is chosen instead of his older brothers to be king of Israel and the progenitor of the Messiah. Thus, through the narrative of the Hebrew Scriptures, God is making abundantly clear the fact that His choice is based upon parameters that only He can see, and it is not at all based upon anything for which we, the chosen ones, can take credit.

Intertwined with the theme of sovereign election, the Bible places in evidence the fact that self-determined human choices are important, and that God holds us accountable for making wise choices. This is clearly the case with Adam, who was given a single prohibition. As a result of his disobedience, the curse of evil, sin, and death fell upon him and all of us as his descendants.

The Prototype

The nation of Israel became a prototype of the individual new covenant believer in their experience of the Exodus, desert wanderings, and Conquest. In particular, the following parallels are noted:

- The experience of the ten plagues by Israel in Egypt corresponds to the experience of **conviction of the bondage to evil, sin, and death** and the desperate need for divine deliverance in the life of the individual whom God is drawing toward Christ.

- The experience of the Passover by Israel in Egypt corresponds to the **exercise of faith** in the covering blood of Jesus Christ on the part of the individual disciple of Christ. In fact, according to

Scripture, the Passover lamb that was slain corresponds to "the Lamb of God, who takes away the sin of the world." [John 1:29, ESV]

- The experience of the Exodus from Egypt for Israel corresponds to the experience of **redemption** out of bondage to evil, sin, and death for the disciple of Christ on account of the atoning work of Jesus Christ.

- The crossing of the Sea of Reeds by Israel corresponds to the experience of **water baptism** by the disciple of Christ, which, in turn, serves as an outward representation of **positional sanctification** wrought by the Holy Spirit. Positional sanctification means that the disciple is declared to be holy and consecrated unto God on the basis of his faith in the atoning sacrifice of Jesus Christ.

- The experience of the Conquest by Israel, by means of which they came to occupy the land of promise, corresponds to **experiential sanctification**, by means of which our positional state of being declared holy and consecrated unto God becomes progressively realized in our experience.

- The tolerance of the residual Canaanites in the land by Israel corresponds to a **failure to carry sanctification to completion** by fully participating in the death of Jesus Christ, by means of which the flesh is made subject to the death of Christ and thereby its power is neutralized.

The Covenant of Conditional Blessing

The **covenant of conditional blessing** is the fifth motif to be discussed in detail later in this chapter.

We employ the phrase of **tears and fire** to characterize the overall trajectory of the Hebrew Scriptures. The suzerain / vassal covenant which Yahweh clearly articulated and firmly established with Israel in the Torah was broken by Israel, resulting ultimately in their banishment from the land of promise. However, as the story of the Hebrew Scriptures approaches its *telos* – that is, its logical and theological conclusion – a remnant of Israel is restored to the land. According to the 8th and 9th chapters of Nehemiah, the people of Israel experienced glorious renewal and revival after the temple had been reconstructed, worship of Yahweh restored, and the walls and gates of Jerusalem had been repaired. This was in accordance with the promise announced through Moses in the concluding chapters of Deuteronomy and confirmed to Solomon in 2 Chronicles 7:14. The tears are those of contrition over sin, and the fire is the outpouring of the Spirit of God to bring about renewal and revival.

Progressive Development of the Integrative Motifs

Figure 5-1 delineates the process whereby each of the fourteen integrative motifs are progressively developed and enriched by the unfolding of revelation in the Hebrew Scriptures. Then they undergo a substantial metamorphosis as they pass through the Christ Event. [76]

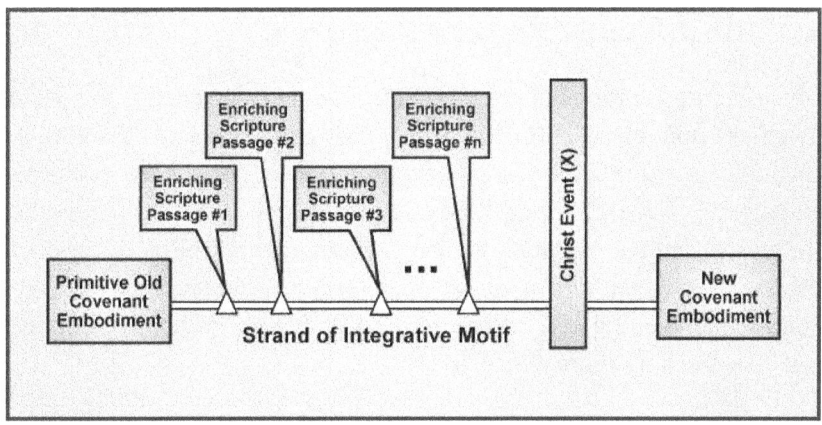

Figure 5-1. The Progressive Development of the Integrative Motifs

Continuities and Discontinuities

A subject of debate among theologians and Bible scholars can be expressed in terms of the following question: what are the areas of continuity from the old covenant into the new, and what are the areas of discontinuity? In other words, which theological, moral, and ethical principles that are clearly set forth in the Hebrew Scriptures carry over and continue to be operative under the new covenant, and which principles ceased to be operative after the Christ Event? For example, most scholars would agree that the dietary laws in the Mosaic system are no longer operative on account of passages such as Mark 7:19 and Acts 10:9-16. However, what about Sabbath-keeping?

I propose that a much more fruitful way to address the continuities / discontinuities issue is to trace each of the fourteen integrative motifs through Scripture as delineated in Figure 5-1. By way of example, this will be done for the following five motifs, which are especially relevant to the WitW study:

- The invasion of evil, sin, and death
- The people of the new way
- The gospel
- Sovereign election and human responsibility
- The covenant of conditional blessing

My discussion of each of these five motifs is sufficiently detailed to serve as an example of how to trace any of the motifs through Scripture in accordance with Figure 5-1. However, the discussion is by no means exhaustive. For each motif, I have selected a few of what I judge to be the most definitive Scriptures to place in evidence how the motif has been shaped over the course of revelation history. However, I leave to the student the exciting task of tracing all fourteen of the motifs through revelation history more exhaustively.

The Invasion of Evil, Sin, and Death

The creation of the cosmos, including the special creation of man, is summarily described in Genesis 1 and 2. In its primeval state, the cosmos is represented as being perfect in Genesis 1:31: "And God saw everything that He had made, and behold, it was very good." [Gen 1:31, adapted from the ESV] An implication of this statement, and what follows in Genesis 3, is that evil, sin, and death were not present in the cosmos at this point.

The Fall of Lucifer

The Fall episode is recorded in the 3rd chapter of Genesis. However, this is not the point that evil, sin, and death actually invaded the perfect cosmos that God had created. That cataclysmic event, the fall of the archangel Lucifer, occurred some time prior to the Fall episode.

The fall of Lucifer is described in two passages, Isaiah 14:12-21 and Ezekiel 28:11-19. In the Isaiah passage, Lucifer is represented as "the king of Babylon," and in the Ezekiel passage he is represented as "the king of Tyre." However, even a superficial reading of these two passages reveals that the attributes of the persons being described are those of an angel rather than a human. Following are key observations from these two passages:

- From the Hebrew text of Isaiah 14:12, the person to whom the passage refers is represented as "Morning Star, son of the Dawn..." From this phrase, the proper name "Lucifer" is derived, which literally means "morning star." He was one of three archangels created by Yahweh Elohim, the other two being Gabriel and Michael.

- The perfection and beauty of Lucifer is described by Ezekiel 28:12b-13.

- The office of Lucifer is described by Ezekiel 28:14 as "an anointed guardian cherub." The implication of the ESV is that Lucifer was one of a number of similar angels. However, the implication of the Hebrew is that he was **the singular anointed guardian cherub**. Evidently, his office was to guard the very throne of Yahweh Elohim. As such, he was the highest ranking archangel, the crown jewel of the angelic creation.

- The prideful rebellion of Lucifer is described by Isaiah 14:13-14 and Ezekiel 28:15-17a.

- Because of his prideful rebellion, Lucifer was evicted from his high office and cast down, as described by Isaiah 14:15-20 and Ezekiel 28:16-19.

The armed revolt and subsequent casting down of Lucifer is also described by the Apostle John in Revelation 12:7-12. As a result, Lucifer becomes Satan and the Devil.

An essential point to observe in the record of Lucifer's fall is that **he brought evil into being by his prideful rebellion**. Having the power to freely choose between submission to the sovereign authority of Yahweh Elohim and rebellion, he chose the latter; and this choice emanated from the prideful assertion of his heart, "I will make myself like the Most High." [Isaiah 14:14, ESV] While it is true that Yahweh Elohim allowed the possibility of evil by creating angels and mankind with free moral agency, Lucifer was the one who **actualized** evil in the cosmos by his own self-determined choice.

> ***The essence of evil is prideful rebellion against the sovereign rule of Yahweh Elohim.***

The prideful rebellion and resulting fall of Lucifer took place at some point prior to the Fall episode recorded in the 3rd chapter of Genesis.

The Fall of Man

According to Genesis 1:26-27, man was created in the image and likeness of Yahweh Elohim, which meant, among other things, that he too had the power of free moral agency. [77] According to the narrative of the 2nd chapter of Genesis, man's being in the divine image and likeness also meant that he had the capacity for fellowship with Yahweh Elohim. Moreover, according to Genesis 1:28-30 and Genesis 2:19, he was assigned the role of regent over the terrestrial creation, this being another aspect of his being in the image and likeness of Yahweh Elohim. As the narrative of the 2nd chapter of Genesis concludes, Adam enjoyed an open and direct relationship with Yahweh Elohim, Eve, his wife, and all of the animals.

Because of the moral free agency with which man was created, and because of his regency over the terrestrial creation, his moral choice had the potential of impacting the entire material cosmos. By definition however, only one sovereign will would determine what is good and evil, and that right was reserved to and exercised by Yahweh Elohim throughout the creative process. This exercise of moral authority by Yahweh Elohim culminated in the pronouncement of Genesis 1:31 that everything "was very good."

The invasion of evil, sin, and death into the heretofore perfect terrestrial sphere is recorded in the 3rd chapter of Genesis. Lucifer, now Satan and the Devil, entered the Garden of Eden in the form of a talking serpent.

Through the agency of the serpent, Satan beguiled Eve into believing "that the tree was good for food, and that it was a delight to the eyes, and that the tree was to be desired to make one wise" [Genesis 3:6, ESV] – that is, to possess moral authority over determining good and evil. As a result, she ate the forbidden fruit and presented some to her husband.

At this critical juncture, Adam was confronted with a dilemma. According to his understanding, if he refused to eat, then Eve would die, and he would be left alone. If he did eat, then they would both die together. What he failed to appreciate was a principle which became codified many centuries later in Numbers 30:3-15; that is, he could have nullified his wife's decision to eat of the forbidden fruit. I am convinced that Adam knew this in his unsullied human conscience, for, as an immutable divine principle,

> God is faithful, and He will not let you be tempted beyond your ability, but with the temptation He will also provide the way of escape, that you may be able to endure it. [1 Corinthians 10:13, ESV]

Tragically, Adam failed to recognize and avail himself of the "way of escape," and he ate of the fruit offered to him by his wife. As a result of **his eating**, not hers, we are told,

> Then the eyes of both were opened, and they knew that they were naked. And they sewed fig leaves together and made themselves loincloths. [Genesis 3:7, ESV]

By his act of eating, Adam embraced Eve's act of prideful rebellion and made it his own. As a couple, they chose to usurp the position that Yahweh Elohim had reserved unto Himself; that is, the moral authority to discern, and thereby to sovereignly determine, good and evil. The effect was immediate, as may be seen in Genesis 3:7-11. In particular, according to the 7th verse, Adam and Eve made their first moral judgment in the observation that they were naked, and that this was not good. Underlying their observation was the awareness of guilt resulting from their prideful rebellion against the singular commandment of Yahweh Elohim. The consequence was schism between the two of them and an attempt to hide from Yahweh Elohim.

According to the Apostle Paul's divinely inspired analysis in Romans 5:12-21, when Adam ate, we all ate with him.

> *As the federal head and progenitor of the entire race, we all sinned at the point in time when he sinned. We all partook of his prideful rebellion, and we have been in rebellion against the rule of God ever since, both by nature and by choice.*

Would Yahweh Elohim punish by death both Adam and Eve for their treasonous act? No, but instead He slaughters animals and provides blood-stained coverings for their naked bodies. By this means, He placed in evidence the singular path to renewed fellowship with Him, which required the death of an innocent substitute. While the attention of Adam and Eve was riveted upon the lifeless animal carcasses lying on the ground before them, His eye was upon the beaten and bleeding form of His Son, hanging upon a Roman cross. Concerning His Son, He addressed the serpent,

> I will put enmity between you and the woman, and between your seed and her seed; He shall strike your head, and you shall strike His heel. [Genesis 3:15, adapted from the ESV]

This pronouncement is designated the *protevangelium* – the first proclamation of the gospel. Thus, the motifs of the seed of the woman, the acceptable sacrifice, and the gospel are tightly intertwined with that of the invasion of evil, sin, and death.

The Flood of Noah

The divine judgment and the fear of god motif is subsumed beneath the invasion of evil, sin, and death. The first cataclysmic judgment in the Book of Genesis is the Flood of Noah.

As we continue to read through the Genesis narrative, the problem of evil, sin, and death multiplies. By the 6th chapter, we are told,

> Yahweh saw that the wickedness of man was great in the earth, and that every intention of the thoughts of his heart was only evil continually. And Yahweh was sorry that He

had made man on the earth, and it grieved Him to his heart.
[Genesis 6:5-6, adapted from the ESV]

And so we are told that Yahweh determined that He would destroy mankind and every living thing by means of a flood, "But Noah found favor in the eyes of Yahweh." [Genesis 6:8, adapted from the ESV]

Why did Yahweh purpose to act in this way? My answer is that He brought about the universal Flood judgment to protect the seed of the woman from being corrupted by the abounding iniquity that was engulfing all of mankind. That seed was being passed through Noah to his son, Shem. Thus, nested within the Flood judgment is Yahweh's gracious deliverance of Noah, his family, and the animals He brought to the Ark to board it with Noah. In Matthew 24:36-44, Jesus likens the judgment that will occur when He returns to that which occurred "in the days of Noah." When He comes, He will gather His elect into a place of protection while He banishes the rest into death.

Noah's Curse Upon Canaan

Genesis 9:18-27 records a noteworthy incident that plays into the story of Noah's descendants many centuries later. Noah became drunk from too much wine, and he lay uncovered in his tent. It would appear that Noah's grandson, Canaan, came upon his grandfather lying naked in the tent, and he reported this to his father, Ham, in a way that was disrespectful of Noah. When Shem and Japheth heard of it, they covered their father with a garment while not allowing themselves to gaze upon his nakedness. Noah's curse is recorded in Genesis 9:24-27:

> When Noah awoke from his wine and knew what his youngest son had done to him, he said, "Cursed be Canaan; a servant of servants shall he be to his brothers." He also said, "Blessed be Yahweh, the Elohim of Shem; and let Canaan be his servant. May God enlarge Japheth, and let him dwell in the tents of Shem, and let Canaan be his servant."
> [Genesis 9:24-27, adapted from the ESV]

By means of this curse, Noah prophetically defines the theological, moral, and ethical trajectories of the races that would emanate from his three sons. In particular, he lays the prophetic foundation for the family of Shem to displace the descendants of Canaan from the land that Yahweh promised to give to Abraham's descendants in Genesis 15:7-21. This would actually occur centuries later in the Conquest episode recorded in the Book of Joshua.

The Tower of Babylon Episode

As we continue to trace the development of the invasion of evil, sin, and death motif in accordance with Figure 5-1, the next important episode is that of the tower of Babylon recorded in Genesis 11:1-9 and illustrated in Figure 5-2. [78] After the Flood, the human population evidently mushroomed. Instead of dispersing to fill the earth, as Yahweh had commanded in Genesis 1:28 and again in Genesis 9:1, they gathered in one place, in "a plain in the land of Shinar and settled there." [Genesis 11:2, ESV]

> Then they said, "Come, let us build ourselves a city and a tower with its top in the heavens, and let us make a name for ourselves, lest we be dispersed over the face of the whole earth." [Genesis 11:4, ESV]

Thus, they defied the command of Yahweh to disperse and fill the entire earth. Moreover,

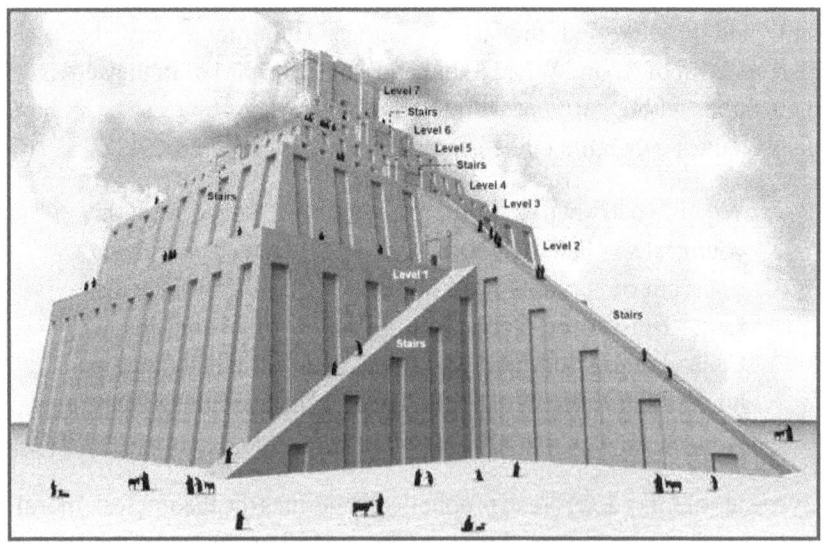

Figure 5-2. The Tower of Babylon

> Yahweh said, "Behold, they are one people, and they have all one language, and this is only the beginning of what they will do. And nothing that they propose to do will now be impossible for them." [Genesis 11:6, adapted from the ESV]

Not only did Yahweh confuse their language, thereby dividing humanity into multiple, distinct language groups, but also He forced their dispersion in accordance with Paul's statement in Acts 17:26:

> And He made from one man every nation of mankind to live on all the face of the earth, having determined allotted periods and the boundaries of their dwelling place... [Acts 17:26, adapted from the ESV]

Once again, as in the Flood episode, Yahweh acted to restrain human iniquity and to protect the seed of the woman from corruption. Moreover, Yahweh's action amounts to a warning against large concentrations of human population in cities, for in such concentrations human iniquity is multiplied.

Destruction of the Cities of the Plain

The second cataclysmic judgment recorded in the Book of Genesis is the destruction of Sodom, Gomorrah, and the other cities allied with them, which were located in the Jordan valley just north of the Dead Sea. The record of this judgment is found in Genesis 19:1-29. Since these were Canaanite cities, their destruction is the first phase of Yahweh's judgment of the descendants of Canaan in accordance with Noah's curse.

Nested within this judgment episode is Yahweh's gracious deliverance of Lot and his two daughters. The Apostle Peter reflects on the evident display of the grace of Yahweh in his 2nd epistle:

> If he did not spare the ancient world, but preserved Noah, a herald of righteousness, with seven others, when he brought a flood upon the world of the ungodly; if by turning the cities of Sodom and Gomorrah to ashes he condemned them to extinction, making them an example of what is going to happen to the ungodly; and if he rescued righteous Lot, greatly distressed by the sensual conduct of the wicked (for as that righteous man lived among them day after day, he

> was tormenting his righteous soul over their lawless deeds that he saw and heard); then Yahweh knows how to rescue the godly from trials, and to keep the unrighteous under punishment until the day of judgment... [2 Peter 2:5-9, adapted from the ESV]

Thus, the great cataclysmic judgments that have occurred in history are intended by Yahweh to instill fear in the human heart, and to motivate men to walk in the way of Yahweh.

The Golden Calf Episode

In accordance with the flow delineated in Figure 5-1, the next passage that adds significantly to our understanding of the invasion of evil, sin, and death is Exodus 32:1-35, which records the golden calf episode. While this is not the first passage in the Torah that mentions the sin of idolatry, it is the paradigmatic passage on the subject in that it represents idolatry in all of its hideous detail.

The literary context of the passage is most striking. During the very time that Moses is communing with Yahweh Elohim at the summit of Mt. Sinai, and he is receiving instructions for the design and construction of the tabernacle, the people of Israel in the valley below are demanding of Aaron,

> Up, make us gods who shall go before us. As for this Moses, the man who brought us up out of the land of Egypt, we do not know what has become of him. [Exodus 32:1, ESV]

The casting and forming of the golden calf was no small project, requiring considerable time and skill to complete. This example of idolatrous workmanship is placed in stark contrast to the God-ordained project of fabricating and constructing the tabernacle and all of its furnishings that is recorded in the extended passage from Exodus 35:4 to the end of the book. Once the fabrication of the calf had been completed, and it had been set up, take careful note of how the people of Israel represented it:

> These are your gods (= *elohim*), O Israel, who brought you up out of the land of Egypt! [Exodus 32:4, ESV]

Accordingly, they ascribed to the golden calf the appellative title, *elohim*, and the very same attribute that Yahweh Elohim had ascribed to Himself:

> I am Yahweh your Elohim, who brought you out of the land of Egypt, out of the house of slavery. You shall have no other gods before me. You shall not make for yourself a carved image... [Exodus 20:2-4, adapted from the ESV]

After they had made this pronouncement, they set apart a day to worship the calf, after which they engaged in revelry, apparently including a sexual orgy.

Take careful note of the parameters of the sin of idolatry:

- Construction of an object to take the place of Yahweh Elohim.

- Representation of that object through language as having divine properties, including the ability to guide and direct human persons.

- Worship of the object.

- Engagement in revelry, often with a perverted sexual component.

> ***These parameters are paradigmatic; that is, they define the actions that constitute and attend the sin of idolatry.***

While it is true that in the golden calf episode a material object was worshiped in the place of Yahweh Elohim, the idol need not be material; instead, it can be a mental construct. That is, it can exist as an ungodly element of the representational world of the human mind. Darwinian evolution exemplifies such an idolatrous mental construct, for it ascribes to the material cosmos the creative attributes and powers that are claimed by Yahweh Elohim as uniquely His.

Prophetic Passages on the Nature of Sin

There are two passages in the prophetic literature of the Hebrew Scriptures which add to our understanding of the nature of sin. The first of these is the 1st chapter of Isaiah and the second is the 16th chapter of Ezekiel. Both of these passages should be read in their entirety and in context. I will offer a number of observations.

As we examine Isaiah 1:1ff, the following observations are noteworthy:

- The prophet employs highly figurative language, replete with metaphors, to represent the seriousness of the sin of the people of Judah and Jerusalem.

- From the 2nd verse, they are like rebellious children. The transliteration of the lexical form of the Hebrew verb translated "rebelled" is *pasha*, which means to rebel or transgress.

- From the 3rd verse, they lack even the sense of an ox or a donkey, both of which respect and are submissive to their owner and master.

- From the 4th verse, they are sinful. The transliteration of the lexical form of the Hebrew word that is translated "sinful" is *chata*, which means to miss the mark or take a wrong path. This word is equivalent in meaning to the Greek *hamartia*, which is translated as "sin" in the Christian Scriptures.

- Also from the 4th verse, they are "laden with iniquity," where the transliteration of the lexical form of the Hebrew word translated "iniquity" is *avon*, which means a systemic evil or corruption of nature.

- Also from the 4th verse, they are the "offspring of evildoers," where the transliteration of the lexical form of the Hebrew word translated "evildoers" is *raa*, which means to be evil or bad.

- Also from the 4th verse, they "deal corruptly," where the transliteration of the lexical form of the Hebrew word translated "corruptly" is *shachath*, which means to go to ruin.

- Also from the 4th verse, they "have forsaken Yahweh," where the transliteration of the lexical form of the Hebrew word translated "forsaken" is *azab*, which means to leave or forsake.

- Also from the 4th verse, they "have despised the Holy One of Israel," where the transliteration of the lexical form of the Hebrew word translated "despised" is *naats*, which means to spurn or treat with contempt.

- Finally, from the 4th verse, they "are utterly estranged," where the transliteration of the lexical form of the Hebrew word translated "estranged" is *zur*, which means to be a stranger.

- From the 5th and 6th verses, the prophet likens the state of the people of Judah and Jerusalem to a person who has been badly beaten and whose wounds have not received medical treatment.

Thus, Isaiah spares no language to place in evidence the various dimensions of the sin of Judah and Jerusalem, and the effect of their sin on their state of moral and ethical health.

The second passage, the 16th chapter of Ezekiel, is an allegorical representation of the idolatry of Jerusalem as the spiritual equivalent of adultery. In this allegory, the city of Jerusalem represents the entire nation of Israel. The theological framework for the allegory is that Yahweh Elohim has taken Israel unto Himself like a husband takes a wife. Moreover, the covenant binding Israel to Yahweh is like the covenant of marriage. Accordingly, for Israel to transgress her covenant with Yahweh is like a wife who turns from her husband and goes after other lovers. In fact, so blatant is Israel's sin that she had become a wanton prostitute!

On account of the hideousness of Israel's sin, Yahweh had no choice but to issue her a certificate of divorce. While the word "divorce" does not occur in the 16th chapter of Ezekiel, the outpouring of the wrath of Yahweh is clearly and emphatically stated in Ezekiel 16:35-52. Moreover, "divorce" is explicitly stated in Isaiah 50:1 and Jeremiah 3:8. Thus, the marriage metaphor, as it applies to the relationship between Yahweh and Israel, was formally broken, but not without remedy.

Chata and *Avon*

These two Hebrew words, which surfaced in Isaiah's indictment of Judah and Jerusalem, deserve some additional comment. With respect to the sin of idolatry, Yahweh states,

> You shall not bow down to them or serve them, for I, Yahweh your Elohim, am a jealous God, visiting the iniquity (= *avon*) of the fathers on the children to the third and the fourth generation of those who hate me, but showing steadfast love to thousands of those who love me

and keep my commandments. [Exodus 20:5-6, adapted from the ESV]

Over against this clear statement, the 18th chapter of Ezekiel in its entirety addresses the issue of each generation being punished for its own sin. In particular, consider this statement by the prophet Ezekiel:

> The soul who sins (= *chata*) shall die. The son shall not suffer for the iniquity (= *avon*) of the father, nor the father suffer for the iniquity (= *avon*) of the son. The righteousness of the righteous shall be upon himself, and the wickedness of the wicked shall be upon himself. [Ezekiel 18:20, ESV]

The apparent contradiction between these two passages hinges on the significance of "visiting" in Exodus 20:5. Recalling that *chata* designates a willful act of falling short or turning in a wrong direction, whereas *avon* designates a systemic evil or corruption of nature, I suggest the explanation put forward in the following paragraphs.

Genetic Transmission of Moral Proclivities. The *avon* of the fathers is **visited** upon their children in the sense that a person's moral proclivities are genetically transmitted to the next generation, even as physical attributes are transmitted. Thus, a father who has a problem with alcoholism, sexual immorality, or other moral weakness should be alert to his children inheriting that same weakness. This is the meaning of Exodus 20:5.

Personal Responsibility. Over against this principle of genetic transmission of *avon*, each person is responsible for his *chata* – that is, his willful acts of falling short or going astray from the right path. In other words, in spite of the fact that I may have inherited from my father a proclivity toward alcoholism, for example, I am still responsible for self-discipline and moderation in the consumption of alcoholic beverages. In other words, I cannot shield myself from guilt before God on account of inherited *avon*, because I am personally responsible for my own *chata*. This is the meaning of Ezekiel 18:20 when read in the context of the entire chapter.

Sexual Orientation Debate. The *chata* versus *avon* issue is especially relevant to the current debate over sexual orientation. The fact that homosexuality is an example of *avon* is indisputable based upon the explicit teaching of passages such as Leviticus 18:22 & 20:13. However, the fact that a proclivity toward homosexuality may reside in a person's DNA does not shield him from responsibility for righteous behavior in his own sexual interactions. Should he give way to his proclivity and practice homosexual intercourse, then this would be a *chata*, and "The soul who sins (= *chata*) shall die." [Ezekiel 18:20a, ESV]

The Death of Jesus Christ

What does the death of Jesus Christ, the Son of God, teach us concerning the invasion of evil, sin, and death? According to Genesis 2:17, sin is a capital offense before God. This is because every sin is a treasonous act of prideful rebellion against the rule of God. In this regard, James 2:10 is especially noteworthy.

> For whoever keeps the whole law but fails in one point has become accountable for all of it. [James 2:10, ESV]

Because of who Jesus Christ is – the Son of God and the Son of Man – His death places in evidence the magnitude of the problem of evil, sin, and death. If we perceive in the death of Jesus only a righteous man dying for the sins of others, we are failing to see that death through the eyes of faith. When Jesus died, He died as both the Son of Man and the Son of God. By virtue of His humanity, He was qualified to stand in our place and take our punishment upon Himself. By virtue of His deity, the magnitude or weight of His death was more than enough to satisfy the requirements of divine justice. We can measure the magnitude or weight of the death of Christ by this: it was equivalent to the eternal death that each and every one of us would have to suffer, had He not died in our place. In fact, the death of Christ was equivalent to the sum total of the eternal deaths that the entire human population of the world for all time would have to suffer in order to make up to God an adequate apology and satisfaction for the capital offense of human sin.

The Teaching of the Apostle Paul

The Apostle Paul certainly had much to say about the problem of evil, sin, and death, but I will select only one passage for consideration here, and that is the 7th chapter of the Epistle to the Romans, which should be read in its entirety and in context.

While there is intense debate over the precise interpretation of this chapter, let us back off and consider the overall trajectory of Paul's argument. Importing his terminology from Romans 8:2, he asserts that there is present in the human personality a law of sin and death. In Romans 7:7-25, he represents this **law of sin and death** as if it were an active agent in the human personality which responds in a pernicious way to the righteous requirements of God as expressed in His moral law. How does the law of sin and death respond to the commandments of God? **By causing an impulse toward disobedience rather than obedience**. In other words, the law of sin and death is another name for the pernicious kernel of prideful rebellion that lurks in the human heart. To use Paul's example in Romans 7:7-8, the prideful rebellion of the human heart responds to the commandment, "You shall not covet," by energizing all manner of covetousness. The same could be said concerning each of the commandments. Returning to the golden calf episode, how did the people of Israel respond to the commandment, "You shall have no other gods before Me?" [Exodus 20:3, adapted from the ESV] By constructing, ascribing divine attributes to, and worshiping the golden calf.

The Teaching of James

There is one more passage that I must consider before concluding this discussion of the invasion of evil, sin, and death; namely, James 1:13-15. To see this passage in its literary context, the entire passage from the 12th verse through the 18th verse should be read. In the focal passage, James teaches us that the wellspring of all temptation – that is, solicitations toward evil – is the human heart. We have only ourselves to blame; not the Devil and certainly not God. The strategy for conquering temptation is, first, to recognize it in its germinal form; that is, when it is just beginning to sprout. Instead of mentally watering and nurturing it, we must ruthlessly pull it up like a noxious weed and put it in the trash!

Concluding Comments Regarding the Invasion of Evil, Sin, and Death

While my discussion of this motif seems lengthy, I have only touched upon a few of the passages of Scripture that inform and illuminate the significance of the problem of evil, sin, and death. You, no doubt, can think of other passages that should be considered; for example, Jesus' teaching in the Sermon on the Mount, which represents sin not only in terms of external behavior but also as internal thoughts and lusts. As you read through Scripture from year to year, you can add your own insights to this discussion.

The People of the New Way

The trajectory of the storyline from the 11th into the 12th chapter of Genesis is most noteworthy. The zenith of mankind's accomplishment after the Flood is represented in the 11th chapter as "a city and a tower with its top in the heavens." Mankind's stated and pridefully rebellious purpose in building the city and the tower was to establish a name for themselves and to defy Yahweh Elohim's explicit command that they should disperse and fill the entire earth. This, then, is the high water mark of the **old way** in which mankind sought to live autonomously and in prideful rebellion against the sovereign rule of God.

After Yahweh confused the language of mankind such that they were divided into distinct language groups and dispersed across the earth, the genealogy of the Shemites is set forth. By this means, the family of Terah, the father of Abram, is introduced.

Yahweh's call of Abram recorded in Genesis 12:1-3 is most remarkable.

> Now Yahweh said to Abram, "Go from your country and your kindred and your father's house to the land that I will show you. And I will make of you a great nation, and I will bless you and make your name great, so that you will be a blessing. I will bless those who bless you, and him who dishonors you I will curse, and in you all the families of the earth shall be blessed." [Genesis 12:1-3, adapted from the ESV]

There are many points in the Genesis narrative when God spoke to men. Previous to Genesis 12:1, God made three speeches which can be considered covenantal in nature and which are recorded in accordance with the formula

> (Divine Name) said (= *amar* = to say or speak), "(A covenantal statement.)"

The first occurs in Genesis 1:28-29 and expresses the primordial, pre-Fall covenant of Yahweh Elohim with Adam and Eve. The second occurs in

Genesis 3:14-22; it includes the post-Fall curses pronounced by Yahweh Elohim upon the serpent, Eve, and Adam. It also includes the *protoevangelium* of Genesis 3:15. The third occurs in Genesis 9:1-17; it is the post-Flood covenant of Yahweh Elohim with Noah and his three sons, Shem, Ham, and Japheth.

In conjunction with the primordial covenant of Yahweh Elohim with Adam and Eve, we are told that "Elohim blessed (= *barak* = to bless) them." Likewise, in Genesis 9:1 we are told, "Elohim blessed Noah and his sons and said to them... "

In contrast with the two prior covenantal episodes which include the pronouncement of blessing, the covenantal statement to Abram is introduced by, "Now Yahweh said to Abram... " As we learn from Umberto Cassuto in his monograph entitled *The Documentary Hypothesis*, [79] the divine names employed in the Torah were not accidental; instead, they were intentionally selected by the narrator, Moses, to express something theologically important. Whereas "Elohim" is an appellative name or title that expresses God's transcendence and His sovereign authority over His creation, "Yahweh" is God's personal name; it expresses His immanence and His covenantal relationship with His people. Accordingly, the use of "Yahweh" in Genesis 12:1 in contrast with "Elohim" in Genesis 1:28-29 and Genesis 9:1-17 is most significant.

> *It dramatizes the fact that, at this particular juncture, after the abject failure of the old way, Yahweh is entering into a personal, covenantal relationship with one man and his descendants. Abram – later, Abraham – would become the pioneer and progenitor of a new way.*

From this point onward, I will refer to the patriarch by the name which Yahweh later conferred upon him; that is, Abraham. Abram means "great father," and Abraham means "father of a multitude."

The Content of the Abrahamic Covenant

Yahweh's covenant with Abraham is the most important covenant in all of Scripture. By means of it, Yahweh sets in motion a plan and program to reverse the curse of Genesis 3:14-22 and to totally obliterate the effects of the invasion of evil, sin, and death. He would accomplish this objective through the family of Abraham. Note the five distinct components of the covenant:

- **Great nation**. "And I will make of you a great nation... "
- **Great name**. "I will bless you and make your name great... "
- **Blessing**. "... so that you will be a blessing."
- **Conditional blessing upon neighboring peoples**. "I will bless those who bless you, and him who dishonors you I will curse... "
- **Families of the earth blessed**. "... and in you all the families of the earth shall be blessed."

Abraham's Immediate Obedience

While the narrative of Genesis does not hide the blemishes in Abraham's character, neither does it hide his strengths. How did he respond to the command of Genesis 12:1? With immediate and unequivocal obedience. Was his obedience at least partly the result of the astounding covenant into which Yahweh had called him? Probably it was. Did Abraham fully understand the implications of the covenant? Probably not, but I believe he understood enough of it to be motivated to obey the call of Yahweh. In particular, I believe Abraham understood that it was to be through him that the seed of the woman promised by Yahweh Elohim in Genesis 3:15 would come to be. Abraham saw that a descendant of his would one day crush the serpent's head, reverse the curse, and obliterate the effects of the invasion of evil, sin, and death. For a man who had previously worshiped idols, his laying hold of Yahweh's promise, packing up his household and all his possessions, and following Yahweh to an as yet undisclosed location is truly remarkable.

The Land Promise

Abraham journeyed southward from Haran until he came to the place called Shechem in the land of Canaan, whereupon we find the first statement of the land promise.

> Abram passed through the land to the place at Shechem, to the oak of Moreh. At that time the Canaanites were in the land. Then Yahweh **appeared** to Abram and said, "To your

offspring I will give this land." [Genesis 12:6-7, adapted from the ESV, emphasis added]

Yahweh Appeared. In Yahweh's first interaction with Abraham, we are told that "Yahweh said (= *amar* = to say or speak)..." In this second interaction we are told that "Yahweh appeared (= *ra â* = to show or appear)..." In both cases, I am curious to know how Yahweh manifested Himself to Abraham. Later, in Genesis 18:1, exactly the same formula is used, and in that case Yahweh took upon Himself a human form; and the context makes it clear that Abraham recognized Him. Accordingly, I am inclined to believe this was probably the case in the Genesis 12:6-7 episode as well.

Confirmation of the Covenant. In accordance with the flow of Figure 5-1, the next Scripture that we need to consider is the 15th chapter of Genesis. We are told, "After these things the word of Yahweh came to Abram in a vision..." After the introductory speech from Yahweh, which is recorded in the remainder of the 1st verse, there ensues a conversation between Abraham and Yahweh that centers on two issues: descendants and land.

Descendants. We noted that the statement of Yahweh's covenant with Abraham recorded in the 12th chapter included the promise that Yahweh would make of him a great nation. In Abraham's mind, this implied a multitude of descendants. But now he was approximately 90 years of age, and his wife, Sarah, was barren. And so Abraham inquires of Yahweh, "O Adonai Yahweh, what will you give me, for I continue childless, and the heir of my house is Eliezer of Damascus... Behold, you have given me no offspring, and a member of my household will be my heir." Yahweh's response was to take him outside and command him, "number the stars, if you are able to number them... So shall your offspring be." The next statement is one of the most important and pivotal statements in all of Scripture:

> And he believed Yahweh, and He counted it to him as righteousness. [Genesis 15:6, adapted from the ESV]

Abraham not only gave mental assent to Yahweh's promise, but he appropriated it as valid and tangible; a promise he could take to the bank, as it were. What kind of faith is this?

> *It is a faith in resurrection, in the ability of Yahweh to call forth life from death.*

Note well Paul's commentary on Abraham's faith in the 4th chapter of Romans:

> He did not weaken in faith when he considered his own body, which was as good as dead (since he was about a hundred years old), or when he considered the barrenness of Sarah's womb. No distrust made him waver concerning the promise of God, but he grew strong in his faith as he gave glory to God, fully convinced that God was able to do what He had promised. [Romans 4:19-21, adapted from the ESV]

Land. According to Genesis 15:7, Yahweh continued the conversation by confirming His promise of the land of Caanan, to which Abraham responded, "O Adonai Yahweh, how am I to know that I shall possess it?" What ensues by way of Yahweh's answer to this question is an ancient **blood covenant ceremony**. In accordance with the protocol for this ceremony, the parties to the covenant would slaughter animals, cut the carcasses in half, and then walk between the pieces, declaring, "Let it be to me as these animals if I fail to abide by this covenant." Was this solemn covenant between Yahweh and Abraham? No, for we are told that Abraham fell asleep, and "dreadful and great darkness fell upon him." As he slept, he beheld a smoking fire pot and a blazing lamp passing between the pieces.

I believe this is the event to which the writer of Hebrews refers in Hebrews 6:13: "For when God made a promise to Abraham, since He had no one greater by whom to swear, He swore by Himself..." In particular, I identify the smoking fire pot with God the Father, and the blazing lamp with God the Son. Thus, the land promise is secured by a solemn covenant between God the Father and God the Son, and the very life of the Triune God was laid on the line by way of collateral!

Testing of Abraham

In accordance with the flow of Figure 5-1, the next passage to which we must turn is the 22nd chapter of Genesis, which records the ultimate test of Abraham's faith. In the opening verses of that chapter, we read as follows:

> After these things Elohim tested Abraham and said to him, "Abraham!" And he said, "Here am I." He said, "Take your son, your only son Isaac, whom you love, and go to the land of Moriah, and offer him there as a burnt offering on one of the mountains of which I shall tell you." [Genesis 22:1-2, adapted from the ESV]

A noteworthy aspect of this passage is that the appellative title, "Elohim," instead of the personal name, "Yahweh," is employed by the narrator. This is in marked contrast with the interactions between God and Abraham recorded in the 12th and 15th chapters, which we have just examined. The use of "Elohim" signals a distance between God and Abraham; God is commanding His servant from His exalted throne in heaven as contrasted with a face-to-face conversation, as between friends. As was the case in Genesis 12:4, Abraham's obedience was immediate and unequivocal.

The writer of Hebrews offers the following commentary on this episode:

> By faith Abraham, when he was tested, offered up Isaac, and he who had received the promises was in the act of offering up his only son, of whom it was said, "Through Isaac shall your offspring be named." He considered that God was able even to raise him from the dead, from which, figuratively speaking, he did receive him back. [Hebrews 11:17-19, ESV]

In other words, the faith that energized and enabled Abraham's obedience in this ultimate test was **his faith in resurrection**. By means of this episode, Abraham enacted the role of God the Father in the ultimate sacrifice of His Son, Jesus Christ. I believe it is this episode to which Jesus referred in His statement to the Jewish leaders, "Your father Abraham rejoiced that he would see my day. He saw it and was glad." [John 8:56, ESV]

In his willingness to sacrifice his son, Isaac, Abraham manifests the faith of Jesus Christ spoken of by the Apostle Paul in Romans 3:22. It is this faith in Yahweh's ability to resurrect the dead that must live in each of us in order for us to follow in the footsteps of Abraham, the progenitor and pioneer of the people of the new way.

> *It is this faith in resurrection that is the distinctive badge of membership in the community of faith, the people of the new way.*

Purposes of the People of the New Way

In keeping with the flow of Figure 5-1, we have examined three seminal passages in Genesis that define the distinctive parameters of the people of the new way motif. It is not my purpose to exhaustively explore all the biblical passages which inform, illuminate, enrich, and develop this important motif. Instead, from this point onward, I will only touch upon a few such passages.

What purposes did Yahweh have in mind in His remarkable call to Abraham to be the pioneer and progenitor of the people of the new way? I have identified three.

To Manifest the Glorious Fruit of the Manifold Wisdom of God. The first purpose is to represent to all the surrounding peoples and nations the glorious fruit of the manifold wisdom of God. Prior to the life and ministry of Jesus Christ, the zenith of the fulfillment of this purpose occurred during the reign of Solomon, as testified by the following passage from 1 Kings:

> And Elohim gave Solomon wisdom and understanding beyond measure, and breadth of mind like the sand on the seashore, so that Solomon's wisdom surpassed the wisdom of all the people of the east and all the wisdom of Egypt. For he was wiser than all other men... and his fame was in all the surrounding nations. He also spoke 3,000 proverbs, and his songs were 1,005. He spoke of trees, from the cedar that is in Lebanon to the hyssop that grows out of the wall. He spoke also of beasts, and of birds, and of reptiles, and of fish. And people of all nations came to hear the wisdom of Solomon, and from all the kings of the earth, who had heard of his wisdom. [1 Kings 4:29-34, adapted from the ESV]

To Serve as a Kingdom of Priests. Yahweh expressed this purpose for the nation of Israel in the following passage from the 19th chapter of Exodus:

> ... Yahweh called to Moses out of the mountain, saying, "Thus you shall say to the house of Jacob, and tell the people of Israel: You yourselves have seen what I did to the Egyptians, and how I bore you on eagles' wings and brought you to Myself. Now therefore, if you will indeed obey My voice and keep my covenant, you shall be My treasured possession among all peoples, for all the earth is mine; and you shall be to me a kingdom of priests and a holy nation..." [Exodus 19:3-6, adapted from the ESV]

That this purpose is not restricted to the nation of Israel, but rather it applies to the entire community of faith, is testified by its reaffirmation in the Christian Scriptures by the Apostle Peter and the Apostle John in the following two passages:

> But you are a chosen race, a royal priesthood, a holy nation, a people for His own possession, that you may proclaim the excellencies of Him who called you out of darkness into His marvelous light. [1 Peter 2:9, adapted from the ESV]

> And they sang a new song, saying, "Worthy is the Lamb to take the scroll and to open its seals, for You were slain, and by Your blood you ransomed people for God from every tribe and language and people and nation, and You have made them a kingdom and priests to our God, and they shall reign on the earth." [Revelation 5:9-10, adapted from the ESV]

To Place in Evidence the Abject Failure of Human Wisdom. This purpose is first placed in evidence by the literary device of juxtaposing the Tower of Babylon episode and the calling of Abraham in the 11th and 12th chapters of Genesis. It is then repeatedly confirmed as we trace the trajectory of the People of the New Way through the Hebrew Scriptures. For example, the 1st Psalm contrasts the way of the righteous, which is the way of wisdom, with the way of the wicked, which is the way of folly. The former leads to life, while the latter leads to ruination and death. The entire Book of Proverbs is a discourse on the way of wisdom versus the way of folly. In His Sermon on the Mount, Jesus contrasts the narrow and difficult way that leads to life versus the broad and inviting way that leads to ruination and death (see Matthew 7:13-14). He concludes the Sermon by contrasting the wisdom of those who hear His word and obey it, versus the folly of those who merely hear but do not practice (see Matthew 7:24-27). Another passage in the Christian Scriptures which further confirms this purpose is from the pen of the Apostle Paul in 1 Corinthians 2:6-16.

Five Lessons of the New Way

I conclude this section on the People of the New Way by identifying the five timeless and normative lessons which Yahweh taught the patriarchs, as recorded in the Book of Genesis.

Proper Relationship With Yahweh. The proper relationship of the People of the New Way with Yahweh is to be characterized by **implicit trust** and **unequivocal obedience**. This is seen especially in the life of Abraham and his grandson, Jacob.

Proper Relationship With Women. Regarding the proper relationship of the patriarchs with their women – wives, daughters, and sisters – the lessons in Genesis are mostly negative. In this connection, it is noteworthy that, ever since the Fall, men tend to oppress and tyrannize women, and women tend to be insubordinate with respect to male leadership.

On two occasions Abraham told a half-truth concerning his wife, Sarah, in order to save his own neck. The first incident is recorded in Genesis 12:10-20, and the second is recorded in Genesis 20:1-18. In both cases, Yahweh used the lips of a pagan king to rebuke Abraham. It is especially noteworthy that the second incident occurred during the one-year period between Yahweh's explicit promise that Sarah would conceive and bear a son in Genesis 18, and the birth of Isaac in Genesis 21.

Isaac followed in the footsteps of his father as he misrepresented his wife to Abimelech in Genesis 26:6-11. Once again, Yahweh used the lips of a pagan king to rebuke Isaac.

Jacob strongly favored Rachel and her children over Leah and hers. This favoritism surfaces in Genesis 29:15-30 and continues unabated through much of Jacob's long life. It is noteworthy that Yahweh deliberately counteracts this favoritism in three ways: first, by enabling Leah to conceive children before Rachel, as recorded in Genesis 29:31-35; second, by causing the royal line of Judah to be through Leah rather than Rachel; and, third, by arranging that Leah, but not Rachel, would be buried in the tomb of the patriarchs located near Hebron (see Genesis 49:31).

According to Genesis 30:21, Leah bore Jacob his only daughter, Dinah. During the time that Jacob and his household resided near Shechem, Dinah left the tent complex unaccompanied, and she went into Shechem to visit with "the women of the land." (Genesis 34:1) The young man, Shechem, the prince of the city, saw Dinah, seized her, and raped her. It is true that Leah's brothers, Simeon and Levi, avenged the violation of their sister by killing all the men of the city, but why had they not protected their sister in the first place? Their fierce rage after the fact was no substitute for their seeing to it that their sister was accompanied in her visit with the women of the city. And, of course, Jacob should have exercised oversight and protected his daughter.

These negative lessons from the lives of the patriarchs teach the following lessons to us, as the men of the new way:

- As leaders, we are responsible for exercising loving oversight of our women.

- All our women, whether wives, sisters, or daughters, are to be protected as precious gifts from the hand of Yahweh.

- Our wives are to be treated differently than our sisters.

Proper Relationship With Brothers. Going back to the very dawn of human history, the calamity of fratricide struck the first family when Cain murdered his brother, Abel. Cain's fratricide resulted from envy; whereas Abel's worship of Yahweh had been accepted, his own worship had been rejected (Genesis 4:1-16).

Centuries later, Ishmael, Abraham's first son by Hagar, was caught making fun of Isaac, his son by Sarah (Genesis 21:8-14). To avoid further trouble, Ishmael and his mother were cast out of the household.

Two generations later, Jacob's favoritism of Joseph resulted in the other brothers being envious (Genesis 37:1-36). In fact, their envy was so intense that they intended to kill Joseph, but instead, they sold him as a slave to a band of Ishmaelite traders for "twenty shekels of silver."

Through a succession of adverse circumstances, Joseph is elevated to the position of vizier over all of Egypt, second in authority to Pharaoh himself. The predicted famine strikes the entire eastern Mediterranean region, and Joseph is in charge of dispensing grain throughout the land of Egypt. The brothers of Joseph journey to Egypt twice to buy grain, and Joseph treats them harshly in order to test them. He recognizes them, but they do not recognize him. During the second visit, Joseph creates a crisis that is centered around his younger brother, Benjamin. This crisis gives rise to a noble speech by Judah, which, in turn, results in Joseph making himself known to his brothers. The essence of Judah's speech was that he would become the slave of Joseph instead of his brother, Benjamin (Genesis 44:18-34); this is an act that goes beyond brotherly kindness. In this connection, we need to be reminded that Judah was a son of Leah, while Joseph and Benjamin were the sons of Rachel.

Judah's speech is the breakthrough which brings resolution to the fratricidal trajectory that begins at Genesis 37:18. In it, he expresses a self-sacrificial love for his half brother, Benjamin. The result is that the twelve brothers embrace brotherly kindness and love as a replacement for a fratricidal spirit.

> *Whereas the natural inclination of the sinful heart of brothers inclines toward fratricide, brothers of the new way are to practice brotherly kindness and self-sacrificing love instead.*

Proper Relationship With Surrounding Peoples. Again, the experiences of the patriarchs are mixed in regard to the proper relationship of the people of the new way to surrounding peoples and nations. Following are seminal passages and lessons.

On account of his nephew, Lot, Abraham intercedes for Sodom, as recorded in Genesis 18:22-33. In so doing, he manifests the kind of magisterial spirit that should characterize the people of the new way in regard to surrounding peoples and nations.

Jacob pitches his tent on a plot of ground he purchased from the people of Shechem, intending on friendly commercial interaction with the people of the land. However, Simeon and Levi upset his plans, and they create a crisis in connection with the Dinah incident discussed previously.

The lesson to be drawn from these incidents is that the people of the new way are to intercede for the surrounding peoples and nations, engage in friendly commercial interaction with them, confront their wickedness with a proper balance of meekness and firmness when necessary, and avoid at all costs assimilation by them.

Sanctification Through Suffering. This fifth and last lesson is beautifully exemplified in the trajectory of Joseph's life, beginning in the 37th chapter of Genesis. We might be motivated to criticize Joseph for his lack of wisdom, and perhaps even a prideful spirit, in his early interactions with his brothers. However, he clearly receives correction through the adverse circumstances that ensue, and he rises to be a prince, set apart from among his brothers in accordance with Jacob's blessing, as recorded in Genesis 49:26. In fact, it is noteworthy that the blessing of the firstborn bypasses Reuben and comes to rest jointly on Judah and Joseph. Whereas the kingship belongs to Judah, the double blessing of the firstborn is conferred upon Joseph, as recorded in the 48th chapter of Genesis and confirmed by 1 Chronicles 5:1-2.

As we devotionally read through the Book of Psalms, we cannot help but note the many passages that address the vital concept of sanctification through suffering. In particular, as I listened through Psalm 119 recently, I was struck by the number of passages within this single psalm that deal with sanctification through suffering.

Summary of the Five Lessons. Let us summarize the five lessons which Yahweh taught the patriarchs:

1. The people of the new way are to respond to Yahweh with implicit trust and unequivocal obedience.

2. The men of the new way are to treat their women – wives, sisters, and daughters – as precious gifts from Yahweh. They are to exercise their God-given leadership role with gentleness and self-sacrificing love.

3. The men of the new way are to avoid giving in to a fratricidal spirit, but instead we are to practice brotherly kindness and self-sacrificing love toward one another.

4. As a kingdom of priests, the people of the new way are to lovingly intercede for the surrounding peoples and nations, confront their wickedness with a balance of meekness and firmness when necessary, engage in friendly commercial interaction, and avoid assimilation at all costs.

5. The people of the new way are to embrace sanctification and spiritual formation through the path of suffering.

While these are the lessons that Yahweh taught the patriarchs according to the narrative of Genesis, they are timeless and normative for the people of the new way. **In fact, they are distinctive features of the way of Christ and the apostles.**

The Gospel

The integrative motif of **the gospel** is intertwined with the people of the new way motif. In fact, it is through the people of the new way that the blessings of the gospel propagate to all mankind. Moreover, as we will see, the integrative motif of the gospel is intertwined with the invasion of evil, sin, and death, the seed of the woman, the prototype, and the covenant of conditional blessing motifs.

In accordance with the flow delineated in Figure 5-1, we now examine some of the seminal passages in which the gospel motif first surfaces, and then a few additional passages which enrich, shape, and develop our understanding of this motif. Our discussion in this section serves as background and introduction to chapter 6, The Two-Part Christian Gospel.

We must keep in mind that we are representing the gospel as singular, but having multiple facets and layers. The ultimate result of the gospel is that the curses pronounced by Yahweh Elohim in Genesis 3:14ff are totally reversed and neutralized, and all the effects of the invasion of evil, sin, and death are obliterated. While an aspect of the gospel is the deliverance of persons from the power of evil, sin, and death, its scope and application greatly transcend individual salvation.

The *Protoevangelium*

As I have already noted in connection with the invasion of evil, sin, and death motif, the gospel motif first surfaces in the context of the curse pronounced by Yahweh Elohim upon the serpent in Genesis 3:15.

> I will put enmity between you and the woman, and between your seed and her seed; He shall strike your head, and you shall strike His heel. [Genesis 3:15, adapted from the ESV]

Judging from how Eve later represents the birth of her sons, it is clear that her understanding of this remarkable statement by Yahweh Elohim was that a man child would come forth from her womb, and he would bring about deliverance from the serpent. However, what Yahweh Elohim had in mind was different. Let us trace the trajectory of the seed of the woman motif through Scripture.

"The Virgin Shall Conceive". Our first stop along the seed of the woman trajectory is Isaiah 7:14, which states,

> Therefore Adonai Himself will give you a sign. Behold, the virgin shall conceive and bear a son, and shall call his name Immanuel. [Isaiah 7:14, adapted from the ESV]

This prophecy is quoted and interpreted by Matthew in his record of the angel's announcement to Joseph as follows:

> Behold, the virgin shall conceive and bear a son, and they shall call his name Immanuel (which means, God with us). [Matthew 1:23, adapted from the ESV]

"The Logos Became Flesh". Our next stop is the 1st chapter of the Gospel of John in which the Apostle John sublimely interprets the true nature of the incarnation of Jesus Christ, the Son of God.

> In the beginning was the Logos, and the Logos was with God, and the Logos was God. He was in the beginning with God. All things were made through Him, and without Him was not any thing made that was made. In Him was life, and the life was the light of men... And the Logos became flesh and dwelt among us, and we have seen His glory,

glory as of the only Son from the Father, full of grace and truth. [John 1:1-4 & 14, adapted from the ESV]

The Devil Destroyer. Our next stop is Hebrew 2:14, which states,

> Since therefore the children share in flesh and blood, He Himself likewise partook of the same things, that through death He might destroy the one who has the power of death, that is, the devil, and deliver all those who through fear of death were subject to lifelong slavery. [Hebrews 2:14-15, adapted from the ESV]

Our final stop along the trajectory of the seed of the woman is Revelation 20:10, which tersely represents the ultimate defeat of Satan as follows:

> ... And the devil who had deceived them was thrown into the lake of fire and sulfur where the beast and the false prophet were, and they will be tormented day and night forever and ever. [Revelation 20:10, ESV]

Paul's Summation. The Apostle Paul offers a sweeping summation of The seed of the woman motif in the 15th chapter of 1 Corinthians.

> Then comes the end, when He delivers the kingdom to God the Father after destroying every rule and every authority and power. For He must reign until He has put all His enemies under His feet. The last enemy to be destroyed is death. For God has put all things in subjection under His feet. But when it says, "all things are put in subjection," it is plain that He is excepted who put all things in subjection under Him. When all things are subjected to Him, then the Son Himself will also be subjected to Him who put all things in subjection under Him, that God may be all in all. [1 Corinthians 15:24-28, adapted from the ESV]

And so the trajectory of the seed of the woman motif emanates from the pronouncement of Yahweh Elohim in Genesis 3:15 through Isaiah's prophecy, to the angel's announcement of the virgin birth to Mary and Joseph, to John's explanation of the incarnation of the Son of God in the 1st chapter of his Gospel, to the ultimate defeat of Satan as described by John in the 20th chapter of Revelation. It was that ultimate defeat that

Yahweh Elohim had in mind in His pronouncement of the *Protoevangelium* in Genesis 3:15.

The Gospel Proclaimed to Abraham

The covenant which Yahweh cut with Abraham, the pioneer and progenitor of the people of the new way, contains the gospel motif. In stating, "in you all the families of the earth shall be blessed," Yahweh signified that the mysterious seed of the woman would pass through the loins of Abraham, and that a descendant of his would bring deliverance from evil, sin, and death to all peoples and nations.

The Apostle Paul clarifies this aspect of the covenant with Abraham in his letter to the Galatians.

> To give a human example, brothers: even with a man-made covenant, no one annuls it or adds to it once it has been ratified. Now the promises were made to Abraham and to his offspring. It does not say, "And to offsprings," referring to many, but referring to one, "And to your offspring," who is Christ. This is what I mean: the law, which came 430 years afterward, does not annul a covenant previously ratified by God, so as to make the promise void. For if the inheritance comes by the law, it no longer comes by promise; but God gave it to Abraham by a promise. [Galatians 3:15-18, ESV]

The Gospel Proclaimed to Israel

The writer of Hebrews represents the gospel proclaimed to Israel as parallel to that proclaimed to us.

> For indeed we have had good news (= gospel) preached to us, just as they also; but the word they heard did not profit them, because it was not united by faith in those who heard. [Hebrews 4:2, NASB]

What was the gospel preached to Israel? It had two parts as follows:

1. Deliverance out of bondage in Egypt; and,

2. Deliverance into rest in the promised land of Canaan after a period of conflict and conquest.

What is the parallel gospel preached to us? It also has two parts as follows:

1. Deliverance out of bondage to evil, sin, and death; and,

2. Deliverance into eternal rest in fellowship with God after a period of conflict and conquest.

And so, the gospel preached to Israel through Moses is, indeed, parallel to the gospel preached to us by Jesus Christ and His apostles.

The Kadesh-barnea Episode. In chapter 3, we discussed at length the effects of Israel's failure to lay hold of Yahweh's promise to deliver them into the land of promise. The ten spies who brought the bad report died immediately, and, except for Caleb and Joshua, that entire generation of Israelites were condemned to die off in the wilderness of Sinai.

Faith in Resurrection. For our present discussion of the Gospel motif, the significance of the Kadesh-barnea episode is this: Israel refused to believe the second part of the gospel preached to them; namely, that Yahweh could or would make good on His promise to deliver them into rest in the land of promise, which corresponds to our refusing to believe that Yahweh can or will deliver us into eternal rest after a period of conflict and conquest.

> *In other words, Kadesh-barnea generation of Israelites lacked the essential ingredient of the faith of their forefather, Abraham, which was his trust in Yahweh's ability to bring about resurrection from the dead.*

The Gospel of the Kingdom

We have already examined Yahweh's remarkable announcement to the people of Israel in the 19th chapter of Exodus in connection with the people of the new way.

> Yahweh called to Moses out of the mountain, saying, "Thus you shall say to the house of Jacob, and tell the people of Israel: You yourselves have seen what I did to the Egyptians, and how I bore you on eagles' wings and brought you to Myself. Now therefore, **if you will indeed obey My**

> **voice and keep My covenant, you shall be My treasured possession among all peoples, for all the earth is Mine; and you shall be to Me a kingdom of priests and a holy nation**. These are the words that you shall speak to the people of Israel." [Exodus 19:3-6, adapted from the ESV, emphasis added]

Who had ever heard of God redeeming and delivering one nation of people out from another nation by means of great signs and wonders, and taking that nation unto Himself to be His treasured possession? Moses never got over this marvelous display of God's glorious grace. Notice the way in which he reflects upon it in the 4th chapter of Deuteronomy.

> See, I have taught you statutes and rules, as Yahweh my Elohim commanded me, that you should do them in the land that you are entering to take possession of it. Keep them and do them, for that will be your wisdom and your understanding in the sight of the peoples, who, when they hear all these statutes, will say, "Surely this great nation is a wise and understanding people." For what great nation is there that has a god so near to it as the Yahweh our Elohim is to us, whenever we call upon Him? And what great nation is there, that has statutes and rules so righteous as all this law that I set before you today? [Deuteronomy 4:5-8, adapted from the ESV]

The Law As Gospel. Because of the teaching of the Apostle Paul in regard to the law of Moses, it is difficult for us now to represent the law as gospel, but truly it was. The essential purpose of the Book of Genesis and the early chapters of Exodus is to set forth the background of the people of the new way, the descendants of Abraham. As those descendants of Abraham, the people of Israel, gathered at the foot of Mt. Sinai, Yahweh Elohim announced that He was taking them unto Himself as His own treasured possession, and He was forming them, by means of the covenant of Sinai, into a kingdom of priests, through whom He would bless all peoples and nations.

A Suzerain / Vassal Treaty. The covenant of Mt. Sinai, with its several components, is set forth according to the pattern of an ancient Hittite suzerain / vassal treaty; that is, a treaty between a king and his people. Such a treaty contained the stipulations of the covenant that the people were required to keep and adhere to in order to receive the blessings of vassalry, of which protection against marauding enemies was paramount. After the stipulations, the covenant stated the blessings that the king would bestow if his people remained faithful to the terms of the covenant, together with the cursings that would attend unfaithfulness. We examine this more fully in the next section, The Covenant of Conditional Blessing. In the context of our discussion of the gospel motif, the point is this: according to the perspective of an ancient suzerain / vassal treaty, the **law of Moses should, in fact, be represented as gospel.**

The Covenant With David. The gospel of the kingdom is further shaped by the covenant that Yahweh cut with David in accordance with the record of the 7th chapter of 2 Samuel.

> Thus says Yahweh Sabaoth, "I took you from the pasture, from following the sheep, that you should be prince over My people Israel. And I have been with you wherever you went and have cut off all your enemies from before you. And I will make for you a great name, like the name of the great ones of the earth. And I will appoint a place for my people Israel and will plant them, so that they may dwell in their own place and be disturbed no more... Moreover, Yahweh declares to you that Yahweh will make you a house. When your days are fulfilled and you lie down with your fathers, I will raise up your offspring after you, who shall come from your body, and I will establish his kingdom. He shall build a house for My name, and I will establish the throne of his kingdom forever. I will be to him a father, and he shall be to Me a son... but My steadfast love will not depart from him... And your house and your kingdom shall be made sure forever before Me. Your throne shall be established forever." [2 Samuel 7:8-16, adapted from the ESV]

The great Messianic 2nd Psalm, which is discussed more fully in chapter 7, The Authority of the King, serves as a poetic commentary on the Davidic Covenant. Note in both the passage quoted above and in the 2nd Psalm how David's son, Solomon, serves as a near-term prefiguration of a greater Son of David who would arise in the future. He would sit upon David's throne in Jerusalem; but His rule would embrace all nations, and His dominion would extend to the ends of the earth.

Prophetic Shaping of the Gospel of the Kingdom

As we trace the trajectory of the gospel of the kingdom through the prophetic literature of the Hebrew Scriptures, it is further shaped and articulated. An important feature of this prophetic shaping and articulation is the **theology of restoration**. Although Israel was unfaithful to the terms of the covenant with Yahweh, and therefore would be made to suffer the terrible consequences specified in the suzerain / vassal treaty, Yahweh would not forsake her utterly, but rather He would bring about a future restoration. This theme is beautifully and poignantly set forth in the following passage from Isaiah:

> "For a brief moment I deserted you, but with great compassion I will gather you. In overflowing anger for a moment I hid my face from you, but with everlasting love I will have compassion on you," says Yahweh, your Redeemer. [Isaiah 54:7-8, adapted from the ESV]

A sublime representation of the glorious future Messianic Kingdom is presented by Micah in the 4th chapter of his prophecy.

> It shall come to pass in the latter days that the mountain of the house of Yahweh shall be established as the highest of the mountains, and it shall be lifted up above the hills; and peoples shall flow to it, and many nations shall come, and say: "Come, let us go up to the mountain of Yahweh, to the house of the Elohim of Jacob, that He may teach us His ways and that we may walk in His paths." For out of Zion shall go forth the law, and the word of Yahweh from Jerusalem. He shall judge between many peoples, and shall decide for strong nations far away; and they shall beat their swords into plowshares, and their spears into pruning hooks; nation shall not lift up sword against nation, neither shall they learn war anymore; but they shall sit every man under his vine and under his fig tree, and no one shall make them afraid, for the mouth of Yahweh Sabaoth has spoken. [Micah 4:1-4, adapted from the ESV]

The historical restoration of Israel recorded in the books of Ezra and Nehemiah serves as prefigurement of the glorious Messianic Kingdom that is set forth in the 20th chapter of the Book of Revelation.

> Then I saw thrones, and seated on them were those to whom the authority to judge was committed. Also I saw the souls of those who had been beheaded for the testimony of Jesus and for the word of God, and those who had not worshiped the beast or its image and had not received its mark on their foreheads or their hands. They came to life and reigned with Christ for a thousand years. [Revelation 20:4, ESV]

Concluding Comments Regarding the Gospel

We have seen that there are several important strands of the gospel motif, and I have traced their trajectory through the entire Bible. However, this discussion has been far from exhaustive. Instead, I have only sketched the development of this important motif, leaving ample space for the student to add detail and his own insights.

However, even this brief sketch has placed in evidence that the scope of the gospel motif is cosmic. One day God will do away with the present heavens and earth, corrupted as they are by evil, sin, and death. And He will create new heavens and earth wherein righteousness dwells. These will be populated by a redeemed worshiping community called forth and made up of people from all nations and ethnic groups. This multitude will enjoy fellowship with God and delight in His glorious grace forever and forever. He will dwell with them and be their God, and they will be His people. The effects of the Fall will be totally obliterated, and the curse pronounced by Yahweh Elohim in Genesis 3:14ff will be utterly reversed and neutralized. This is the ultimate focus and goal of the gospel.

Sovereign Election and Human Responsibility

Of all the integrative motifs, this one is the most perplexing and difficult to understand. How does the sovereign grace of God interact with human responsibility? If God is absolutely sovereign over everything that takes place in the cosmos, then how can any of His creatures be truly free to choose for themselves? Human free agency and the sovereignty of God seem to be mutually exclusive. How can they coexist in the same cosmos?

Because this subject area is so perplexing, I have written Appendix F for the express purpose of shedding some light upon it and making it more understandable. Therefore, I encourage you to carefully read Appendix F before continuing your study of this motif.

God's Firm Foundation

It seems to me that sovereign election and human responsibility is unlike the other motifs in another respect. While we see **evidence** of God's elective choice in the narrative of the Hebrew Scriptures, we must wait for the teaching of the apostles – especially Paul – before we can even begin to make sense of this motif. I am reminded of the following passage in the second letter to Timothy in which Paul places the concept of sovereign election alongside human responsibility in the following profound statement:

> But God's firm foundation stands, bearing this seal: "Yahweh knows those who are His," and, "Let everyone who names the name of Yahweh depart from iniquity." [2 Timothy 2:19, adapted from the ESV]

Paul's language in this verse suggests that he is visualizing the chief cornerstone of a great building – perhaps a temple – which bears this engraving: "Yahweh knows those who are His," and, "Let everyone who names the name of Yahweh depart from iniquity."

Please allow me to change the symbolism as follows: let us visualize a lofty monumental gate structure that stands at the entrance into God's eternal kingdom. It consists of two great pillars, one on either side, which support a massive stone that forms the top of the gate structure. The pillar on one side is engraved with, "Yahweh knows those who are His," and the pillar on the other side is engraved with, "Let everyone who names the name of Yahweh depart from iniquity." The stone above is engraved with "Sovereign Election and Human Responsibility." The first pillar reminds us that election is a choice which God makes, and it is not conditioned on anything for which the chosen one can take credit. And the pillar on the other side reminds us that God's chosen ones are responsible for being righteous and holy because God has fastened His love upon them.

This great monumental gate structure is visible through the mists of time from the dawn of revelation history. We see numerous examples of God choosing some and refusing others, but it is only after we move past the Chi Event in Figure 2-1 that we are able to read the inscriptions on the two pillars.

From what passage in the Hebrew Scriptures did Paul derive the language of 2 Timothy 2:19? If you have a study bible, you can probably see a rather long list of possible passages in the Hebrew Scriptures that are associated with this passage in 2 Timothy. The single passage with seems to me to be the best candidate is the 16th chapter of Numbers, which records the Korah rebellion episode. "Yahweh knows those who are His" is derived from the 5th verse, and "Let everyone who names the name of Yahweh depart from iniquity" is derived from the 26th and 27th verses.

This chapter in Numbers is most significant because it is all about choices. Korah was a relative of Moses and Aaron, and, by his own free choice, he put himself forward as being equal in stature to them. Why shouldn't he be able to lead Israel, and why did Moses and Aaron appropriate the role of leaders for themselves? Through the entire passage, God makes abundantly clear that He had, indeed, chosen Moses and Aaron, and He had not chosen Korah and his associates. In the Korah rebellion episode, sovereign election and human responsibility violently collide with disastrous results for Korah and his associates.

The Divine Plan of Salvation

Because the sovereign election and human responsibility motif is different from all the others in the way it unfolds through revelation history, I am going to deal with it differently as well. Continuing with the monumental gateway metaphor suggested above, let us stand between the two pillars, where we can clearly read their inscriptions, and let us gaze backward in time from that vantage point. In fact, let our gaze be focused at a point in eternity past to which the Apostle Paul refers in this awesome passage in the 8th chapter of Romans:

> And we know that for those who love God all things work together for good, for those who are called according to His

purpose. For those whom He **foreknew** (= *proginosko*) He also **predestined** (= *proorizo*) to be conformed to the image of His Son, in order that He might be the firstborn among many brothers. And those whom He predestined he also **called** (= *kaleo*), and those whom He called He also **justified** (= *dikaioo*), and those whom He justified He also **glorified** (= *doxazo*). [Romans 8:28-30, adapted from the ESV]

In this brief passage, Paul unfolds for us a cosmic view of the divine plan of salvation. This statement by Paul is awesome because each of the five key verbs, which are emphasized in the quotation above, are expressed in the **aorist active indicative tense**. What is the significance of this? The aorist tense in the *koine* Greek of the Christian Scriptures signifies an event that is lifted out of time and given timeless significance. [80] It is as if God intentionally orchestrated the development of the *koine* Greek language to include a verb tense that represents His perspective on things. As our discussion in this section unfolds, the fact becomes evident that the actions signified by the five key verbs in our focal passage **took place in the counsels of eternity past!**

I hope you are gaining a deeper appreciation for why we must approach the sovereign election and human responsibility motif differently from all the others. Even though we see evidence of this motif beginning in Genesis, we cannot appreciate its significance unless and until God grants us a heavenly perspective on His grand plan of salvation. And it is exactly this kind of perspective that the Holy Spirit enabled Paul to express in the language of our focal passage. So let us now attempt to unpack each of the key verbs as a means to understand the full significance of the sovereign election and human responsibility motif.

Those Whom He Foreknew. As indicated in the quotation of our focal passage, the lexical form of the Greek verb which is translated "foreknew" is *proginosko*, which means to know beforehand. Where might we turn in Scripture to appreciate the significance of God's knowing us beforehand? I believe the cardinal passage on this subject is found in the poetic literature; namely, the 139th Psalm.

> O Yahweh, you have searched me and known me!
>   You know when I sit down and when I rise up;
>   You discern my thoughts from afar.

> You search out my path and my lying down
> > and are acquainted with all my ways.
> Even before a word is on my tongue,
> > behold, O Yahweh, You know it altogether.
> You hem me in, behind and before,
> > and lay Your hand upon me.
> Such knowledge is too wonderful for me;
> > it is high; I cannot attain it...
> For You formed my inward parts;
> > You knitted me together in my mother's womb.
> I praise You, for I am fearfully and wonderfully made.
> Wonderful are Your works;
> > my soul knows it very well.
> My frame was not hidden from You,
> > when I was being made in secret,
> > > intricately woven in the depths of the earth.
> Your eyes saw my unformed substance;
> > in Your book were written, every one of them,
> > > the days that were formed for me,
> > > > when as yet there was none of them.
> [Psalm 139:1-16, adapted from the ESV]

In this beautiful psalm, David unfolds the concept of the **omniscience** of God – the fact that He knows all things fully and perfectly, past, present, and future. In the 13th through the 16th verses, David makes clear that God's omniscience is in nowise bound by time. That is, He knew David in an intimate and relational way long before David was born. In fact, we can say with confidence that God's intimate, relational knowledge of David **existed in the mind of God in the counsels of eternity past**.

Thus, David's rich poetry in the 139th Psalm powerfully informs and illuminates the significance of the **foreknowledge** of God.

Another passage from the Hebrew Scriptures which reflects the foreknowledge of God is found in the 31st chapter of Jeremiah:

> Thus says Yahweh:
> > "The people who survived the sword
> > > found grace in the wilderness;
> > when Israel sought for rest,
> > > Yahweh appeared to him from far away.

> I have loved you with an everlasting love;
>> therefore I have continued my faithfulness to you."
> [Jeremiah 31:2–3, adapted from the ESV]

Yahweh's foreknowledge of His elect is a relational kind of knowledge and includes the dimension of approval, love, and even delight. He delights in His people, not based on what we are, but based on what we are becoming through the operation of His glorious grace.

He Also Predestined. As indicated in the quotation of our focal passage, the lexical form of the Greek verb which is translated "predestined" is *proorizo*, which literally means to mark out beforehand. The text of our focal passage makes clear two points in regard to God's action of marking out beforehand:

- This act is logically predicated upon His act of foreknowing.

- The object of His marking out beforehand is that those marked out would be conformed to the image of His Son.

The Book of Life. This present discussion is an appropriate context in which to bring up the **book of life** or **the Lamb's book of life**. This book is mentioned in connection with the Great White Throne judgment in Revelation 20:15, 21:27 & 22:19. Those whose names are written in this book will enter into the eternal kingdom of God, and those whose names are not written in the book will be cast into the lake of fire, where...

> They will suffer the punishment of eternal destruction, away from the presence of Yahweh and from the glory of His might, when He comes on that day to be glorified in His saints, and to be marveled at among all who have believed, because our testimony to you was believed. [2 Thessalonians 1:9-10, adapted from the ESV]

The book of life is mentioned or alluded to in ten passages of Scripture, of which the following are examples:

- Exodus 32:30ff records Moses' prayer of intercession for the people of Israel after the golden calf episode. In the 32nd verse, as part of this prayer, he requests that his name be blotted out of the book of life if Yahweh is unwilling to forgive the sin of His people.

- Luke 10:1ff records the commissioning of the seventy disciples whom Jesus sent ahead into all the places through which He was about to pass on His way to Jerusalem. After they returned to the Lord with rejoicing, Jesus told them, "Nevertheless, do not rejoice in this, that the spirits are subject to you, but rejoice that your names are written in heaven." [Luke 10:20, ESV]

- In Philippians 4:3, Paul speaks of those at Philippi, "whose names are in the book of life."

- In Revelation 3:5, Jesus affirms that He will never blot the name of one who conquers out of the book of life.

- In Revelation 13:8 and Revelation 17:8, John speaks of those whose names were not written in the book of life; they will worship the Antichrist and his image.

Except for that cohort of people who are alive during the period of time spoken of by the Apostle John in 13th and 17th chapters of Revelation, the only action regarding the names in the book of life mentioned in all of Scripture is blotting out, erasure, or **removal**. Accordingly, I propose the following:

- In the case of that specific cohort of people who will worship the Antichrist and his image, **it appears that their names were never written in the book of life**.

- In the case of everyone else, his name is written into the book of life on a provisional basis; should he pass from this life without ever having received the grace of God in salvation, his name will be removed from the book.

The book of life is another awesome concept which allows us to view things from a divine perspective. Even as David states in Psalm 139:16 that all the days ordained for him were written down in the counsels of eternity past, in like manner, the name of every human being is recorded in the Lamb's book of life in the counsels of eternity past, with the exception of those who will worship the Antichrist or his image. And each one who rejects the grace of God in salvation by his own self-determined choice is removed from the book.

Those Whom He Predestined He Also Called. As indicated in the quotation of our focal passage, the lexical form of the Greek verb which is translated "called" is *kaleo*, which means to call. But what kind of call is this? We need to keep in mind that this verb, like each of the other four key verbs in our focal passage, is expressed in the aorist, active, indicative tense, which means that this action, like each of the others, is lifted out of the context of time and conferred with timeless significance. Those whom God knew intimately and relationally, He marked out to be conformed to the image of His Son, and those whom He thus marked out, He **called** before the foundation of the world. And that divine call rings forth from the counsels of eternity past, reverberates down through the corridors of time, and then intersects with and impacts upon the life of each one being called at some definite point on the knife edge of time. And at this precise intersection, the divine call takes the particular form of the power-packed message about Christ mentioned by Paul in Romans 10:17:

> So faith comes from what is heard, and what is heard comes through the message about Christ. [Romans 10:17, HCSB]

And, in the lives of the elect, that divine call activates, energizes, and imparts the faith of Jesus Christ whereby we are justified in accordance with Romans 3:21-26.

And thus we come to this question: is the call of God resistible or irresistible. With respect to the elect, it is irresistible. And yet, the call of God is not coercive. In the language of Appendix F, God **causes** the elect to respond affirmatively to the message about His Son, but He doesn't **make** them respond this way. From the perspective of the one being called, the decision to respond affirmatively to the call of God is seen as a self-determined and freely made choice. And yet, to that one, deliverance from the power of evil, sin, and death is seen to be entirely the product of the lavish grace of God.

> For by grace you have been saved through faith. And this is not your own doing; it is the gift of God, not a result of works, so that no one may boast. [Ephesians 2:8–9, ESV]

Someone is bound to ask this question: what about the non-elect? This is a most profound question, at it pokes at an unfathomable mystery. In regard to this mystery, I am reminded of the following passage from the 11th chapter of Romans:

> Oh, the depth of the riches of both the wisdom and knowledge of God! How unsearchable are His judgments and how inscrutable his ways! For who has known the mind of Yahweh, or who has been His counselor? Or who has given a gift to Him that he might be repaid? For from Him and through Him and to Him are all things. To Him be glory forever. Amen. [Romans 11:33-36, adapted from the ESV]

The Potter Metaphor. To answer the question about the non-elect, I turn to the potter metaphor that surfaces in Paul's discourse on election in the 9th chapter of Romans.

> You will say to me then, "Why does He still find fault? For who can resist His will?" But who are you, O man, to answer back to God? Will what is molded say to its molder, "Why have you made me like this?" Has the potter no right over the clay, to make out of the same lump one vessel for honorable use and another for dishonorable use? What if God, desiring to show His wrath and to make known His power, has endured with much patience vessels of wrath prepared for destruction, in order to make known the riches of His glory for vessels of mercy, which He has prepared beforehand for glory – even us whom He has called, not from the Jews only but also from the Gentiles? [Romans 9:19-24, adapted from the ESV]

The potter metaphor, which Paul employs here to illustrate God's elective choice of some for salvation, derives from two passages in the Hebrew Scriptures. The first of these is Isaiah 64:8-12 and the second is Jeremiah 18:1-11.

The technology of pottery manufacture is complex, including the following important elements:

- Selection of clays.

- Addition of binding and tempering materials, such as straw and lime.

- Thorough mixing of the clay with additives.

- Formation of the vessel on the wheel according to a design that exists in the mind of the potter.

- Curing the vessel in a dark, damp space, such as a cave, until the clay is leather hard.

- Firing the vessel to harden the clay, even to the point of metallic hardness.

- Application of surface treatment, including incising, burnishing, painting, and glazing.

Paul would have us recognize that each person is the product of God's handiwork for some specific purpose, even as the potter manufactures a vessel according to a specific design and for a specific purpose. Moreover, according to our focal passage, God has manufactured two categories of pottery; namely, **vessels of mercy** which are destined for glory, and **vessels of wrath**, which are destined for destruction. To objectify these two categories, I employ the following equivalence:

Vessels of mercy = bowls

Vessels of wrath = jugs

These two categories of vessels are illustrated in the two panels of Figure 5-3. Whereas the bowls have been broken and mended, the jugs are graceful in shape and perfectly whole. As indicated in the figures, the vessels of mercy (= bowls) voluntarily receive the grace of God in response to His call, while the vessels of wrath (= jugs) voluntarily reject the grace of God when exposed to the proclamation of the gospel. Each of these diametrically opposing self-determined choices are perfectly in accord with the nature and character of the bowls and the jugs.

The Need for Both Bowls and Jugs. It would be natural for us to allow this question to surface in our minds: wouldn't the world be a better place if there were only bowls and no jugs? However, from the passage in the 9th chapter of Romans quoted above, it seems clear that, in order for God to put on display all the dimensions of His glorious grace, both His mercy and His wrath must be manifested. In fact, mercy has no meaning

Figure 5-3. Vessels of Mercy = Bowls and Vessels of Wrath = Jugs

without wrath, and *vice versa*. Therefore, as in the parable of the Wheat and the Weeds of Matthew 13:24-30, both the bowls (= vessels of mercy) and the jugs (= vessels of wrath) must exist side by side until the final judgment.

"**Those Whom He Called He Also Justified.**" Because justification on the basis of the faith of Jesus Christ is so central to the content of the gospel of God, our discussion of this subject is reserved for chapter 14. Based upon what we have already seen, the power-packed call of God imparts and energizes the faith of Jesus Christ in the spirit of the elect. Then, in accordance with Paul's teaching in Romans 3:21-26, God declares the person to be justified – to be made right in God's eyes. Having been justified by faith, we enter a state of peace with God in accordance with Romans 5:1-5. In other words, the state of animosity and hostility that previously existed between us and God has been totally resolved so that God is able to embrace us as His sons and daughters – in fact, beloved members of His household.

"**And Those Whom He Justified He Also Glorified.**" Our glorification is the final state of the process we call **sanctification**, whereby we are progressively conformed to the image of Jesus Christ, the Son of God. Whereas from our perspective this is a lengthy, arduous, and even painful **process**, from God's eternal perspective it is an **event** that He determined and secured in the counsels of eternity past. It appears to be the case in the economy of God that the glory that is to be revealed in each of us is a function of the extent to which we participate in the fellowship of the sufferings of Christ. Such is the implication of the following passages from 2 Corinthians, Philippians, and 1 Peter:

> Therefore we do not give up. Even though our outer person is being destroyed, our inner person is being renewed day by day. **For our momentary light affliction is producing for us an absolutely incomparable eternal weight of glory.** So we do not focus on what is seen, but on what is unseen. For what is seen is temporary, but what is unseen is eternal. [2 Corinthians 4:16-18, HCSB, emphasis added]

> But everything that was a gain to me, I have considered to be a loss because of Christ. More than that, I also consider everything to be a loss in view of the surpassing value of knowing Christ Jesus my Lord. Because of Him I have suffered the loss of all things and consider them filth, so that I may gain Christ and be found in Him, not having a righteousness of my own from the law, but one that is through the faith of Christ – the righteousness from God based on faith. My goal is to know Him and the power of His resurrection and the **fellowship of His sufferings, being conformed to His death,** assuming that I will somehow reach the resurrection from among the dead. Not that I have already reached the goal or am already fully mature, but I make every effort to take hold of it because I also have been taken hold of by Christ Jesus. Brothers, I do not consider myself to have taken hold of it. But one thing I do: Forgetting what is behind and reaching forward to what is ahead, **I pursue as my goal the prize promised by God's heavenly call in Christ Jesus.** [Philippians 3:7-14, adapted from the HCSB, emphasis added]

> Dear friends, don't be surprised when the fiery ordeal comes among you to test you as if something unusual were happening to you. **Instead, rejoice as you share in the sufferings of the Messiah, so that you may also rejoice with great joy at the revelation of His glory.** If you are ridiculed for the name of Christ, you are blessed, because the Spirit of glory and of God rests on you. [1 Peter 4:12-14, HCSB, emphasis added]

Concluding Comments Regarding Sovereign Election and Human Responsibility

Whereas from God's perspective our salvation was altogether determined and secured in the counsels of eternity past, from our perspective it involves a long and sometimes painful sequence of human choices that begins with the critical choice of receiving the grace of God as expressed in the Christian gospel, and then working out the implications and applications of that choice over the course of a lifelong pilgrimage in accordance with the following injunction from the Apostle Paul:

> So then, my dear friends, just as you have always obeyed, not only in my presence, but now even more in my absence, work out your own salvation with fear and trembling. For it is God who is working in you, enabling you both to desire and to work out His good purpose. [Philippians 2:12-13, HCSB]

To persist in that lifelong pilgrimage entails patient endurance, and one of my favorite passages in this regard is the following from Hebrews:

> 11:39 All these were approved through their faith, but they did not receive what was promised, since God had provided something better for us, so that they would not be made perfect without us. 12:1 Therefore, since we also have such a large cloud of witnesses surrounding us, let us lay aside every weight and the sin that so easily ensnares us. Let us run with patient endurance the course that is marked out for us, keeping our eyes on Jesus, the source and perfecter of our faith, who for the joy that lay before Him endured a cross and despised the shame and has sat down at the right hand of God's throne. [Hebrews 11:39 – 12:2, adapted from the HCSB]

As a benediction to conclude this discussion of sovereign election and human responsibility, consider these words from the Apostle Peter:

> Praise the God and Father of our Lord Jesus Christ. According to His great mercy, He has given us a new birth into a living hope through the resurrection of Jesus Christ from the dead and into an inheritance that is imperishable,

uncorrupted, and unfading, kept in heaven for you. 5 **You are being protected by God's power through faith for a salvation that is ready to be revealed in the last time.** [1 Peter 1:3-5, HCSB, emphasis added]

Peter's language in the 5th verse beautifully represents the interaction between the sovereign elective grace of God and human responsibility in our successfully executing the Christian pilgrimage and attaining the "salvation that is ready to be revealed in the last time." Our successful pilgrimage is accomplished by God's power, and not by our power. But God's power works through the intermediate agency of our faith – that is, the faith of Jesus Christ that is given and sustained by the ministry of the Holy Spirit. However, our responsibility is to **exercise that faith** at every step of the way, looking to God to unleash the power of His Spirit to substantially actualize the glorious realities set forth in His word in our experience as delineated in Figure 3-1. As we appropriate and embrace His precious and magnificent promises, we become partakers of His nature and we escape the corruption that is in the world through lust (2 Peter 1:4).

The Covenant of Conditional Blessing

God has enacted a number of covenants with mankind over the course of revelation history. I would suggest that these fall into the following three categories:

- **Implied**. An example of an implied covenant is that between Yahweh Elohim and Adam. So long as Adam obeyed Yahweh Elohim by not partaking of the fruit of the tree of the knowledge of good and evil, he would enjoy fellowship with his Maker in the Garden of Eden.

- **Conditional**. A conditional covenant has stated terms together with stated results that would accrue if the terms were met. The covenant that Yahweh Elohim enacted with Israel at Mt. Sinai is the prime example of a conditional covenant, and it is the subject of the discussion that follows.

- **Unconditional**. An unconditional covenant has a stated outcome that Yahweh Elohim promises to bring about without regard to human obedience or lack thereof. His covenant with Abraham, that is first announced in the 12th chapter of Genesis, and then confirmed in the 15th chapter by means of a solemn blood covenant ceremony, is the prime example of an unconditional covenant.

Statement of the Covenant

The covenant of conditional blessing that Yahweh Elohim enacted with the people of Israel may be stated as follows: if you remain faithful to My covenant, then I will bless you in the land; if you rebel against and disobey My covenant, then you will be cursed.

Suzerain / Vassal Treaty

As was mentioned in connection with the gospel motif, the Mosaic covenant enacted by Yahweh Elohim with the people of Israel at Mt. Sinai corresponded to the format of an ancient Hittite suzerain / vassal treaty. Such a treaty contained the following three principal components:

1. A set of laws that the vassal was required to obey.

2. Prescribed benefits that the suzerain would bestow upon the vassal, conditioned upon his obedience.

3. Prescribed punishments that would be inflicted by the suzerain upon the vassal in case of disobedience.

Review of the Mosaic covenant as recorded in Exodus, Leviticus, and Numbers places in evidence that these three components are all present. The covenant of conditional blessing motif, which is the subject of this discussion, embodies components (2) and (3). In accordance with Figure 5-1, this covenant is now traced through Scripture. For the sake of efficiency of presentation, the covenant of conditional blessing motif will be referred to as the CCB motif in the discussion which follows.

First Intimation

The first intimation of this motif surfaces in Exodus 15:22-26 in connection with the waters of Marah episode; this is when Yahweh presents Himself as Yahweh Rapha – the One who heals.

> There Yahweh made for them a statute and a rule, and there He tested them, saying, "If you will diligently listen to the voice of Yahweh your Elohim, and do that which is right in

His eyes, and give ear to His commandments and keep all His statutes, I will put none of the diseases on you that I put on the Egyptians, for I am Yahweh Rapha, your healer." [Exodus 15:25-26, adapted from the ESV]

First Substantial Discourse

Exodus 23:20ff is the next passage in the Torah which contributes substantially to the definition of the CCB motif. Following is the opening statement in this discourse:

> Behold, I send an angel before you to guard you on the way and to bring you to the place that I have prepared. Pay careful attention to him and obey his voice; do not rebel against him, for he will not pardon your transgression, for my name is in him. But if you carefully obey his voice and do all that I say, then I will be an enemy to your enemies and an adversary to your adversaries. [Exodus 23:20-22, ESV]

This passage continues with Yahweh promising material blessings that would attend obedience to the terms of His covenant. He concludes with a command to completely annihilate the Canaanite population of the promised land lest they become a snare and a solicitation toward idolatry.

Second Substantial Discourse

The entire 26th chapter of Leviticus is devoted to stating the blessings that would result from the people of Israel remaining faithful and obedient to the terms of the covenant enacted with them by Yahweh Elohim at Mt. Sinai, and the cursings that would attend their breaking faith and rebelling against the terms of the covenant.

In this case, the blessings not only include the divine force multiplier which would enable them to be victorious over their enemies (see Leviticus 26:8), but also all manner of material blessings. By means of these, not only would the Israelites be well provided for, but also people from the surrounding nations would be drawn to them. In accordance with the covenant of Abraham, Israel would be a blessing to all the surrounding nations.

However, should they chose to rebel against and disobey the covenant, then not only would they be defeated by their enemies, but also all manner of adversity would befall them in the material realm. The end result of their rebellion would be that Yahweh Elohim would remove them from their land and disperse them among the nations.

The discourse concludes with the promise that Yahweh Elohim would not utterly destroy them, but rather that He would remain true to His unconditional promises to Abraham, Isaac, and Jacob. If they humbled themselves, confessed their sins, and sought the forgiveness of Yahweh Elohim, then He would restore them to their land.

Third Substantial Discourse

Most of the Book of Deuteronomy records Moses' speeches to the new generation of Israelites while they were encamped on the plains of Moab opposite Jericho. Nearly 40 years had passed since the previous generation had witnessed the glory of Yahweh Elohim atop Mt. Sinai, and they had embraced His covenant, enacted through His servant, Moses. However, because that generation had refused to trust the promise of Yahweh Elohim to give them the land of Canaan, they failed to enter the land from Kadesh-barnea. As a result of their apostasy, that entire generation had been condemned to die off in the wilderness. Only Caleb and Joshua had survived.

Thus, the purpose of Moses' speeches recorded in Deuteronomy was to prepare and equip the new generation of leaders and fighting men to carry out the conquest of Canaan. For this reason, I like to characterize this entire book as a **theology of conquest**. Moses' instruction was patently simple: If they were careful to remain faithful to the covenant with Yahweh Elohim enacted at Mt. Sinai, then they could be assured of the divine force multiplier promised in Leviticus 26:8. In other words, they would be an invincible military force; none of the Canaanite nations would be able to stand against them. However, if they rebelled against the covenant, then they would be defeated.

The entire 28th chapter of Deuteronomy amounts to a recapitulation of the 26th chapter of Leviticus. The 29th chapter records a renewal of the covenant of Mt. Sinai with the new generation, including further exhortation to remain faithful to it. The 30th chapter records the promise of restoration and revival of the nation, conditioned upon their returning to Yahweh Elohim in contrition, confession, and repentance.

Chain of Prophetic Proclamation

Figure 5-4 delineates the chain of prophetic proclamation that spans the entire 1,000-year period from the time of Moses to the time of Ezra and Nehemiah. Allow me now to touch upon each of the salient Scripture passages along this chain.

Moses. In concluding his speech to the people of Israel recorded in the Book of Deuteronomy, Moses states the following:

> I call heaven and earth to witness against you today, that I have set before you life and death, blessing and curse. Therefore **choose life**, that you and your offspring may live, loving Yahweh your Elohim, obeying His voice and holding fast to Him, for He is your life and length of days, that you may dwell in the land that Yahweh swore to your fathers, to Abraham, to Isaac, and to Jacob, to give them. [Deuteronomy 30:19-20, adapted from the ESV, emphasis added]

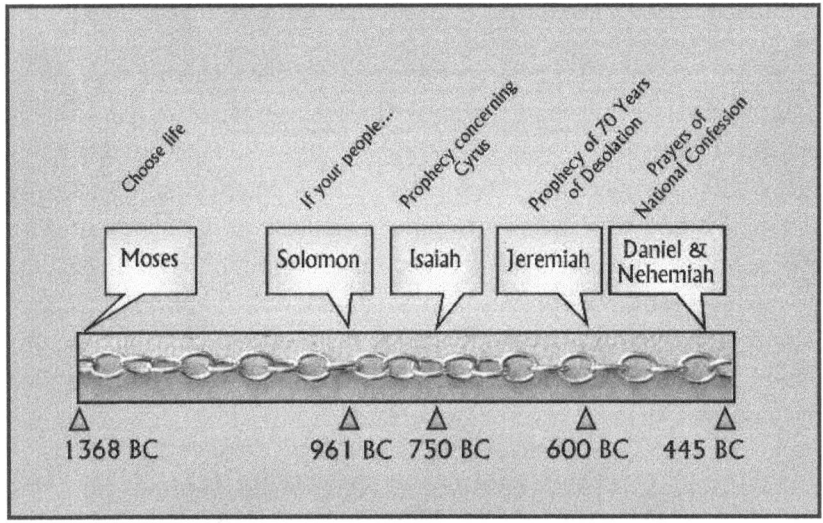

Figure 5-4. Prophetic Chain

Solomon. The trajectory of Israel's failure to keep the covenant with Yahweh is traced through the Early Prophets until we come to the time of David and Solomon. The entire Book of Judges is characterized by repeated cycles of apostasy, judgment, defeat and oppression by enemies, and gracious deliverance by Yahweh. Finally, under the leadership of David, who is described by Yahweh as a man after His own heart, Israel finally begins to realize and occupy the domain originally promised to Abraham in Genesis 15:18-21.

While David purposed to build a magnificent temple in honor of the name of Yahweh, Nathan the prophet informed him that he was not the one to build the temple, but rather his son would do so. This is recorded in the 7th chapter of 2 Samuel, a passage we have already considered. As recorded in the 22nd chapter of 1 Chronicles, David prepared a design for the temple, and he accumulated large quantities of the materials that would be needed for its construction.

After Solomon had completed construction of the temple to the name of Yahweh, he offered a prayer of dedication that is recorded in 1 Kings 8:12ff and 2 Chronicles 6:12ff. It is the record in 2 Chronicles upon which we focus.

As you trace through Solomon's dedicatory prayer, you will note that he makes repeated reference to the curses pronounced by Moses at the conclusion of Deuteronomy. And he pleads for Yahweh to be merciful and gracious in responding favorably to prayers offered by the people of Israel. Yahweh responds to Solomon's plea as follows:

> Then Yahweh appeared to Solomon in the night and said to him: "I have heard your prayer and have chosen this place for Myself as a house of sacrifice. When I shut up the heavens so that there is no rain, or command the locust to devour the land, or send pestilence among My people, **if My people who are called by My name humble themselves, and pray and seek My face and turn from their wicked ways, then I will hear from heaven and will forgive their sin and heal their land.** Now My eyes will be open and My ears attentive to the prayer that is made in this place. [2 Chronicles 7:12-15, adapted from the ESV, emphasis added]

This promise is the basis for the theology of restoration, the objective of which is the revival and restoration of Israel after a period of chastening on account of her manifold sins and transgressions.

Cyrus. Isaiah's remarkable prophecy concerning Cyrus is recorded in Isaiah 44:28 – 45:7. Isaiah's prophetic ministry began during the reign of Uzziah, king of Judah (ca. 767-740 BC), and ended during the reign of Hezekiah, king of Judah (ca. 715-686 BC). Cyrus the Great conquered Babylon in 539 BC, and in the 1st year of his reign (ca. 538-537 BC), he issued the decree allowing the Jews to return to their homeland. This decree is recorded in Ezra 1:2-4. Therefore, Isaiah's prophecy concerning Cyrus predates the issuance of the decree by at least 150 years.

Jeremiah. Jeremiah's prophetic ministry began toward the end of the reign of Josiah, king of Judah (ca. 640-609 BC), and it continued through the conquest of Jerusalem by the Babylonians in 586 BC. His prophecy of the 70 years of desolation for Judah and Jerusalem is stated in Jeremiah 25:11, and the text of the letter Jeremiah sent to the exiles in Babylon is recorded in Jeremiah 29:1-23. The beginning of the 70-year period is keyed to the first deportation, which occurred in 605 BC. Therefore, the end of this period would be 535 BC; that is, after Cyrus conquered Babylon and approximately the time of his decree to allow the Jews to return to their homeland.

Daniel. Daniel's prayer of confession and intercession on behalf of his people is recorded in the 9th chapter of the Book of Daniel. The motivation for Daniel's prayer, as explicitly stated in Daniel 9:2, was Jeremiah's vision of the 70 years of Jerusalem's desolation. This prophecy was stated in the letter which Jeremiah addressed to the exiles. The text of the letter is recorded in the 29th chapter of the Book of Jeremiah.

Nehemiah. Nehemiah's prayer of confession and intercession is recorded in Nehemiah 1:4-11. It was motivated by the report of Hanani concerning the state of Jerusalem.

> The remnant there in the province who had survived the exile is in great trouble and shame. The wall of Jerusalem is broken down, and its gates are destroyed by fire.
> [Nehemiah 1:3, ESV]

"If My People..." The prayer of Daniel coupled with that of Nehemiah evidently satisfied the condition prescribed by Yahweh in 2 Chronicles 7:14. The decree of Artaxerxes, which authorized Nehemiah to restore and rebuild Jerusalem, was issued in 445 BC. (It is noteworthy that the date of this decree marks the beginning of the Vision of the Seventy Weeks recorded in Daniel 9:24-27.)

The end of the chain of Figure 5-4 corresponds to the national revival which is recorded in the 8th chapter of the Book of Nehemiah. It is noteworthy that the outpouring of the Spirit of Yahweh to bring about this spiritual renewal of the people of Israel occurred only after the walls and gates of Jerusalem had been restored.

The Wisdom Literature. The Wisdom Literature – especially Job, Psalms, and Proverbs – are permeated with passages that contribute to the enrichment of our understanding of the CCB motif. In particular, the epic story of Job places in evidence the intersection of sanctification through suffering with the covenant of conditional blessing. As clearly manifested in Job's experience, the operation of the covenant of conditional blessing does not translate to a life that is filled with material comfort and prosperity. Instead, as we are instructed by the writer of Hebrews, we must "not regard lightly the discipline of Yahweh, nor be weary when reproved by Him. For Yahweh disciplines the one He loves, and chastises every son whom He receives." [Hebrews 12:5-6, which is derived from Proverbs 3:11-12, adapted from the ESV] Thus, through the testimony of the writers of the Wisdom Literature, **the blessing of Yahweh** translates to true spiritual prosperity and heavenly riches, not merely to material prosperity and comfort in this life.

Of the many passages in the Book of Psalms which provide commentary on the CCB motif, Psalms 34:12-16 is especially noteworthy because it is quoted by the Apostle Peter in 1 Peter 3:8-12. Also, as I recently listened through Psalm 119, I was struck by the number of passages in this psalm which enrich our understanding of the CCB motif.

New Covenant of Conditional Blessing

I will now seek to place in evidence the fact that the CCB motif continues under the new covenant inaugurated by Jesus Christ. In keeping with the flow of Figure 5-1, I will briefly touch upon several passages in the

Christian Scriptures which are either explicitly or implicitly conditional in nature.

1 John 1:9. In this verse, the Apostle John states,

> If we confess (= *homologeo*) our sins, He is faithful and just to forgive us our sins and to cleanse us from all unrighteousness. [1 John 1:9, ESV]

Note that the Greek word translated as "confess" is *homologeo*, which literally means "to say the same thing." In other words, to confess means to represent our sin as God does, or to agree with God concerning His representation of our sin.

The classic example of confession in Scripture is seen in 2 Samuel 12:13 when David confessed his sin of adultery and murder before Nathan the prophet. David's prayer of confession is recorded in the 51st Psalm.

The purpose of confession is not only to receive forgiveness from God, but, more importantly, to restore fellowship with God. So long as we harbor unconfessed sin, our communion with God is broken. This means that we cannot be filled with His Spirit, and therefore we have no divine power for facing the adversities of life or for performing ministry.

What is the implication of the conditional promise of 1 John 1:9? If, and only if, we represent our sins and transgressions as God does will He forgive us, cleanse us from all unrighteousness, and restore our fellowship with Himself. However, if we refuse to represent our sins and transgressions as He does, then He will withhold forgiveness and cleansing, and we will remain divorced from fellowship with Him.

Matthew 7:24-27. While the word "if" does not occur in this passage, conditionality is clearly present.

> Everyone then who hears these words of Mine and **does them** will be like a wise man who built his house on the rock. And the rain fell, and the floods came, and the winds blew and beat on that house, but it did not fall, because it had been founded on the rock. And everyone who hears these words of Mine and **does not do them** will be like a foolish man who built his house on the sand. And the rain fell, and the floods came, and the winds blew and beat

against that house, and it fell, and great was the fall of it. [Matthew 7:24-27, ESV]

What is the point of this passage? If we not only absorb Jesus' teachings and give mental assent to them, but if we also practice them, then our way will be firmly established, and we will be able to withstand the storms that life brings against us. However, if we merely absorb Jesus' teachings and give mental assent to them, but if we fail to practice them, then our way will not be firmly established, and we will collapse when subjected to the storms of life.

John 15:7. In this verse, Jesus states a remarkable promise concerning prayer.

> If you abide in Me, and My words abide in you, ask whatever you wish, and it will be done for you. [John 15:7, ESV]

A similar prayer promise is found in Matthew 17:20 and Luke 17:6, of which the Matthew passage is quoted below:

> For truly, I say to you, if you have faith like a grain of mustard seed, you will say to this mountain, "Move from here to there," and it will move, and nothing will be impossible for you. [Matthew 17:20, ESV]

I conclude from these three passages that having faith to believe God will answer our prayers is subsumed beneath abiding in Christ and having His word abiding in us. In other words, if we are abiding in Christ, and if His faith and His word are abiding in us, then we will also trust that God will answer our prayers. However, if we are not abiding in Christ, and if His faith and His word are not abiding in us, then there is no guarantee that God will hear and answer our prayers. As I make this assertion, I am mindful of the fact that however much we endeavor to abide in Christ, and have His faith and His word abide in us, we inevitably do so imperfectly and incompletely. And so God hears and answers our prayers, not on the basis of any merit of ours, but on the basis of His grace and His mercy.

1 Peter 3:8-12. This passage includes a quotation from Psalm 34:12-16, and it is a clear restatement of the oft-repeated formula in the Hebrew

Scriptures that Yahweh blesses those who walk in His way, and He opposes those who stubbornly refuse to walk in that way.

> Finally, all of you, have unity of mind, sympathy, brotherly love, a tender heart, and a humble mind. 9 Do not repay evil for evil or reviling for reviling, but on the contrary, bless, for to this you were called, **that you may obtain a blessing**. For
>
> > "Whoever desires to love life and see good days,
> > > let him keep his tongue from evil and his lips from speaking deceit;
> > let him turn away from evil and do good;
> > > let him seek peace and pursue it.
> > For the eyes of Yahweh are on the righteous,
> > > and his ears are open to their prayer.
> > But the face of Yahweh is against those who do evil."
>
> [1 Peter 3:8-12, adapted from the ESV, emphasis added]

Note carefully the emphasized phrase in the 9th verse; this passage tells us how to live under the blessing of Yahweh. Thus, according to the Apostle Peter, the covenant of conditional blessing continues to operate under the terms of the new covenant enacted through the shed blood of Christ, just as it did under the old covenant enacted at Mt. Sinai.

> ***If you desire to live under the blessing of Yahweh, then walk in His way. If you refuse, then you can anticipate that He will oppose you, and you will live under His curse.***

"To him who overcomes..." Each of the letters that the risen Christ addresses to the seven churches in Asia Minor concludes with this formula: "To him who conquers..." The English phrase, "him who conquers," is represented in the Greek by a single word, *nika*, which literally means "the victor," or the one who overcomes, prevails, subdues, or conquers. As we examine the seven specific things which Christ promises to give to the ones who overcome, they all represent the eternal fruits of salvation. This succession of promises culminates in Revelation 21:7, which states that a place in the eternal city, the New Jerusalem, will be granted to the one who overcomes. However, those who do not overcome, "the cowardly, the faithless, the detestable, the murderers, the sexually immoral, sorcerers, idolaters, and all liars, their portion will be in the lake that burns with fire and sulfur, which is the second death." (Revelation 21:8, adapted from the ESV)

What does Christ mean by this? Clearly, from these passages in the Book of Revelation, the glorious, eternal fruits of salvation are granted, not to those who merely give mental assent to the gospel of salvation in Jesus Christ, but rather to those who resolutely follow in His way. Throughout the Christian Scriptures the life of the disciple is likened to a marathon race or to a great athletic contest. The following passage from the pen of the Apostle Paul provides insight into what Jesus means by the phrase, "to him who overcomes":

> Do you not know that in a race all the runners run, but only one receives the prize? So run that you may obtain it. Every athlete exercises self-control in all things. They do it to receive a perishable wreath, but we an imperishable. So I do not run aimlessly; I do not box as one beating the air. But I discipline my body and keep it under control, lest after preaching to others I myself should be disqualified. [1 Corinthians 9:24-27, ESV]

Clearly, Paul recognized a certain conditionality with regard to the eternal fruits of salvation, just like there is conditionality in a marathon race or in an athletic contest. Not all those who enter a race cross the finish line first, and not all those who enter the arena emerge as victors. This is how I would express what it means to overcome: the person who is truly in Christ, and in whom the faith and word of Christ are truly abiding, will persevere to the end; he will overcome all the obstacles and adversities that God allows to come against him to test the genuineness of his faith; he will, with patient endurance, finish the course marked out for him.

Concluding Comments Regarding the Covenant of Conditional Blessing

I conclude this section on the CCB motif by quoting a passage from the Book of Hebrews in the way I have memorized it.

> And all these, having gained approval on account of their faith, died without receiving that which was promised, God

having prepared something better for us, so that only together with us would they be made perfect. Therefore, since we are surrounded with such a great cloud of witnesses, let us also lay aside every encumbrance that would slow us down and that besetting sin which so readily entangles our feet to trip us up, and let us run with patient endurance the course that is marked out for us, looking off and away unto Jesus, the source and perfecter of faith, who for the joy set before Him endured the cross, despising its shame, and has sat down at the right hand of the throne of God. [Hebrews 11:39 – 12:2, adapted from the ESV]

Thus, Jesus Christ, Himself, is the ultimate example of what He means by "the one who overcomes."

Questions for Discussion

1. Select three passages from the Christian Scriptures that instruct us that the Torah remains, in some sense, the fountainhead of wisdom for the disciple of Christ. In your own words, discuss what these passages teach you concerning the relevance of the Torah to the disciple of Christ. (**Hint**: explore the Sermon on the Mount in the 5th through the 7th chapters of Matthew, the first three chapters of Romans, and the 8th chapter of Romans.)

2. Select three of the integrative motifs which are the most meaningful to you and which are other than the five motifs discussed above. In your own words, discuss the utility of each in helping you to apply the wisdom of the Torah to your own life and ministry.

3. In your own words, discuss the ways in which the Christian gospel is rooted in the wisdom of the Torah.

4. Select two passages from the Christian Scriptures that express the CCB motif, either explicitly or implicitly. Your two passages should be different from those discussed above. Discuss the significance of each passage. (**Hint**: For one of your passages, consider Matthew 25:31-46.)

Notes & Reflections

Use the space below to record additional insights and commentary resulting from your studies thus far.

Chapter 6.
The Two-Part Christian Gospel

Chapter Overview

The two-part Christian gospel sets forth God's purpose and program for completely obliterating the effects of the invasion of evil, sin, and death into the cosmos. It consists of two equally important, mutually complementary, and interconnected aspects or components, which are the **gospel of the kingdom of God** and the **gospel of God**. The summary presented in Table 6-1, which continues for several pages, includes the essentials of these two aspects of the Christian gospel. There are a number of Scripture passages for you to look up and read in context. Following the Scripture passages in Table 6-1 are five questions to guide your study and reflection.

The purpose of this chapter is not to present a comprehensive, in-depth analysis of the Christian gospel, but rather to serve as a gateway and introduction to Parts Two and Three of the WitW study, in which each of the aspects are studied and discussed at length. In the process of introducing Parts Two and Three, I will endeavor to cast a vision of the glory and magnificence of the gospel, which, like the very nature and character of God Himself, transcends the power of human language to adequately represent it. In fact, the Christian gospel is like a many-faceted diamond, exquisite in beauty, brilliance, and clarity. While being complex and rich, it is also simple to the extent that a child can understand its essence.

Learning Objective

The learning objective for this chapter is to impart an overall understanding of the Christian gospel; that is, the good news of salvation which is made possible by the atoning death, burial, and resurrection of Jesus Christ. While we naturally focus on the benefits of salvation that accrue to each of us individually, the scope of the gospel is cosmic and universal.

One manifestation of the superficial understanding of Scripture possessed by the average disciple of Christ is the fact that he is likely to have difficulty articulating the Christian gospel. Exacerbating this issue is the fact that the gospel has not been accurately and fully proclaimed in most churches for almost two centuries. In fact, the gospel preached and taught by Christ and the apostles has been seriously corrupted. Thus, the purpose of this chapter – indeed, the entire WitW study – is to overcome these difficulties toward the goal that the disciple of Christ is equipped, not only to explain the gospel, but also, and more importantly, to practice it in his life and ministry.

Discovering the Christian Gospel

In chapter 4 we discussed the proper method for discovering the biblical author's intended meaning from a given passage or book. In fact, we first discussed some general principles of biblical interpretation derived from Scripture itself. Then we discussed specific principles that apply to each of four kinds of biblical literature: namely, narrative, Hebrew poetry, didactic or teaching literature, and apocalyptic literature.

In chapter 5 we identified fourteen motifs or themes that surface in the Torah – the five books of Moses – and which are progressively developed as we read through the Bible from Genesis to Revelation. The progressive development of each of the motifs is delineated in Figure 5-1, which emphasizes the fact that as a given motif passes through the Christ Event – designated by the Greek letter Chi (**X**) in Figure 2-1 – it acquires a new covenant embodiment. Two of the motifs are **the invasion of evil, sin, and death** and **the gospel**, both of which we traced through Scripture in accordance with Figure 5-1. That discussion provides necessary background for our discussion of the two-part Christian gospel. Therefore, if you feel the need to refresh your understanding of those two motifs, it would beneficial for you to review the discussion in chapter 5.

The Importance of Discovering the Christian Gospel

It would be entirely appropriate and correct to assert that the entire Bible is gospel – that is, good news of salvation whereby God will one day obliterate all the effects of the invasion of evil, sin, and death into the cosmos. However, for us to properly understand the gospel in order to effectively share it with other people and to practice it in our lives and ministries, I think you would agree that we need to distill its essence from Scripture. How should we go about this task? I suggest that the following five questions will guide and help us discover the essence of the gospel as we read through Scripture:

1. Regarding any given biblical passage, why is the passage good news?

2. Are there promised blessings specified in the passage; if so, what are they, and why are they beneficial?

3. Are there conditions specified for receiving the promised blessings; if so, what are they?

4. Does the passage touch on an obedient lifestyle by way of application; if so, what does it require us to practice?

5. Finally, which aspect of the Christian gospel is in view: the gospel of the kingdom of God, or the gospel of God, or are both equally in view?

As emphasized in chapter 4, it is critical that we read and interpret Scripture in context, and so I will now endeavor to guide you through a process of discovery as we, together, seek an understanding of the essence of the Christian gospel. This process will entail our examining a number of Scripture passages which are listed in Table 6-1. Each passage is like a piece of a puzzle, and our task is to assemble the pieces into an entire picture that represents the Christian gospel in all its magnificence.

Introduction to Table 6-1

Table 6-1 presents a summary of our thought process in discovering the essence of the Christian gospel. The first part of the table focuses on Scriptures which seem to relate to the entire gospel – that is, both its aspects. The second part of the table is divided into two columns, where the column on the left lists Scriptures that seem to relate to the gospel of the kingdom of God, and the column on the right lists Scriptures that seem to relate to the gospel of God. At the beginning of both the first and second parts of the table, keynote Scriptures are listed that are especially noteworthy.

For example, the keynote Scripture for the first part of the table is Revelation 14:6-7, which addresses the **eternal gospel** announced by an angel during the times of the end. And what is the eternal gospel? That we should "Fear God and give Him glory, because the hour of His judgment has come. Worship the Maker of heaven and earth, the sea and springs of water." Regarding this passage, let us now attempt to answer the five questions.

1. As we read through the Book of Revelation, John repeatedly emphasizes the fact that the "inhabitants of the earth," to which the eternal gospel is addressed, are disinclined to repent of their prideful rebellion against God, fear Him, give Him glory, and worship Him as Creator of all things – the responses to the eternal gospel called for in the passage. However, the implication of the passage that I believe John would have us see is this: all those who **do respond** to the wave upon wave of judgments by repenting of their prideful rebellion against God, fearing Him who is the author of those judgments, giving Him glory, and worshiping Him will be saved.

2. As stated above, the blessing of eternal salvation is not literally stated in the passage, but is implied by it.

3. The conditions specified in the passage are the three responses to the eternal gospel: fear God, give Him glory, and worship Him.

4. This passage does not touch on an obedient lifestyle, except as regards the three responses identified above.

5. The passage seems to relate to the entire Christian gospel, although the three required responses intersect more with the gospel of the kingdom of God than with the gospel of God.

For each of the passages listed in the first and second parts of Table 6-1, attempt to answer the five questions as a means for discovering the aspect of the Christian gospel that is in view in the passage.

The third part of Table 6-1 summarizes each of the two aspects of the Christian gospel under the following eight headings: (1) Roots, (2) Emphasis, (3) Scope, (4) Confrontation, (5) Focus, (6) Response, (7) Perversions, and, (8) Reflections.

Table 6-1. Summary of the Two-Part Christian Gospel

The Christian Gospel = The Eternal Gospel
Keynote Scripture: **Revelation 14:6-7** – Then I saw another angel flying high overhead, having the **eternal gospel** to announce to the inhabitants of the earth – to every nation, tribe, language, and people. He spoke with a loud voice: **"Fear God and give Him glory**, because the hour of His judgment has come. **Worship** the Maker of heaven and earth, the sea and springs of water."
Other Scriptures: **Romans 8:19-21** – For the creation eagerly waits with anticipation for God's sons to be revealed. For the creation was subjected to futility – not willingly, but because of Him who subjected it – in the hope that the creation itself will also be set free from the bondage of corruption into the glorious freedom of God's children. **Colossians 1:20** – ... Through Him to reconcile everything to Himself by making peace through the blood of His cross – whether things on earth or things in heaven. **Titus 2:11-14** – For the grace of God has appeared with salvation for all people, instructing us to deny godlessness and worldly lusts and to live in a sensible, righteous, and godly way in the present age, while we wait for the blessed hope and appearing of the glory of our great God and Savior, Jesus Christ. He gave Himself for us to redeem us from all lawlessness and to cleanse for Himself a people for His own possession, eager to do good works. **Titus 3:4-7** – But when the goodness of God and His love for mankind appeared, He saved us – not by works of righteousness that we had done, but according to His mercy, through the washing of regeneration and renewal by the Holy Spirit. He poured out this Spirit on us abundantly through Jesus Christ our Savior, so that having been justified by His grace, we may become heirs with the hope of eternal life.

Table 6-1. Summary of the Two-Part Christian Gospel – Cont.:

The Christian Gospel = The Eternal Gospel
Other Scriptures – Cont.:
Hebrews 6:17-20 – Because God wanted to show His unchangeable purpose even more clearly to the heirs of the promise, He guaranteed it with an oath, so that through two unchangeable things, in which it is impossible for God to lie, we who have fled for refuge might have strong encouragement to seize the hope set before us. We have this hope as an anchor for our lives, safe and secure. It enters the inner sanctuary behind the curtain. Jesus has entered there on our behalf as a forerunner, because He has become a high priest forever in the order of Melchizedek.
Hebrews 7:24-25 – But because He remains forever, He holds His priesthood permanently. Therefore, He is able to save to the uttermost all those who come to God through Him, since He always lives to intercede for them.
<u>Introduction</u>:
The Christian gospel consists of the following two complementary and interconnected aspects: the **gospel of the kingdom of God** dominates the Synoptic Gospels and the Book of Acts; and the **gospel of God** is introduced by the Gospel of John, and it dominates the writings of Paul, especially the Epistle to the Romans.

The Gospel of the Kingdom of God	The Gospel of God
<u>Keynote Scripture:</u>	<u>Keynote Scriptures:</u>
Mark 1:14-15 – After John was arrested, Jesus went to Galilee, preaching the good news of the kingdom of God: "The time is fulfilled, and the kingdom of God has come near. **Repent** and **believe** in the good news!"	**John 1:10-13** – He was in the world, and the world was created through Him, yet the world did not recognize Him. He came to His own, and His own people did not receive Him. But to all who did **receive** Him, He gave them

Table 6-1. Summary of the Two-Part Christian Gospel – Cont.:

The Gospel of the Kingdom of God	The Gospel of God
	Keynote Scriptures – Cont.: the right to be children of God, to those who **believe** in His name, who were born, not of blood, or of the will of the flesh, or of the will of man, but of God. **Romans 10:9** - If you **confess** with your mouth, "Jesus is Yahweh," and **believe** in your heart that God raised Him from the dead, you will be saved.
<u>**Key Verbs:**</u> ■ Repent ■ Believe	<u>**Key Verbs:**</u> ■ Confess ■ Receive ■ Believe
<u>**Unfolding Revelation:**</u> **Deuteronomy 30:1-20** – "When all these things happen to you – the blessings and curses I have set before you – and you come to your senses while you are in all the nations where Yahweh your Elohim has driven you, and you and your children return to Yahweh your Elohim and obey	<u>**Unfolding Revelation:**</u> **Genesis 3:15** – I will put hostility between you and the woman, and between your seed and her seed. He will strike your head, and you will strike his heel. **Genesis 15:6** – Abram believed Yahweh, and He credited it to him as righteousness.

Table 6-1. Summary of the Two-Part Christian Gospel – Cont.:

The Gospel of the Kingdom of God	The Gospel of God
Unfolding Revelation – Cont.: Him with all your heart and all your soul by doing everything I am giving you today, then He will restore your fortunes, have compassion on you, and gather you again from all the peoples where Yahweh your Elohim has scattered you... This command that I give you today is certainly not too difficult or beyond your reach. It is not in heaven so that you have to ask, 'Who will go up to heaven, get it for us, and proclaim it to us so that we may follow it?' And it is not across the sea so that you have to ask, 'Who will cross the sea, get it for us, and proclaim it to us so that we may follow it?' But the message is very near you, in your mouth and in your heart, so that you may follow it. See, today I have set before you life and prosperity, death and adversity. For I am commanding you today to love Yahweh your Elohim, to walk in His ways, and to keep His commands, statutes, and ordinances, so that you may live and multiply, and Yahweh your Elohim may bless you in the land you are entering to possess...	Unfolding Revelation – Cont.: **Jeremiah 31:31-40** – "Look, the days are coming" – this is Yahweh's declaration – "when I will make a new covenant with the house of Israel and with the house of Judah. This one will not be like the covenant I made with their ancestors when I took them by the hand to bring them out of the land of Egypt – a covenant they broke even though I had married them" – Yahweh's declaration. "Instead, this is the covenant I will make with the house of Israel after those days" – Yahweh's declaration. "I will put My teaching within them and write it on their hearts. I will be their God, and they will be My people..." **John 3:16-19** – For God loved the world in this way: He gave His One and Only Son, so that everyone who believes into Him will not perish but have eternal life. For God did not send His Son into the world that He might condemn the world, but that the world might be saved through Him. Anyone who believes into

Table 6-1. Summary of the Two-Part Christian Gospel – Cont.:

The Gospel of the Kingdom of God	The Gospel of God
Unfolding Revelation – Cont.: **Psalm 2:1-12** – Why do the nations rebel and the peoples plot in vain? The kings of the earth take their stand, and the rulers conspire together against Yahweh and His Anointed One: "Let us tear off their chains and free ourselves from their restraints." The One enthroned in heaven laughs; Adonai ridicules them. Then He speaks to them in His anger and terrifies them in His wrath: "I have consecrated My King on Zion, My holy mountain." I will declare Yahweh's decree: He said to Me, "You are My Son; today I have become Your Father. Ask of Me, and I will make the nations Your inheritance and the ends of the earth Your possession. You will break them with a rod of iron; You will shatter them like pottery." So now, kings, be wise; receive instruction, you judges of the earth. Serve Yahweh with reverential awe and rejoice with trembling. Pay homage to the Son or He will be angry and you will perish in your rebellion, for His anger may	Unfolding Revelation – Cont.: Him is not condemned, but anyone who does not believe is already condemned, because he has not believed into the name of the One and Only Son of God. **Acts 16:29-33** – Then the jailer called for lights, rushed in, and fell down trembling before Paul and Silas. Then he escorted them out and said, "Sirs, what must I do to be saved?" So they said, "Believe upon the Lord Jesus, and you will be saved – you and your household." Then they spoke the message of the Lord to him along with everyone in his house. He took them the same hour of the night and washed their wounds. Right away he and all his family were baptized. **Romans 3:21-26** – But now, apart from the law, God's righteousness has been revealed – attested by the Law and the Prophets – that is, God's righteousness through the faith of Jesus Christ, into all who believe, since there is no distinction. For all sinned and fall short of the glory of God.

Table 6-1. Summary of the Two-Part Christian Gospel – Cont.:

The Gospel of the Kingdom of God	The Gospel of God
Unfolding Revelation – Cont.: ignite at any moment. All those who take refuge in Him are happy. **Zechariah 9:9** – Rejoice greatly, Daughter Zion! Shout in triumph, Daughter Jerusalem! Look, your King is coming to you; He is righteous and victorious, humble and riding on a donkey, on a colt, the foal of a donkey. **Acts 2:37-39** – When they heard this, they came under deep conviction and said to Peter and the rest of the apostles: "Brothers, what must we do?" "Repent," Peter said to them, "and be baptized, each of you, in the name of Jesus Christ for the forgiveness of your sins, and you will receive the gift of the Holy Spirit. For the promise is for you and for your children, and for all who are far off, as many as the Lord our God will call." **Acts 10:43** – All the prophets testify about Him that through His name everyone who believes into Him will receive forgiveness of sins.	Unfolding Revelation – Cont.: They are justified freely by His grace through the redemption that is in Christ Jesus. God presented Him as a propitiation through faith in His blood, to demonstrate His righteousness, because in His restraint God passed over the sins previously committed. God presented Him to demonstrate His righteousness at the present time, so that He would be righteous and declare righteous the one who has the faith of Jesus. **Romans 8:28-30** – We know that all things work together for the good of those who love God: those who are called according to His purpose. For those He foreknew He also predestined to be conformed to the image of His Son, so that He would be the firstborn among many brothers. And those He predestined, He also called; and those He called, He also justified; and those He justified, He also glorified. **Romans 10:17** – So faith comes from what is heard, and what is heard comes through the message about Christ.

Table 6-1. Summary of the Two-Part Christian Gospel – Cont.:

The Gospel of the Kingdom of God	The Gospel of God
Unfolding Revelation – Cont.: **Acts 13:29-38** – When they had fulfilled all that had been written about Him, they took Him down from the tree and put Him in a tomb. But God raised Him from the dead, and He appeared for many days to those who came with Him from Galilee to Jerusalem, who are now His witnesses to the people. And we ourselves proclaim to you the good news of the promise that was made to our ancestors. God has fulfilled this for us, their children, by raising up Jesus... Therefore He also says in another passage, You will not allow Your Holy One to see decay. For David, after serving his own generation in God's plan, fell asleep, was buried with his fathers, and decayed. But the One God raised up did not decay. Therefore, let it be known to you, brothers, that through this man forgiveness of sins is being proclaimed to you... **Acts 14:15-18** – "Men! Why are you doing these things? We are men also, with the same nature as you, and we are proclaiming	Unfolding Revelation – Cont.: **1 Corinthians 15:1-8** – Now brothers, I want to clarify for you the gospel I proclaimed to you; you received it and have taken your stand on it. You are also saved by it, if you hold to the message I proclaimed to you – unless you believed for no purpose. For I passed on to you as most important what I also received: that Christ died for our sins according to the Scriptures, that He was buried, that He was raised on the third day according to the Scriptures, and that He appeared to Cephas, then to the Twelve. Then He appeared to over 500 brothers at one time; most of them are still alive, but some have fallen asleep. Then He appeared to James, then to all the apostles. Last of all, as to one abnormally born, He also appeared to me. **Ephesians 2:8-10** – For you are saved by grace through faith, and this is not from yourselves; it is God's gift – not from works, so that no one can boast. For we are His workmanship, created in Christ Jesus for good works,

Table 6-1. Summary of the Two-Part Christian Gospel – Cont.:

The Gospel of the Kingdom of God	The Gospel of God
Unfolding Revelation – Cont.: good news to you, that you should turn from these worthless things to the living God, who made the heaven, the earth, the sea and everything in them. In past generations He allowed all the nations to go their own way, although He did not leave Himself without a witness, since He did what is good by giving you rain from heaven and fruitful seasons and satisfying your hearts with food and happiness." Even though they said these things, they barely stopped the crowds from sacrificing to them. **Acts 17:22-31** – Then Paul stood in the middle of the Areopagus and said: "Men of Athens! I see that you are extremely religious in every respect. For as your worship, I even found an altar on which was inscribed: TO AN UNKNOWN GOD. Therefore, what you worship in ignorance, this I proclaim to you. The God who made the world and everything in it – He is Lord of heaven and earth and does not live in shrines made by hands. Neither is He served by human	Unfolding Revelation – Cont.: which God prepared ahead of time so that we should walk in them. **Hebrews 4:2** – For indeed we have had good news preached to us, just as they also; but the word they heard did not profit them, because it was not united by faith in those who heard. **Note**: In chapter 5 this verse was unpacked in the course of discussing The Gospel motif. There we noted that the gospel preached to Israel had two parts: (1) deliverance from bondage in Egypt; and, (2) deliverance into rest in the promised land after a period of conflict and conquest. The parallel gospel preached to us also has two parts: (1) deliverance from bondage to evil, sin, and death; and, (2) deliverance into eternal rest after a period of conflict and conquest. **2 Peter 1:3-11** – His divine power has granted to us everything required for life and godliness through the true knowledge of Him who called us according to His own glory and excellence.

Table 6-1. Summary of the Two-Part Christian Gospel – Cont.:

The Gospel of the Kingdom of God	**The Gospel of God**
Unfolding Revelation – Cont.: hands, as though He needed anything, since He Himself gives everyone life and breath and all things. From one man He has made every nationality to live over the whole earth and has determined their appointed times and the and the boundaries of where they live. He did this so they might seek God, and perhaps they might reach out and find Him, though He is not far from each one of us. For in Him we live and move and exist, as even some of your own poets have said, 'For we are also His offspring.' Being God's offspring then, we shouldn't think that the divine nature is like gold or silver or stone, an image fashioned by human art and imagination. Therefore, having overlooked the times of ignorance, God now commands all people everywhere to repent, because He has set a day when He is going to judge the world in righteousness by the Man He has appointed. He has provided proof of this to everyone by raising Him from the dead."	Unfolding Revelation – Cont.: By these He has granted to us His precious and magnificent promises, so that by them you may become partakers of the divine nature, having escaped the corruption that is in the world by lust. For this very reason, make every effort to supplement your faith with moral excellence, moral excellence with experiential knowledge, experiential knowledge with self-control, self-control with patient endurance, patient endurance with godliness, godliness with brotherly affection, and brotherly affection with self-sacrificing love. For if these qualities are yours and are increasing, they will keep you from being useless or unfruitful in the knowledge of our Lord Jesus Christ. The per-son who lacks these things is blind and shortsighted and has forgotten the cleansing from his past sins. Therefore, brothers, make every effort to confirm your calling and election, because if you do these things you will never stumble.

Table 6-1. Summary of the Two-Part Christian Gospel – Cont.:

The Gospel of the Kingdom of God	The Gospel of God
	Unfolding Revelation – Cont.: For in this way, entry into the eternal kingdom of our Lord and Savior Jesus Christ will be richly supplied to you.
Questions for Discussion: Read each Scripture passage listed above in its context, and then discuss the following questions: ■ In an overall sense, why is the passage good news? ■ Are there promised blessings specified in the passage; if so, what are they, and why are they beneficial? ■ Are there conditions specified for receiving the promised blessings; if so, what are they? ■ Does the passage touch on obedient lifestyle by way of application; if so, what does it require us to practice? ■ Which aspect of the Christian gospel (= eternal gospel) is in view: the gospel of the kingdom of God, or the gospel of God; or are both equally in view?	
The Gospel of the Kingdom of God	The Gospel of God
Roots. The gospel of the kingdom of God is rooted in the suzerain / vassal treaty enacted by Yahweh Elohim with Israel at Mt. Sinai. It is confirmed in the covenant of Yahweh with David,	**Roots**. The gospel of God is rooted in the *protoevangelium* of Genesis 3:15. It is announced in Yahweh's covenant with Abraham in Genesis 12:1ff, confirmed by the solemn blood

Table 6-1. Summary of the Two-Part Christian Gospel – Cont.:

The Gospel of the Kingdom of God	**The Gospel of God**
Roots – Cont.: and it is announced through the prophecies of the Hebrew Scriptures.	Roots – Cont.: covenant ceremony of Genesis 15:1ff, and subject to the new covenant announced in Jeremiah 31:31ff.
Emphasis. The gospel of the kingdom of God emphasizes the truth, righteousness, and justice of God in His rule over men and nations.	**Emphasis**. The gospel of God emphasizes the sovereign grace of God in obliterating the effects of evil, sin, and death and granting eternal life to those who love and fear Him.
Scope. The scope of both the gospel of the kingdom of God and the gospel of God is both cosmic and eternal; that is, it embraces all time and space.	
The Gospel of the Kingdom of God	**The Gospel of God**
Confrontation. The gospel of the kingdom of God directly confronts the core of human iniquity, which is prideful rebellion against Christ's righteous rule as king of the cosmos.	**Confrontation**. The gospel of God directly confronts human bondage to evil, sin, and death.
Focus. The gospel of the kingdom of God is focused upon Jesus Christ as King of kings and Lord of lords as presented through the narrative of the Synoptic Gospels, especially Matthew's Gospel.	**Focus**. The gospel of God is focused upon the atoning death, burial, and resurrection of Jesus Christ, which makes possible God's gracious gifts of righteousness, regeneration, sanctification, glorification, and eternal life.

Table 6-1. Summary of the Two-Part Christian Gospel – Cont.:

The Gospel of the Kingdom of God	The Gospel of God
Response. The proper human response to the gospel of the kingdom of God is to **repent** and **believe** in accordance with the keynote passage, Mark 1:14. This entails a turning from prideful rebellion with wholehearted repentance and submission to Christ's kingly rule.	**Response**. The proper human response to the gospel of God is to **receive** and **believe** in accordance with the keynote passage, John 1:12. This entails a whole-hearted embracing of Jesus Christ as both Savior and Lord.

Perversions. Perversions of the Christian gospel (= eternal gospel) generally fall into the following two broad categories:

- **Antinomianism**, which literally means **against law**. Those who subscribe to antinomianism believe that obedience to the law of Moses, or any command of Scripture for that matter, is entirely optional. One needs only to trust in the gospel for salvation, which is entirely a gift of God's grace. In fact, saving faith is reduced to mere mental assent to the facts of the gospel. Paul's question in the opening verses of the 6th chapter of Romans expresses the essence of antinomianism:

   > What should we say then? Should we continue in sin so that grace may multiply? Absolutely not! How can we who died to sin still live in it?

- **Legalism**, which is the case of **too much law**. Those who subscribe to some form of legalism add requirements to the gospel which a person must practice in order to be genuinely saved. While the legal requirements may have changed, the essence of legalism today is the same as that which gave rise to the Jerusalem Council recorded in the 15th chapter of Acts.

Table 6-1. Summary of the Two-Part Christian Gospel – Cont.:

Reflections. The Christian gospel, like God Himself, transcends human language – even the inspired language of Scripture. It was settled in the councils of eternity past as the plan by which God would conclusively conquer the mystery of inequity, the spirit of Babylon; obliterate evil, sin, and death from the cosmos; and bring into being a new heaven and a new earth in which righteousness and truth would dwell.

The Christian gospel is revealed in Scripture by means of two different but mutually complementary motifs – the **gospel of the kingdom of God** and the **gospel of God**. These are like two musical motifs or themes in a great classical symphony. As we trace our way through Scripture, one and then the other is emphasized, and at some points they are blended or synthesized. In the Scripture passages quoted above, we have observed the majestic dance between these two motifs or themes.

In this life, the outcome of the Christian gospel, consisting of both the above aspects, is a lifestyle which reflects the nature and character of God; that is, one which is characterized by truth, humility, righteousness, and holiness. This summarizes what we mean by **walking in the way of Christ and the apostles**.

As part of the **Omega Event**, God will do away with the present heavens and earth, which are indelibly corrupted by evil, sin, and death; and He will bring into being a new heaven and a new earth in which righteousness dwells and which fully reflect His glory.

In God's eternal kingdom, the ultimate outcome of the Christian gospel is a new race of humanity – the **elect** or the **saints** – headed by Jesus Christ and conformed to His image.

This new race of humanity will inhabit the new heaven and the new earth; and they will enjoy the glory of God through all of eternity.

The Bible is the personal communication from the Infinite Personal God to His elect, His saints; its purpose is to equip and enable them

Table 6-1. Summary of the Two-Part Christian Gospel – Cont.:

Reflections – Cont.:
to maintain their hope, fervent to the end, and to overcome all adversity in this life.
The purpose of the Synoptic Gospels (Matthew, Mark, and Luke) is to present the good news that the kingdom of God is at hand because the King has come. A vital aspect of the narrative in all four Gospels is the presentation of Jesus' credentials as the One who is qualified to stand as a lawgiver like Moses; to speak, teach, and perform miraculous signs as the Prophet spoken of by Moses in Deuteronomy 18:18-19; to sit on the throne of His forefather David; to minister as the suffering Servant of Yahweh; and who is, in fact, the uniquely begotten Son of God. The kingdom parables which are presented in the Synoptic Gospels describe the kingdom of God and its governing principles.
A vital aspect of the narrative of the Book of Acts is the presentation of the preaching of the Apostles as they expanded the kingdom of God by obeying and implementing the Great Commission mandate of Matthew 28:18-20. Thus, we find recorded in the Book of Acts the manner in which the Apostles presented the gospel of the kingdom of God to the people of the Greco-Roman world of the 1st century AD, including both Jews and Gentiles.

Introduction to the Christian Gospel

In the 5th chapter, we traced the development of five of the fourteen integrative motifs; namely, **the invasion of evil, sin, and death**, **the people of the new way**, **the gospel**, **sovereign election and human responsibility**, and **the covenant of conditional blessing**. With this background, the fact becomes evident that the Christian gospel is not really new, but rather it is the expression of God's ongoing program for obliterating the effects of the invasion of evil, sin, and death into the cosmos.

As set forth in Table 6-1, the Christian gospel consists of two equally important, mutually complementary, and interconnected aspects or components.

Introduction to the Gospel of the Kingdom of God

This is the gospel preached by Christ and the apostles as recorded in the Synoptic Gospels and the Book of Acts. However, as set forth in Table 6-1, it is actually rooted in the Sinaitic Covenant – that is, the suzerain / vassal treaty enacted by Yahweh Elohim with the people of Israel through Moses – and it is confirmed in the Davidic Covenant of 2 Samuel 7. It emphasizes our turning from our prideful rebellion, submitting to the kingly rule of Jesus Christ, and thereby becoming citizens of His kingdom. The gospel of the kingdom of God appeals most strongly to the Jewish mind.

> *God confers upon those who thus submit to His righteous rule all the glorious rights and privileges that pertain to citizenship in His kingdom.*

Introduction to the Gospel of God

This is the gospel introduced by the Apostle John in his Gospel and expounded by the Apostle Paul, chiefly in his epistle to the Romans, but also in his other epistles. However, as set forth in Table 6-1, it is actually rooted in the *protoevangelium* of Genesis 3:15 and the covenant that Yahweh cut with Abraham in accordance with the 12th and 15th chapters of Genesis. Its scope and purpose includes the obliteration of all the effects of the invasion of evil, sin, and death into the cosmos, and it includes the provisions God has made to release mankind individually and corporately from bondage to evil, sin, and death. The gospel of God appeals most strongly to the Gentile mind.

The Gospel of the Kingdom of God

The **gospel of the kingdom of God** is the focus of Part 2 of the WitW study. The gospel of the kingdom of God flows directly from the Great Commission as expressed in Matthew 28:18-20. The emphasis of the gospel of the kingdom of God is our repenting of our prideful rebellion, our submitting to the kingly rule of Jesus Christ, and our voluntarily following Him as His disciples.

The Way of Christ and the Apostles

For the disciple to follow Jesus necessitates that he learn to walk in the way of Christ and the apostles. As we explained in our discussion of the people of the new way in the 5th chapter, the concept of **the way** is ancient. As this concept comes down to us, it designates a **pattern of conduct** or a **manner of life**. In Matthew 28:20 Jesus defined what it means to be His disciple as follows:

> ... teaching them to observe **all** that I have commanded you.
> [Matthew 28:20a, ESV, emphasis added]

In other words, the lifestyle of the disciple of Christ must conform to the commandments of Christ. Because the way of Christ and the apostles is counterintuitive, the disciple must be taught how to walk in that way. In the 10th chapter of Part 2, we discuss the seven disciplines of the Christian life. These seven disciplines provide an outline of what the disciple's life should look like. However, the seven disciplines are not a new set of legal requirements that we must keep in order to be truly saved. Rather, they represent the fruit of the faith of Jesus Christ dwelling and operating in the spirit of the disciple.

The Gospel of God

The **gospel of God** is the focus of Part 3 of the WitW study. The gospel of God is the good news of the provisions God has made for delivering us from bondage to evil, sin, and death through the atoning death, burial, and resurrection of Jesus Christ. In the course of discussing the gospel motif in chapter 5, I unpacked Hebrews 4:2 (one of the Scriptures included in the right column of Figure 6-1) to place in evidence the fact that the gospel of God actually has two aspects:

1. Deliverance from bondage to evil, sin, and death.

2. Deliverance into eternal rest after a period of conflict and conquest.

By means of the precious and magnificent promises God has vouchsafed to us on the basis of the atoning death, burial, and resurrection of his Son, we are becoming partakers of the divine nature and are thereby enabled to actually walk in the way of Christ and the apostles.

> *In other words, all the spiritual resources and power we need in order to walk in the way of Christ and the apostles derive from the gospel of God.*

The Four-Faced Living Creatures

The four-faced living creature visions of Ezekiel the prophet and John the apostle are relevant to the two-part structure of the Christian gospel. The four faces, according to the order in John's vision, were as follows:

- Lion, signifying kingship
- Ox, signifying servitude
- Man, signifying humanity
- Eagle, signifying divinity

As we study the two passages of Scripture where these visions are recorded, we note differences in the details of the visions, but the four faces are common to both. So, what is the significance of the four faces with reference to the gospel? John's order is especially noteworthy in this regard. We are convinced that the four faces signify four facets of the person, life, and ministry of Jesus Christ: that is, the face of the lion signifies that He is the King of Israel as revealed primarily in the Gospel of Matthew; the face of the ox signifies that He is the Suffering Servant of Yahweh as revealed primarily in the Gospel of Mark; the face of the man signifies that He is the Son of Man as revealed primarily in the Gospel of Luke; and the face of the eagle signifies that He is the Son of God as revealed primarily in the Gospel of John.

Perversions of the Christian Gospel: A Brief Summary

Before turning to the discussion of the gospel of the kingdom of God in Part 2, it is important that we at least touch upon the two most important perversions of the Christian gospel; these are both discussed at greater length in Part 2 of the WitW study, chapter 15. At this point in our study, I present only a very brief summary.

In the days of the Apostle Paul, the two cardinal perversions of the Christian gospel were **antinomianism** and **legalism**. Both of these perversions entail a misrepresentation of the Christian disciple's relationship with the Torah, which we discussed in chapter 3. Moreover, they both involve a corruption of the normative relationship between belief and behavior in the life of the disciple.

Antinomianism

The antinomian heresy asserts that there is **no law** bearing upon the behavior of the disciple of Christ. Accordingly, this perversion of the gospel can be described as **lawlessness**, in regard to which Jesus' stern warning in the following passage is frightening:

> On that day many will say to me, "Lord, Lord, did we not prophesy in your name, and cast out demons in your name, and do many mighty works in your name?" And then will I declare to them, **"I never knew you; depart from me, you who practice lawlessness."** [Matthew 7:22-23, adapted from the ESV, emphasis added]

The modern counterpart to the antinomianism of the 1st century is reflected in the lordship salvation controversy that became public and widespread in the early 1990s. The antinomian side of this controversy maintains that saving faith consists only of a **mental assent to the facts of the gospel**, and that obedience to the commands of Jesus Christ is entirely optional. The opposing position, advanced chiefly by John MacArthur, maintains that obedience to the commands of Christ is an integral part of saving faith.

It is because of the antinomian heresy, that has corrupted the presentation of the gospel for over a century, that I emphasize the gospel of the kingdom of God and its implications in the WitW study.

Legalism

In the 1st century AD, the second perversion was principally embodied in the teachings of the **Judaizers**, who demanded that all disciples should be circumcised and should be required to obey the law of Moses. The modern counterpart to legalism is the attachment of certain works requirements as being essential to saving faith. For example, traditional Roman Catholic dogma holds that a person cannot be saved except by consistent practice of the system of religious works prescribed by the church, including baptism and partaking of the Eucharist. Within the sphere of Protestant denominations, involvement in ministry, pursuit of Christian education, and avoidance of certain taboos may acquire legalistic status; that is, be regarded as essential to salvation. Taboos, such as avoidance of alcoholic beverages, tobacco, mixed bathing, dancing, or movie attendance, are often unique to a given geographic region, or even to a given community of disciples.

Proclaiming the Christian Gospel

I have asserted that the form of the Christian gospel that has been proclaimed for nearly two centuries is incomplete in that the kingly rule of Christ, and our obedient submission to His rule, has not been adequately emphasized. In fact, one of the chief purposes of the WitW study is to restore a full understanding of the Christian gospel. Accordingly, it seems entirely fitting that I offer a model for proclaiming the Christian gospel that accords with this full understanding. I have decided that the best way to accomplish this is to update the Bridge Model for proclaiming the gospel, which is presented in Appendix G.

After studying Appendix G, you may be tempted to complain that the Bridge Model is overly complex. In fact, that was my reaction when I was first exposed to it. However, the Bridge Model has proven to be effective. Moreover, it is comprehensive in that it addresses all the logical steps that are needed to guide a person from a state of unbelief and callousness regarding his perilous condition to a state where he is prepared to at least consider repenting of his prideful rebellion against the rule of God, submitting to that rule, and embracing the salvation which Jesus Christ has purchased for us at such a horrendous cost.

Therefore, I urge you to carefully study Appendix G, and then use it as a pattern or guide for evangelistic conversations with friends, relatives, and associates.

Questions for Discussion

1. In your own words, define the Christian gospel, including its several interrelated and intertwined aspects.

2. In your own words, discuss why the entire gospel must be embraced as an integrated whole.

3. In your own words, summarize the two principal perversions of the Christian gospel, including the dangers associated with each. Include in your summarization any personal experiences with either perversion.

4. After carefully studying Appendix G, discuss its applicability to your own life and ministry. As part of your discussion, critically evaluate this model gospel proclamation.

Notes & Reflections

Use the space below to record additional insights and commentary resulting from your studies thus far.

Endnotes

1. Figures are numbered internal to each chapter with the chapter number followed by a hyphen and the figure number. Thus, the figure number inherently reveals where it is located.

2. For a description of Daystar Institute, refer to *Introduction to the Daystar Institute of Biblical Theology & Leadership Development*, which may be requested by phone or email using the contact information provided on the copyright page of this document.

3. The 10 – 40 window refers to a latitude band from 10° north to 40° north and extending from western Africa to eastern Asia. Most of the unevangelized population of the world lives within this window.

4. Students who are interested in pursuing the relevance and importance of representational thinking may refer to Briggs (2005) entitled *Knowing the Fear of the Lord: An Introduction to Representational Theology*.

5. Refer to Briggs (2008b), ch. 4.

6. Refer to Blackaby & King (2008).

7. Worldview = *weltanschauung* = a comprehensive conception or apprehension of the world, especially from a specific standpoint.

8. Hermeneutics is a technical term that designates the science and art of interpretation – that is, the act of deriving meaning from a text.

9. For your convenience, the initial definitions presented in this paragraph are repeated in the Glossary, Appendix A.

10. Refer to Appendix B for a discussion of the methods of biblical and exegetical theology.

11. **Ministry identity** is a technical term that designates that arena of ministry in which a person's talents, skills, and spiritual gifts enable him to operate with great fruitfulness and impact. Usually, this arena of ministry corresponds with a person's passion and

interest. In other words, we enjoy operating according to our ministry identity.

12 Refer to the 3rd chapter, p. 29ff, for an unfolding of the extended passage, Hebrews 3:7 – 4:13.

13 Refer to Briggs (2008b) for discussions of recent developments in the fields of linguistics, archaeology & biblical history, and biblical studies that support the assertion that the Bible is true narrative.

14 Refer to Briggs (2008b), pp. 21-32, for a discussion of the properties of true narratives.

15 Refer to Grenz & Franke (2001), pp. 254-255.

16 Refer to Appendix A for a definition of determinative.

17 Refer to the discussion of The Invasion of Evil, Sin, and Death in chapter 5.

18 Refer to Funk, et al. (1997).

19 Refer to Appendix A for a definition of **represent**.

20 Refer to Capon (2002), p. 15.

21 Refer to Piper (2003).

22 Refer to Appendix A for a definition of **glory**.

23 Refer to Trinity Hymnal (2005), p. 869.

24 Piper (2003), p. 28.

25 Refer to Appendix A for a definition of **idolatry** and **grace**.

26 Refer to Appendix A for a definition of **paradigmatic**.

27 Refer to Schaeffer (1982).

28 An **appellative** name is a title, as contrasted with a proper or personal name.

29 Referring to Van Gemeren (1997), p. 405, No. 466, "the pl. has reference to intensification or absolutization or exclusivity (say, God of gods); it is less commonly considered a pl. of majesty."

30 In Ephesians 6:10ff Paul employs the same terminology to refer to the minions of Satan, who rule over the corrupt and rebellious world order in this present age of darkness.

31 Refer to the discussion of Sovereign Election and Human Responsibility in chapter 5. Also, refer to Appendix F.

32 Refer to Appendix A for a fuller definition of **redeem**.

33 Refer to Appendix A for a fuller definition of **propitiation**.

34 Refer to Appendix A for a definition of the **millennium**.

35 Refer to Appendix A for definitions of **sanctify** and **holy**.

36 Refer to Appendix A for a definition of **glory**.

37 Refer to Briggs (2008b), pp. 5-47 for an answer to this question.

38 Refer to Jesus' teaching concerning fruitless branches in the 15th chapter of John and Paul's teaching concerning living in accordance with the flesh in the 8th chapter of Romans.

39 Refer to the section entitled Guarding the Heart later in this chapter for further discussion of how to gain victory over the flesh.

40 Refer to the discussion of The Covenant of Conditional Blessing in chapter 5 for more detail.

41 Graphic by Karbel Multimedia. Copyright © 2011, Logos Bible Software. Used by permission.

42 Refer to Appendix A for a definition of **cherubim**.

43 Refer to Appendix A for a definition of **worship**.

44 HCSB Study Bible (2010), p. 1648.

45 Refer to Luke 23:34.

46   Refer to Acts 7:60.

47   A parallel passage is found in Mark 7:21ff.

48   Paraclete is a transliteration of the Greek *parakletos*, which means one called alongside to render aid. Refer to John 14:16, 14:26, 15:26 & 16:7 where *parakletos* is translated either Helper or Counselor.

49   Refer to the Glossary in Appendix A for the definition of semi-Pelagianism.

50   Refer to Piper (2005), pp. 27-29.

51   We will have occasion to return to this episode in chapter 11 in connection with our discussion of The Household or Family.

52   Refer to 1 Samuel 14:49.

53   Refer to Appendix A for a definition of **canon.**

54   Refer to Piper (1999), pp. 181-183.

55   For a more exhaustive treatment of this subject, refer to Briggs (2009b).

56   Refer to Collins (2002) for a detailed discussion of the identification of Thutmosis IV as the Pharoah of the Exodus.

57   Alter (1981), pp. 25ff.

58   For example, the *Gilgamish* and *Enuma Elish* epics of ancient Mesopotamia. An epic is a story of the exploits of a single heroic character.

59   Alter (1981), p. 27.

60   Alter (1981), p. 20ff.

61   Kass (2003), ch. 13, p. 389ff.

62   Refer to Alter (1981), ch. 3, p. 47ff.

63 Alter employs this story to illustrate how biblical narrative is constructed. See Alter (1981), ch. 1, pp. 3-22.

64 Refer to Alter (1981), ch. 4, p. 63ff.

65 Refer to Klein, et al. (1993), p. 226.

66 In the Hebrew Scriptures, the English word "God" usually translates the Hebrew word *Elohim*, which is an appellative name or title that signifies God's transcendence.

67 Yahweh is God's personal, covenant name. The paradigmatic passage in which God introduces himself by this name is that which relates the Burning Bush episode in Exodus 3:1ff. In particular, God's formal introduction of himself to Moses occurs in Exodus 3:13-15.

68 In the sphere of biblical interpretation, a **pericope** is a paragraph-length passage of biblical text which presents a unit of thought suitable for explanation and exposition.

69 Refer to Kaiser (1981), pp. 48-49.

70 Refer to Appendix A for a definition of **exegesis**.

71 Refer to Ryken (2004), pp. 5-9.

72 Refer to the discussion in chapter 6, The Two-Part Christian Gospel.

73 Refer to Piper (1999), pp. 197-199.

74 For a substantial discussion related to the Marriage Metaphor refer to the discussion of the Household or Family in chapter 11.

75 I postpone the discussion of this motif to chapter 11, entitled Household of the King. In particular, refer to the section of this chapter entitled Sphere of Civil Government.

76 The Christ Event is designated by the Greek letter Chi (**X**) in Figure 2-1.

77 Refer to Appendix F for a careful but readable analysis of the meaning of human free agency.

78 Graphic by Karbel Multimedia. Copyright © 2011, Logos Bible Software. Used by permission.

79 Refer to Cassuto (2006), pp. 18-49.

80 *Koine* means common. In other words, *koine* Greek was the language of commercial, political, and legal discourse. In fact, *koine* Greek was the *lingua franca* of the Greco-Roman world of the 1st century AD.

Walking in the Way of Christ & the Apostles

Study Guide Series (SGs)

Part 1 – Foundational Concepts. These concepts are foundational to equip the Christ-follower to have and to be governed by the mind of Christ.

1. The Way of God
2. The Storyline of the Bible
3. Biblical Reality
4. Discovering the Meaning of Scripture
5. Torah: The Fountainhead of Wisdom
6. The Two-Part Christian Gospel

Part 2 – The Gospel of the Kingdom of God. Here we explore the ways in which the Christian gospel confronts the prideful rebellion of the human heart and exalts Christ as King over all.

7. Authority of the King
8. Called by the King
9. Meaning of Discipleship
10. Disciplines of the Kingdom
11. Household of the King
12. Second Coming of the King

Part 3 – The Gospel of God. This final set explores how the Christian gospel affords a complete solution to human depravity and the threefold problem of evil, sin, and death.

13. Introduction to the Gospel of God
14. Reason for the Gospel of God
15. Content of the Gospel of God
16. Perversions of the Gospel of God
17. Application of the Gospel of God

Theological Readers (TRs)

TR1 – Part 1: Foundational Concepts
TR2 – Part 2: The Gospel of the Kingdom of God
TR3 – Part 3: The Gospel of God
TR4 – Resources and Appendices

Connect with us at www.DaystarInstituteNM.us, or
Contact us via email at WalkingintheWayUSA@gmail.com